NINETEENTH CENTURY RAILWAY HISTORY THROUGH THE ILLUSTRATED LONDON NEWS

ILN *engraving at its best: an excellent depiction of the footplate of a Midland Railway 2-4-0, although it was used to illustrate an article on 10 January 1891 about a strike in Scotland*

NINETEENTH CENTURY RAILWAY HISTORY THROUGH

THE ILLUSTRATED LONDON NEWS

ANTHONY J. LAMBERT

DAVID & CHARLES

Newton Abbot   London   North Pomfret (Vt)

Publisher's note
The Publisher acknowledges with grateful thanks the permission given by the proprietors of *The Illustrated London News* to reproduce the extracts from the issues of the last century. It should be noted that *The Illustrated London News* continues to be published reporting on life and events of the 1980s.

British Library Cataloguing in Publication Data

Lambert, Anthony J.
    Railway history through the Illustrated
    London news.
    1. Railways – Great Britain – History
    I. Title
    385'.0941   HE3018

    ISBN 0-7153-8521-6

Typeset by Typesetters (Birmingham) Ltd
and printed in Great Britain
by Redwood Burn Limited, Trowbridge, Wilts
for David & Charles (Publishers) Limited
Brunel House Newton Abbot Devon

Published in the United States of America
by David & Charles Inc
North Pomfret Vermont 05053 USA

CONTENTS

Publisher's Preface   6
Introduction   7
Construction and Openings   10
London   26
Viaducts and Bridges   39
Politics and Economics   55
Stations   62
Locomotives and Propulsion Systems   65
Locomotive Works and Engine Sheds   74
Signalling   80
Accidents and Disasters   88
Carriages   93
Ships and Docks   99
Royalty   105
Train Services   106
Battle of the Gauges   113
Personalities   117
Railwaymen   120
Abortive Schemes   121
Civil Unrest   125

PUBLISHER'S PREFACE

As this book so vividly demonstrates, we are fortunate that *The Illustrated London News* (the first periodical to make regular use of pictures) was thoroughly railway minded during the great periods of railway building and consolidation. Its columns tell us much not only about the railways themselves, but the trains that ran on them and the people and goods that were conveyed in those trains. Many details are brought to life that otherwise would have been forgotten. The railway is shown as a thing of great intrinsic interest, and its place in the countryside and in society are also often vividly brought to life. We indeed learn not merely about the attitudes of the public to railways but about the very way the Victorians thought and behaved overall.

Most people interested in railways must be familiar with at least one or two fine engravings from *The Illustrated London News*. They have been produced in numerous other railway works, some of them appearing time after time. But until now it has been hard to review the whole scope. Even if you are lucky enough to have a house large enough to accommodate a run of the bound volumes, far larger than any contemporary coffee-table book, it is difficult to make use of the treasures within them.

Here, then, is a book that has long deserved publishing, a substantial, carefully-selected cross-section through different periods of railway history. You will find many famous events duly recorded and enjoy new perspectives. The combination of the carefully reproduced original engravings, selections from the original text and Anthony Lambert's commentary almost add up to a picture history of Britain's railways in its own right, but its real value lies in the clarity of detail and the capturing of contemporary attitudes and excitements. It is a book that will have a particularly-treasured spot on my own shelves and which is likely to be taken down and browsed through and referred to frequently for the rest of my life. I hope it gives you equal value.

DAVID ST JOHN THOMAS

Brunel House
Newton Abbot

Sheep and cattle for Christmas arriving at Tottenham station on the Eastern Counties Railway on 22 December 1855. Although Tottenham was a town when the railway arrived in 1840, its period of major growth had yet to come.

INTRODUCTION

The Illustrated London News first appeared in 1842, and broke with previous newspaper tradition in having a substantial number of illustrations in each issue; to help to promote the first issue on 14 May, 200 men paraded the streets of London with placards that read 'The Illustrated London News 30 Engravings Price 6d'. Newspapers had included illustrations before but not as a regular feature. The paper's founder, a Nottingham printer named Herbert Ingram, had noticed that sales of the *Weekly Chronicle* had increased whenever a picture had been used. Ingram had arrived in London at the beginning of 1842, determined to increase sales of 'Old Parr's Life Pills' which he had sold well in Nottingham as a remedy for the wide range of ills that many Victorian medicines and pills were purported to cure. He had promoted the pills in conjunction with his brother-in-law and claimed that they had enabled a Shropshire countryman, Thomas Parr, to live to 152 and father a child at 105; as one would expect of an ill-educated nation, the Victorians generally were a gullible lot. (A painting of 'Old Parr' hangs in the Library at Powis Castle, owned by the National Trust.)

Ingram's original idea was to produce an illustrated paper of crime stories, but Henry Vizetelly, a wood engraver who had provided an illustration of 'Old Parr' to market the pills, persuaded him to expand the idea to include news of all kinds. Ingram was won over to the idea and set about implementing it. He recruited artists and journalists, and an able writer named Frederick Bayley as editor. The first issue contained sixteen pages and thirty-two engravings with subjects ranging from the war in Afghanistan to a fancy dress ball at Buckingham Palace. It sold 26,000 copies and by the end of 1842 sales had reached 60,000 an issue. A 'scoop' was achieved before the Great Exhibition of 1851 with the publication of Joseph Paxton's plans for the Crystal Palace before even Prince Albert had seen them; in his capacity as President of the Society of Arts, Prince Albert played a prominent role in promoting the exhibition. This coup increased sales to 130,000. The tax on newspapers was abolished in 1855, boosting sales to 150,000, and by 1861 the taxes on advertising and paper had also disappeared. Sales in 1863 were over 300,000 a week.

These figures must be seen in comparison with circulation figures for other leading papers: in 1861, *The Times* at 3d sold only 70,000 copies and none of the penny dailies could rival the *ILN*. The ½d *Evening News* was not founded until 1894, and the *Daily Mail*, which was to revolutionise journalism by the rewriting of reports in a more racy or salacious style ('written by office-boys for office-boys' as Lord Salisbury put it), did not appear until 1896. There were more closely related competitors; Vizetelly himself left the *ILN* to found the *Illustrated Times* but he sold out to Ingram who closed it down.

Another rival, the *Pictorial Times*, lost its promoter £20,000 before being sold to Ingram. The *ILN* shrugged off potential competitors with remarkable ease.

Part of the explanation for this must be the calibre of the writers whom the paper employed: R. L. Stevenson, J. M. Barrie, Arthur Conan Doyle, Rudyard Kipling, Rider Haggard, Thomas Hardy and George Meredith, amongst others. The quality of some of the early illustrations certainly left something to be desired, but at a time when there were no other publications of the kind available with such a high pictorial content, this did not matter too much. Initially engravings were printed from hand-engraved blocks made of box tree which not only allowed delicate carving but was also extremely durable. The life expectancy was about 300,000 impressions on the massive steam-driven printing presses. The quality of the illustrations improved quite dramatically when the use of photography enabled the engravers to work from an image transferred on to the wood. Metal half-tone blocks, usually of copper, replaced wood towards the end of the nineteenth century as photographs on glossy paper became the norm.

What were the character and features of the Britain that the *ILN* sought to portray and record? The Battle of Waterloo in 1815 ended twenty-eight years of intermittent wars which left Britain supreme politically. But it marked the beginning of a time of political and social unrest that was only appeased by the prolonged period of growing prosperity which roughly followed the end of the 'Hungry Forties' and the Great Exhibition in 1851. Economically progress was not as swift as might be inferred from the rapid spread of the railway system between 1825 and 1848 during which time 4,600 miles of railway had been opened in Britain, or in comparison with the rates of growth in the third quarter of the century; exports, for example, in 1842 were slightly lower than they had been in 1815 when the country's trade would still be affected by the war. A form of bulk transport that was quicker and cheaper than the canals was required to fulfil the conditions necessary for an economic 'take-off'; this the railways naturally provided, but it was not until the network had reached most large industrial centres, ports and markets that the full benefit could be felt by manufacturing industry. Equally, much industrial development had already occurred by the time the Duke of Wellington witnessed the opening of the Liverpool & Manchester Railway in 1830: Abraham Darby III's iron bridge had been carrying traffic across the River Severn for 51 years; coal production had reached 25 million tons per annum; iron output had topped ¾ million tons; and there were many cotton mills employing over a thousand workers.

But the social conditions of Britain in 1842 reflected a society divided in a way that now seems quite extraordinary in our more egalitarian western world. Urban growth, and burgeoning mineral rights and mining royalties endowed the few landed families fortunate enough to possess land enjoying such potential with fabulous wealth. This divide had always been present, of course, but the Industrial Revolution served to accentuate it, besides creating a new class of industrial parvenus, and the squalid conditions of many quarters of towns and cities made the plight of poverty *seem* worse than it was in a rural context. One of the main consequences of urbanisation was to increase the capacity for public expression of grievances and insurrection; rural revolts, by the logic of geography, require a stronger impulse and co-ordination to develop the momentum that could so easily be raised amongst the urban proletariat.

Riots and disturbances were almost endemic between the end of the Napoleonic Wars and the mid-century, largely due to frustrated demands for parliamentary reform and universal male suffrage. In common with many uprisings throughout history, there was a correlation between them and industrial and agricultural distress; the potency of the reform movement was emasculated by the steady growth in the economy and rising real wages after 1851. Many reactionaries believed that the railways would exacerbate dissent in society; a perceptive observer in Manchester wrote in 1830 with the opening of the Liverpool & Manchester Railway that 'Parliamentary Reform must follow soon after the opening of this road. A million of persons will pass over it in the course of this year, and see that hitherto unseen village of Newton; and they must be convinced of the absurdity of its sending two members to Parliament, whilst Manchester sends none.' In reality the railway can hardly be credited with this particular reform, since it came but two years later with the Great Reform Bill and the impetus for it predated the railway. Nonetheless the spirit of the quote holds good, and was certainly the cause of some people's fear about the consequences of the first truly public form of transport. Besides broadening man's experience and the stimulus given to the development of ideas by travel, news itself could travel more swiftly to the sedentary. Early morning trains left the capital with papers for the provinces, thereby reducing the sense of remoteness that must have obtained even with the brisker coach services to London over the turnpike roads. The Post Office quickly realised the potential of railways; in 1838 railway carriages with both sorting facilities and an apparatus for collecting and dropping mail bags while on the move were introduced.

The inevitable result of this accelerated communication of person, news or idea was a growing sense of national identity, the development of a larger consciousness that facilitated the formation of organisations that looked to the country rather than the region or town for their support. Although Chartism petered out in the 1840s and early attempts at forming national trade unions were largely fruitless, the former in particular directed the nation's attention to the condition of the working classes,

creating a concern that was to occupy the minds of the more enlightened and humane reformers, politicians and writers. The 'condition of England question' was the spur to Disraeli's *Sybil*, sub-titled 'The Two Nations', the writings of Charles Kingsley, Elizabeth Gaskell, Charles Dickens and some of Elizabeth Barrett Browning's poems; it fostered the 'Young England' movement within the Tory party which attracted Disraeli and envisaged an alliance between the aristocracy and the workers against the Whig middle classes. They would have applauded the sentiments expressed by Canon Parkinson and quoted in Asa Briggs' *Victorian Cities*: 'There is far less *personal* communication between the master cotton spinner and his workmen, the calico printer and his blue-handed boys, between the master tailor and his apprentices, than there is between the Duke of Wellington and the humblest labourer on his estate.' Although an essentially romantic outlook, it had its positive outcome in early legislation to mitigate the worst excesses in the factories and mines – the employment of women and children in appalling conditions.

But if the condition of the majority of the population would horrify today's susceptibilities, and the fear of disorder was ever present, the Britain of 1842 was vibrant with potential. That potential was to be realised in an unparalleled increase in the nation's output and a real increase in wealth for most workers, at least until the mid-1870s. The railways played an indispensable role in reducing transport costs and making possible the creation of larger factories.

It is difficult to exaggerate the importance of *The Illustrated London News* for railway historians. Although there were two early magazines devoted to railways – Herepath's *Railway Magazine* (1835–1903) and the *Railway Times* (1837–1914) – they dealt primarily with the commercial side of railways, eschewing much of interest to today's historian. The *ILN* naturally looked to a wider market and consequently embraced a broader outlook on the railway scene, examining such subjects as signalling, propulsion systems, locomotives and carriages. This variety is extraordinary: in what contemporary weekly or daily publication aimed at the general reader could one find articles of such ostensibly specialist interest? Information was presented in lay terms for the general reader, although the depth in which some articles examined their subjects is impressive and makes the *ILN* of the nineteenth century a much more useful mine of information than its equivalents today.

It may be a surprise to today's reader that a general publication should devote so much of its space to railways. Although the *ILN* was obviously 'railway minded', it is hardly to be wondered at that so much importance should be attached to a relatively new creation that was very evidently changing the entire character of life in Britain, and would eventually do so for the world. It is not easy for us to appreciate the excitement that must have been felt about the possibilities opened up by the prospect of cheap travel at speeds that only a decade or two before would have been thought impossible. Those with more perceptive minds would have realised the potential that the railway created for economic expansion on an unprecedented scale, and even for the development of resources overseas, particularly in India where the first public line opened in 1853. The construction and equipment of thousands of miles of railway overseas using British skills, was one of the most enduring achievements of a period remarkable for its enterprise and industry. The enormous export trade in locomotives, carriages, signalling equipment and even castings for bridges and station roofs is one of the least celebrated elements of Victorian international trade. Even when the *ILN* was formed in 1842, Thomas Brassey was building one of France's first railways, the Paris & Rouen; Brassey was to build six further railways in France before moving on to construct railways in Belgium, Holland, Spain, Italy, Canada, Norway, Sweden, Denmark, Switzerland, Turkey, Austria, India, Australia and South America. The foremost overseas contractor he may have been, but many followed in his footsteps.

The *ILN* began publication just before the Railway Mania of 1844–6 and naturally documented most of the major developments of the network. Its coverage was slightly biased towards the south but dispatching illustrators to record the opening of a line in Hampshire was obviously cheaper than an assignment in the Highlands. There were, of course, exceptions, such as Ireland which received surprising coverage for its distance from London.

Second only to articles on new lines and accidents was the attention paid to new methods of propulsion, some of them so impractical that it is difficult to conceive how contemporaries can have taken them seriously. Yet the *ILN* was not above poking fun at the poor innocent, as evidenced by its relation in 1850 of a story concerning a man from Meltham, near Huddersfield, who had never seen a railway. He 'lately went to the Standege [sic] Tunnel, on the Huddersfield and Manchester Railway, and ascended an eminence, from which he witnessed a train at full speed. The following is his account of it: "Hod (I had) been standing there very little when I saw a long black thing coming as sharp as leetning, and puffing and reeking loik mad; un as soin as iver it saw me, it sets up a great scream, un run into a hoile." '

Curiously the *ILN* devoted little space to steam locomotives, in marked contrast to the other forms of proposed traction. It may be that the gradual development of the steam locomotive was not newsworthy, or too complex for the average reader. Whatever the reason, more attention was given to signalling systems which were probably perceived as having a more direct bearing on the safety, and therefore interest, of the *ILN*'s readers.

Although there would have been no doubt in most people's minds in 1842 that the country would sooner or later have a railway network, only a relatively few lines were operative in 1842. The London & Birmingham Railway had been open for four years, providing London with a route to Liverpool and Manchester over the Grand Junction Railway. Almost exactly a month after the first issue of the *ILN*, Queen Victoria would take her first journey by train, from Slough to Paddington; the Great Western Railway to Bristol had been open for less than a year. The total mileage open had not yet reached 2,000; in the last year of peace, 1913, the GWR alone had a route mileage of 2,678 exclusive of joint lines, and the total was over 23,000 miles. The North Eastern Railway owned almost as many wagons as British Rail – 119,000 compared with BR's 137,589 (1979), although admittedly the tremendous increase in the efficiency of freight handling makes an absolute comparison a little arbitrary. By World War I, the network was effectively complete, only the odd few miles being constructed after the war. Neither passenger nor goods traffic levels after World War I were to regain their pre-war level of 1,294m passengers carried and 520m tons of freight (both 1912).

The 60 years spanned by the majority of the extracts in this book represent the years of railway supremacy. Trams and omnibuses had challenged its monopoly of urban transport by World War I, but for longer journeys there was no alternative but the railway. The few motor cars were slow and unreliable and offered nothing in the way of comfort that most railways provided in the Edwardian era. An inspection of some of the carriages in the National Railway Museum affords an idea of how luxurious train travel was for those who could afford a first-class ticket. Of course, the speeds of inter-war expresses were much improved and the standards of comfort and service remained high; but never again did the railways enjoy a monopoly of public transport, a monopoly that was seldom abused because of the Victorians' concern to maintain competition between the companies. The railways were in slow retreat, compelled by indifferent governments to campaign for a 'Square Deal' and an integrated policy for the nation's transport that would establish more equal competition between the forms of transport. In contrast, these extracts from the *ILN* provide a fascinating insight into the buoyant optimism of the Victorian age, a time when staggering amounts were invested in railway construction schemes on a scale that makes today's motorways seem small beer. From our standpoint of faltering and uncertain progress, it is small wonder that we should look back at the achievements and confidence of the Victorians with a mixture of admiration and disapprobation.

*　　　　*　　　　*

In a few instances, extracts from publications contemporary with the *ILN* have been chosen; in the case of the *Pictorial Times*, it was bought out by the *ILN*.

CONSTRUCTION AND OPENINGS

In a publication that was more of a newspaper than a review magazine, it was inevitable that a substantial proportion of the space given to railways should be devoted to new schemes. Obviously there were far too many for the ILN to give more than a mention to most, at least until the pace of construction slackened from the 1860s. Some issues would contain a column or two of railways for which plans had been deposited, about which little or nothing more would be heard, whatever their fate.

The choice of railway lines for closer examination can sometimes be described as idiosyncratic. One would expect a London-based publication to concentrate upon lines which directly affected the capital and for there to be relatively fewer reports on developments north of the border, if only because of the expense of gathering them; but it is difficult to explain two and a half pages on the Great Northern Railway's Lincoln to Honington line. Opened in April 1867, the railway did provide a more direct route from London to Lincoln and was one of three lines promoted by the GNR to thwart the Great Eastern Railway's efforts to gain access to the Yorkshire coalfield. But its significance hardly warranted so much space. The explanation may lie in now-forgotten friendships or commercial interests; even the ILN felt some need to justify its close attention: 'We have thus carefully mentioned these features, as we confess to a feeling of surprise at finding so charming a district in the much-maligned county of Lincoln.'

Interestingly, as much attention is given to Irish matters as to Scottish developments, which is surprising given the importance attached by railway companies to traffic between the two countries and the concern of many of the ILN's readers about communications with their grouse moors or salmon rivers. Few illustrations were ever included in the ILN of the ceremony that marked the official commencement of construction, the cutting of the first sod (or turf to be more refined), yet for the issue of 30 May 1863 a relatively obscure line in West Cork was chosen for the depiction of this occasion. The ILN justified their inclusion by saying that the two events (a new line was opened on the same day) were 'of great importance to the western part of the county of Cork'. Whether the majority of the ILN's readership would have taken much interest in them is doubtful.

Artists' licence in the drawings usually manifested itself in the exaggeration of the scale of earthworks, doubling the depth of cuttings or height of viaducts. Sometimes this was combined with a poor grasp of perspective and proportions between objects, so it may not always have been an intentional distortion to impress the reader.

The commentary was as particular about the inclusion of all the important personalities concerned as The Tatler in reporting a society gathering. The almost obsequious deference that was shown towards the upper echelons of society surfaces in some passages, and descriptions of new lines paid as much attention to the country seats and manor houses and their incumbents along the way as to the sources of the line's traffic or its raison d'être.

The Lancaster & Carlisle Railway opened in several stages: the lines from Lancaster to Kendal Junction (later Oxenholme) and the two-mile section of the Kendal & Windermere Railway as far as Kendal were opened on 21 September 1846; the ceremonial opening of the whole line was held on 15 December 1846 and a special train ran from Lancaster to Carlisle. A special was operated on the 16th, carrying guests returning south, and public services commenced on the 17th. The weather, which the ILN describes as severe, encouraged speculation about the climb up Shap Fells; light snow covered the higher ground and sheets of ice were hanging down the sides of Shap cutting. The locomotive was a Trevithick-Allan 2-2-2 Dalemain, named after the residence of the L&C's chairman, and was preceded as far as Shap by a sister engine Greystoke in case assistance was needed on the climb. It was not, and Dalemain breasted the summit at 22½mph. During the speech briefly referred to in the passage on 'The Contractors' Dinner', John Stephenson predicted that 'some improvement may be made in the construction of the engines which will make it practicable to go up 1 in 75 at 30mph, or even twice that speed'. In fact a train went up at 35mph in the first week; 60mph was not achieved until 16 November 1936 when Princess Elizabeth went up at an average of 64.5mph between Tebay and Shap Summit box. The bridge over the River Lune at Lancaster, depicted in one of the illustrations, was replaced in 1866 when the

original three laminated-timber arches were rebuilt in wrought iron. A footpath has always been provided across the bridge since this was a condition of Lancaster council's approval.

OPENING OF THE LANCASTER AND CARLISLE RAILWAY, ON TUESDAY LAST

Tuesday last was the day appointed for the opening of this new line of Railway. Accordingly, the Castle Station, at Lancaster, by eleven o'clock, was a scene of unusual bustle and excitement; and numbers of individuals, in spite of the severity of the weather, were grouped in the old church-yard, and on the terrace of the Castle, to view the public ceremony, by the Directors of the Lancaster and Carlisle Railway, throwing open to the distant cities of the north those advantages which their more southern neighbours have long enjoyed. The necessary arrangements being completed, the Directors' train, consisting of six first-class carriages, and three second-class carriages, moved slowly from the Castle Station, across two high embankments, to the Lune Viaduct, a work of extreme difficulty, consisting of eight stone and brick arches, of fifty-three feet span. As a specimen of strength and lightness, this structure is not surpassed on the Line; and its three laminated timber arches give it a highly ornamental appearance from the town: the whole was completed in about twelve months.

Hest Bank comes next, a small bathing village on the borders of Morecambe Bay, which lies on a wide expanse of sandy desert for many a mile, bounded by the hills of Westmorland. The train then proceeded at a more rapid rate through some deep cuttings, past Carnforth and Holme Stations, to Milnthorp Station, along an embankment of great length. This station is very substantial, and will be the best, in point of accommodation, on the Line. Beyond Sedgwick, after passing an embankment, and through some heavy rock cutting, the train stopped at Oxenholme Station, within two miles of Kendal, at the junction of the Kendal and Windermere Railways. A fine view of the town of Kendal was enjoyed from this station: the winter sun lit up the church spires, and blue roofs of the white houses which lay

Lancaster Station

in the vale beneath; whilst, far beyond, rose the white-capped mountains of the west – the giants of the Lake. After a few minutes' delay, the whistle of the engine gave notice of starting; and the precaution was here taken of sending a pilot engine a few hundred yards a head.

For the next mile or two, occasional glimpses were obtained of the town of Kendal, and its old Castle; the train then passed round Hay Fell, and away over Docker Garths Viaduct, commonly called Fiddler's Gill, a work of beauty and greatness (the middle arch being about 80 feet high); and then, past Lowgill Station, over an embankment 90 feet high, to the proposed junction of the North Western Railway; and onward, round the base of Dillicar Fell, at an elevation of 200 feet from the river, which lies at the foot of the embankment; a large amphitheatre of

hills rises on every side, and the path seems at an end; but the skill of the Engineers (Messrs. Locke and Errington) carried this line over many a place deemed impracticable – round the foot of hills, across rivers, over vallies, &c.

Crossing Brown Beck by a Viaduct of red freestone, and the river Berbeck by another large viaduct, the rise to the summit at Shap commences. The cutting here is the deepest, hardest, and most expensive on the line, and varies from 50 to 61 feet in depth. The works were first commenced here in June, 1844. The summit at Shap is 900 feet above the level of the sea. Around, is a region of bare hills and cheerless scenes, making quick travelling a comfort. But Clifton Moor Station is passed, and the train passes over the river Lowther, by the *Lowther Viaduct*, a noble work, and next in

importance to the bridge across the Lune. It is unrivalled for boldness and beauty of proportion; and consists of 7 semi-circular arches of 60 feet span, supported on piers, 8 feet in thickness at the top, and increasing to 18 feet 6 inches at the base. Its total length is about 500 feet. The scenery here is a perfect contrast to the region passed. Lowther Park, with its thick and massive woods – the clear winding river, 100 feet below – the stern grandeur of the distant mountains, just tinted with the last farewell rays of the setting sun – formed a beautiful picture.

A short mile from here is *Eamont Viaduct*, crossing the dark and wooded banks of the Eamont, with five arches of 50 feet span each, and 70 feet high. An embankment beyond commands a fine view of Brougham Hall, the residence of Lord Brougham; its stately park and large pleasure-grounds looked gloomily with their winter's clothing. At Penrith, the train was met by another from Carlisle; and, after gazing for a short time at the ruins of its old Castle, they each proceeded onward to Carlisle. The county, for some miles, is flat and uninteresting, with the exception of Borrock Lodge, which stands on the borders of a vale of remarkable loveliness. A high embankment passes Wreay Hall and village, noted for the beauty of its Chapel. Further on is Newbiggin Bridge – a neat wooden erection, built for the convenience of the proprietor of Newbiggin Hall, H. A. Aglionby, Esq.

The train reached Carlisle between four and five o'clock. A splendid dinner was served in the Athenaeum, to the Directors and their friends; the confectionery and most of the table ornaments having been

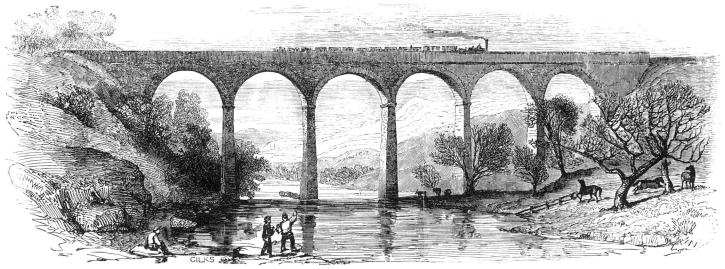

Lowther Viaduct

forwarded from Liverpool.

A trial trip, from Carlisle to Lancaster, was made yesterday week. The Directors in the train, we learn from the *Carlisle Journal*, were Mr. John Dixon and Mr. G. H. Head, who were joined at Penrith by Mr. E. W. Hasel (Chairman of the Directors), Mr. H. Howard, of Greystoke Castle, and Lieutenant-Colonel Maclean. They were accompanied by Mr. T. C. Heysham, Mr. P. Dixon, Mr. Steel, of the *Carlisle Journal*, Mr. Larmer, Resident Engineer, Mr. Collister, Resident Engineer of the Caledonian Railway, Mr. Mould, Mr. Hemberow, Mr. Green and two or three other gentlemen connected with the works. The train consisted of the engine, tender, and three carriages. It proceeded at the rate of upwards of 30 miles an hour, and would have reached Penrith (18 miles) in about 35 minutes, but for a slight accident when about two miles from that place. It caused a delay, however, of upwards of an hour, when the train again proceeded on its way – reaching Lancaster (70 miles) in about three hours of actual travelling – the Directors having stopped at several places to inspect the works.

In the evening, the Directors, engineers, and friends, dined together at the King's Arms Inn, and next morning, were joined at breakfast by Captain Coddington, the Government Inspector, who had just arrived from London. A little after eight o'clock, they started with a train of four carriages on the return to Carlisle. The day was excessively cold, with rain, sleet, snow, and frost, by turns. At times, the rails presented the appearance of long lines of ice, and were extremely slippery. The difficulty on such a day was the ascent of the great incline on Shap Fells, one of the severest gradients on any railway in England: the whole party watched this with no little interest; and it must have been highly satisfactory to both Engineers and Directors, when Captain Coddington, who stood upon the engine and timed its progress, announced that the ascent had been made, notwithstanding the unfavourable state of the rails, at the rate of 20 miles an hour – although the engine was an old one, and not of the most powerful class. All the heavy works – the bridges, viaducts, cuttings, and embankments – were minutely inspected by Captain Coddington, who expressed himself, at the end of the journey, as highly pleased with the whole of the works, declaring that the public might travel upon the

Newbiggin Bridge

Line with the most perfect safety; and, immediately afterwards, gave the Directors a certificate to that effect. We may mention here, that the Line is double throughout, with the exception of about two miles, near Lowther. This portion will be made double in a month, or less. The Line is remarkably easy nearly throughout – the exception being a short distance where it has been recently ballasted; and it passes through a country which can scarcely be surpassed for picturesque beauty and wildness of scenery.

[ILN Dec. 19 1846]

OPENING OF THE LANCASTER AND CARLISLE RAILWAY

The article continued the following week:
Leaving the summit, we enter a cutting through limestone rock, and before it approaches Shap Village, the Line runs through a circle of large boulder stones, said to be the inner circle of an ancient Druidical Temple.

The Line now proceeds on the east side of the town of Shap, along a heavy cutting through limestone rock, and passing under an elegant skew-bridge, erected at an angle of 45°.

The Line next descends along the flat portion of the Line called Shap Mines; and following the valley of the stream, the Line again runs under the turnpike-road; and thence passing Thrimby, through a thick plantation.

Here the character of the scenery is considerably altered – the bare, rugged, and sterile mountains being succeeded by fertile pastures and picturesque prospects.

The Kendal turnpike-road is crossed for the last time, by a skew-bridge at Clifton, near the entrance to Lowther Park, in which, hidden by a forest of huge oaks, stands Lowther Castle, the seat of the Earl of Lonsdale.

The scenery between Shap and Clifton is very attractive – Cross Fell, Saddleback, Skiddaw, and the other hills in the Lake District, appearing to great advantage.

We are now carried along the Lowther Embankment, and about 50 miles from Lancaster and 20 miles from Carlisle we cross the river Lowther on a magnificent viaduct, 100 feet above the stream. Its arches, six in number, are of 60 feet span each; its total length, 500 feet. It is the largest and one of the most beautiful objects of art on the Line.

A mile and a half from the Lowther Viaduct, the Line crosses the Eamont on a viaduct of great beauty, consisting of Five semi-circular arches of 50 feet span each. Its height is 70 feet, and its extreme length upwards of 300 feet.

Westmoreland is now left in the rear, and we enter "Canny Cumberland," – the two counties being divided by the stream which we have just crossed. We immediately enter a large cutting, containing 180,000 cubic yards, and the Line then runs nearly level to the town of Penrith: the Station closely adjoining ruins of the ancient Castle.

From Penrith, the Line enters the valley of the Petteril, through which it pursues almost a direct course to Carlisle, joining the Newcastle and Carlisle Railway at the London-road Station, where the line is 36 feet above the level at Morecambe Bay, and 852 feet below the Shap summit.

Besides the principal viaducts enumerated, the works on the Line comprise 15 turnpike-road bridges, 64 occupation-road bridges, 86 occupation bridges, 47 cattle creeps, and 60 level crossings.

We have abridged this outline from the *Carlisle Journal*. We add a few engineering details: –

Total quantity of gunpowder used upon the works – 4133 barrels, of 100 lbs each, or 184 tons. Coils of fuze, 61,044; length of fuze used, about 416 miles.

On the Kendal district alone (five miles) the holes drilled for blasting amount to 41 miles.

Number of nights worked, 152,147.

Horses night work, 10,500.

Rock, 844,000 cubic yards. Independent of this rock, there has been at least 400,000 cubic yards of sand requiring blasting, making the rock work nearly one-seventh of the whole excavations.

Greatest number of men employed upon the works, 9,615.

Greatest number of horses employed upon

the works, 790.

The number of days' work executed on the Line is equivalent to the work of three millions of men for one day.

The excavations average nearly 100,000 yards per mile.

Making deductions for the time lost by the men, and the unusually wet country through which the Line passes, the working time in which the Line has been completed is fifteen months.

THE CONTRACTORS' DINNER

We have engraved one of the festal commemorations of the Opening of the Railway – viz., the sumptuous Dinner given by the Contractors, Messrs. Stephenson, Mackenzie, and Co. The entertainment took place in the Assembly Room of the Crown and Mitre Inn and Coffee House. This beautiful apartment was elaborately embellished for the occasion. At the upper end of the room, behind the President's chair, was displayed a mantle of white silk, emblazoned with the Royal arms, and arched with laurel and flowers. On each side appeared an illumination, the initials "V.A.," and surmounted by the order of the Star and Garter, within wreaths of evergreen. Against the wall, at the lower end of the room, was displayed an elegant flag, emblazoned with the incorporated arms of the towns of Lancaster and Carlisle, typical of the union of these two important towns by railway. Against the walls, on each side, were ranged silk flags bearing the titles of all the Railways for which Messrs. Stephenson, Mackenzie, and Brassey are Contractors, about a dozen in number, and constituting in the aggregate upwards of 800 miles of railway communication. In addition to these decorations, appeared a number of other devices, illuminated by Royal crowns, stars, &c.; wreaths of evergreens gemmed with roses, and inclosing loyal and other mottoes. With the lustre of the illuminations, aided by the light of three chandeliers depending from the ceiling, the room presented a most brilliant appearance. The dinner, supplied by Mr. Jarman and Mrs. Wells, host and hostess of the hotel, was of the most costly description.

The dessert, wines, &c., were excellent. Mr. Scarisbrick, the celebrated organist of Kendal, presided at the pianoforte. The chair was occupied by John Stephenson, Esq.; G. Mould, Esq., officiating as Vice.

The number of guests exceeded 200, comprising not only the heads of the various departments engaged in the con-

Bridge over the Lune, from the churchyard, Lancaster

struction of the Railway, from the resident engineers and contractors downwards, but a considerable number of influential strangers interested in other lines, and many representatives of the trade of Carlisle, Kendal, Lancaster, Preston, &c.

At the lower end of the room was an orchestra, occupied by an instrumental band from Cobden's establishment, Cross Hall, near Chorley, and also by a party of glee singers, chiefly from Preston, conducted by Mr. Edward Scarisbrick, of Carlisle.

We regret that we have not space to report the very interesting after-dinner proceedings. After the customary loyal toasts had been duly honoured, the healths of the Chairman and Directors, the Engineers-in-Chief, the Secretary, and the Resident Engineers, of the Railway Company were drunk with great applause; and the toast of "Messrs. John Stephenson and Co." was received with immense cheering.

Mr. Stephenson's reply modestly glanced at the difficulties which he had overcome in the construction of the Railway. He concluded by observing it was consoling and satisfactory to mark the progress of science, and he trusted that the time would come, and that ere long,

when passengers could travel right through to Forfar. (Cheers.) The communication by iron rails between England and Scotland would be a great benefit to both countries; and, as an humble individual, he felt proud to have been the means of amalgamating both sides of the Sark by the Trunk Line, part of which had yesterday been opened. (Cheers.) He could only say he felt obliged for the kindness of the Company, in speaking of him and his partners as they had done. He only regretted he could not reply adequately to their compliments, for he would repeat that he would rather make a railway than a speech any day. (Loud cheers.)

Mr. Mould, Mr. Horn, and other speakers, in their addresses, entered into the details of the great work; so that the day's proceedings were stored with a vast amount of practical information, instead of the complimentary common-place which usually characterises post-prandial eloquence.

[ILN DEC. 26 1846]

OPENING OF THE SOUTH EASTERN RAILWAY – TO BOULOGNE AND BACK IN A DAY

This important railway, which has hitherto been open as far as Ashford only, is now completed to Folkestone, to which point the public were first conveyed on Wednesday last. The company having purchased the harbour of Folkestone, one of their objects is to establish a steam communication direct from the port to Boulogne, in addition to that which, when the line is completed, will be effected from Dover to Calais. To demonstrate the case with which this may be done, and at the same time to show the practicability of a trip from London to France and back in a day, an experimental journey was performed on Saturday last, the result of which was perfectly satisfactory.

At six o'clock a special train, containing the directors and their guests, started from the London-bridge station, which arrived at Folkestone temporary station, a distance of 82 miles from town, in two hours and 40 minutes, having stopped at five stations by the way. In Folkestone harbour the Water Witch steamer, commanded by Captain Hayward, was lying ready, and, as soon as the different passengers could be got on board, she started for Boulogne.

Among the gentlemen congregated on board the vessel were several Members of Parliament, and other distinguished persons who take a warm interest in the promotion of science. By half-past twelve all the passengers had landed, and a copy of the London papers of that morning, containing the debates in Parliament of the previous night, were presented by the chairman of the directors to the astonished authorities of the place, who had come down to the pier to meet their English visitors. The whole population of the town and neighbourhood had poured out to witness the embarkation, and the very extensive piers of the harbour were crowded with spectators – a dense mass of people, high and low, rich and poor, in every costume and colour possible even to French imagination – blue, pink, red, black, brown, green, and pretty faces without end. The same scene was continued on the way from the harbour to the shore, where, in a saloon over the baths, a collation had been prepared for the visitors. This was a splendid room, beautifully decorated, and capable of holding, perhaps 500 persons. A band

First Folkestone train passing the Bletchingley Tunnel

was in attendance, and played the English and French national airs. The entertainment did credit to the town by whom it was provided. The chair was occupied by Mr. Baxendale. On his right was M. Malinet, the *premier adjoint du Maire*. On his left was the Sous-prefet of Boulogne, and opposite were Count de Steffi, Colonel Sausot, and other leading inhabitants of the place. The eating and drinking having subsided, the chairman then gave "The health of Louis Philippe," which was received with the most deafening cheers, particularly from the English present. – Colonel Sausot (Colonel of the National Guard, and formerly Colonel of Bonaparte's Guides) then gave "The Queen of England, the People of England, and perpetual Peace between the two Nations." This gave the French

The prospect of day trips to France from London was opened up by the completion of the South Eastern Railway line to Folkestone. It seems odd to use an illustration of Bletchingley Tunnel for the opening of the final section between Ashford and the Channel port; Bletchingley is situated between Redhill and Godstone on the first part of the line to be opened, on 31 May 1842. The opening of the last section took place on 28 June 1843, although to a temporary station at Folkestone. Not only has the artist developed the cutting at Bletchingley into sheer cliffs towering above the line, but the train is working on the wrong line. The tunnel was 1,327yd long.

an opportunity of returning the compliment, which they did with all due gallantry and enthusiasm. – Mr. Baxendale, having returned thanks for "The health of the Directors," stated that, when the new iron steamers were put on the station, the people of Boulogne would be able to receive the London newspapers of the same day in four hours and a half after their publication. (Cheers.) – The health of the mayor having been drunk, the guests returned to the steam-vessel, escorted as before by a gazing and cheering multitude. They had remained two hours and ten minutes at Boulogne. The steamer got under way at forty minutes after two, and arrived in Folkestone harbour at half-past six. At five minutes past ten it arrived in London, stopping at eight stations to put down passengers. This trip, therefore, was performed in sixteen hours, allowing about two hours and a quarter at Boulogne. A steamer is being constructed by Maudslay and Field for Captain Hayward, which will do the distance to Boulogne (27 miles) in fine weather in two hours, so that the whole journey from London to Boulogne may in favourable circumstances be performed in four hours and a half. Thus persons leaving at six A.M., and returning to town at ten P.M., could (allowing for delays) spend at all events five or six hours at Boulogne.

[ILN July 1 1843]

Elsenham Station

Chesterford Station

Wendon Station

THE EASTERN COUNTIES RAILWAY – OPENING OF THE LINE TO CAMBRIDGE AND ELY

The views illustrating the opening of the branch line from the Eastern Counties Railway to Cambridge and Ely, and the line from Norwich to Ely, which appear in this number of our journal, represent the principal points in the new line. In a former number we gave illustrations of the principal points of the line then opened, so that our subscribers will now be in possession of a perfect illustrated itinerary of several hundreds of miles of railway through a country comparatively little known to those who live at any distance from it, yet full of interest, and worthy to be visited by the traveller, the artist, the agriculturist, and the man of general business.

On Tuesday last, at ten minutes before nine o'clock, a train of thirteen double carriages, with an open carriage, in which were the band of the Coldstream Guards, conveyed the worthy Chairman of the Eastern Counties Railway, the Directors and their friends, a host of men of science, engineers, and others, the Earl of Roden, and Lord Braybrook, the Bishop of Norwich, and many members of the House of Commons, from the London terminus, at Shoreditch, to Ely and Cambridge; and on the same morning, at half-past ten o'clock, a smaller train of carriages left Norwich, conveying many of the principal inhabitants, and the gentry of the county of Norfolk, to Ely, to meet the London train, and thence proceed in company with it to Cambridge, to partake of the banquet there prepared by the liberal hospitality of the Directors. We shall mention the places through which the trains passed, which will show the line of country creating the connection between the distances, and describe some of the points as fully as our limits will allow.

The first station, after leaving Shoreditch, through which the London train passed, is Stratford; a suburb of the Great Metropolis, of which the appearance conveys to those about to enter our vast emporium of commerce, science, arts, learning, and riches, but little idea of its magnificence and wealth. Indeed this is the worst entrance into London: the houses are mean, the inhabitants, though

Cambridge Station

The openings described refer to the lines from Bishop's Stortford to Cambridge and from Norwich to Cambridge, through Wymondham and Thetford. The former was built by the Eastern Counties Railway, the latter by the Norwich & Brandon (amalgamated with the Yarmouth & Norwich in 1845 to form the Norfolk Railway). Both were built to the eccentric 5ft gauge adopted by Braithwaite, the engineer of the ECR, and opened on 30 July 1845. The station building at Cambridge, depicted in the illustration, was described as a 'long, flat and handsome brick building . . . consisting of a double series of arcades'; one side enclosed the trains on the only platform provided while the other covered road coaches and carriages. The 'shade of Walton' referred to Isaak Walton (1593–1683), best known for his Compleat Angler. *The remarks about the carriages running as smoothly as balls on a billiard table was tempting providence; within a week a Norwich express derailed near Littlebury, killing one person and ripping up the track for 200yd.*

most industrious and respectable, are unfortunately not opulent. There is little to admire, and nothing to emprize. Lea Bridge, the next station, is somewhat picturesque. All Cockney fishermen find something here to recollect. The shade of Walton still hovers on the banks of the river, and the reminiscences of early times revive. At Tottenham the appearance of the country mends still more; the topographer recalls to mind the Cross which the piety of his ancestors erected on the spot within a short distance of where the railway passes, and the general aspect of the country is rural and pleasing.

The next station is Marsh Lane, which to describe would be an idle task; and then comes Edmonton, where, once the "Merrie Devil" played the strange pranks recorded by the early dramatist; and next to this is Waltham, situated in a pleasing country, famous for its "Cross," and more famous still for its ancient Abbey, in the vaults of which repose the bones of hundreds of the slain in Hastings, and among them the last remains of the ill-fated Harold. At Broxbourne, the next station, the appearance of the surround-

ing country is very delightful; there is little of the hill and dale, by which magnificent scenery is formed, but there is much to be admired both by the artist and the general spectator. The line then passes through the stations of St. Margarets, Ware, and Hertford. The name of Ware revives the recollections of John Gilpin and his adventurous ride, which Cowper has made immortal—

Said John, it is my wedding day,
    And folks would gape and stare,
If wife should dine at Edmonton
    And I should dine at Ware.

Here, also, a few years ago, and here, also, may still remain, for ought we know to the contrary, the great bed which attracted the attention of visitors in days gone by. At Hertford, the county town, are held the assizes, and on the outskirts is the College of the East India Company for the education of its civil officers.

The railway next passes the stations at Brydon, Burnt Mill, Harlow, and Sawbridgeworth – all pleasing villages standing in a good country, well wooded and watered, and luxuriant in its produce.

And then comes to Bishop Stortford, at the distance of thirty-two miles and a quarter from Shoreditch, and the old terminus of the branch line now carried on to Ely. The distance between this place and London was performed in the short space of one hour and a quarter, although the train stopped ten minutes at Broxbourne; so that the pace was upwards of thirty miles an hour. Here it is that the newly laid down rails commence; and highly to the credit it is of the engineer, Mr. Robert Stephenson, and of the contractors, that the work has been executed in so admirable a manner; during the whole transit of the train, no jolting, no undulating motion was perceptible; the engine and the carriages ran as smoothly as balls on a billiard-table, and not an oscillation was felt. Leaving Bishop Stortford station, the train passed on by Standstead station, close to the pleasant village of that name, by Elsenham and Newport stations; all built in the Elizabethan, or Tudor, style of architecture, neat and commodious; the houses of the last-named village presenting their white sides and fronts to the spectator, and standing out well from the green landscape by which they are surrounded. The scenery here is very delightful – a perfect English landscape, trim, neat, and highly cultivated; a village church – an ancient mansion – on the right hand, Short Grove Hall, the seat of Mr. Smith, a gentleman highly respected in his neighbourhood, and a fine specimen of an English squire. At Wendon station, or rather just before it is arrived at, the railway passes through an embankment of chalk, and a cutting of some length, the only thing of the kind throughout the whole line. At Littlebury are two specimens of tunnelling, the long one about a quarter of a mile, or rather more, in length; the other, shorter. The entrances are good specimens of the bold and early style of arch, over which are, as in our illustration, the armorial bearings of the noble house of Neville and Griffin, Lords Braybrooke.

We next come to Chesterford, a small village, in which is the celebrated inn kept by Mr. Edwards, well known, and long frequented, by the aristocratic visitors to Newmarket Races, the turnpike-road to which here branches off to the right of the line, which passes over the old London road.

Whittlesford, Ickleton, and Thetford, are the only places now between Chesterford and the town of Cambridge which

Ickleton Station

Brandon Station

Littlebury Tunnel

Norwich Station

require mention. The stations at these places are of the same character as the small stations along the line. The country here loses its picturesque appearance, and is flat and without interest, till the spectator comes in sight of Cambridge. The first thing which strikes the eye on approaching this ancient and time-honoured town and University, is the celebrated chapel of King's College, erected in the reign of Henry VI., and endowed most richly with broad lands and rich manors by that saintly, but unfortunate monarch. Here—

Grateful Science still adores
Her Henry's holy shade;

and here still exists the noblest specimen of Gothic architecture, of its class, in Europe. The four turrets which surmount the corners of the building, are conspicuous at a great distance. The University Church of St. Mary's is also seen from the Railway: a heavy square tower, without ornament or elegance, rises in the view, and attracts the eye.

The train reached the station at Cambridge at half-past eleven o'clock, having passed over fifty-seven and a quarter miles in two hours and forty minutes, the rate of speed, allowing for stoppages, being more than twenty-eight miles an hour!

It was in this town, that something more than two hundred years ago, lived the celebrated Hobson (from whose peculiar mode of doing business, comes the saying, "Hobsons choice – this or none"), the greatest carrier and post-master of his day, in England. The old man lies buried in the town, honoured by an epitaph by Milton:—

Here lieth one who did most truly prove
That he would never die while he could
      move;
So hung his destiny, never to rot,
While he might still jog on and keep his
      trot.

Here, also, lies the most celebrated coach-man of modern times, the well-known Richard Vaughan, whose *soubriquet* involves the naming of a place not mentionable to ears polite. Alas! what would these men say, could they now behold the railway, and witness the speed of the locomotive engine, with which compared, their utmost efforts would be but the crawling of a caterpillar.

[ILN AUGUST 2 1845]

Opening of the West Cornwall Railway – The Penzance Station [ILN SEPT 4 1852]

This scene would still be recognisable today as Penzance, with the well-known sea wall curving around the harbour which has appeared in so many photographs taken 'over the wall'. The West Cornwall Railway was originally conceived as broad gauge but applied for and was granted sanction to *retain the narrow (standard) gauge which had already been adopted by the Hayle Railway; the latter was to be rebuilt as part of the WCR and extended to Truro and Penzance. The reason for the change of mind over the gauge was the dilatory progress of the Cornwall Railway,* *ultimately to open between Plymouth and Truro in May 1859. The standard gauge line between Penzance and Redruth opened on 11 March 1852 and the line was extended to Truro Road on 25 August.*

THE GRAND CENTRAL RAILWAY STATION AT BIRMINGHAM

We now engrave the façade of this important structure, a view of the interior of which appeared in our Journal of last week.

The present Illustration shows the main front of the Station and Hotel, which is a handsome building in the Italian style, 312 feet long, and consists of a centre and right and left wings. The centre, which projects about twenty feet from the wings, is 120 feet long, and four stories in height. The lower story is composed of an arcade, divided by Doric pilasters into ten arches, and deriving richness of effect from each pilaster being flanked by piers of rusticated masonry. This story is built entirely of Derbyshire stone. Above the arcade runs a boldly-moulded plain cornice, above which, corresponding with the arcade, are ten handsome windows with pedimented heads, and at the foot of each is an elegant balcony. The first floor is divided from the second by a string-course, above which is another line of windows, with square heads and cornices. Above this is another string-course and a range of smaller and less ornamented square-headed windows, placed immediately under the principal cornice, which is remarkable for its breadth of treatment combined with fulness of detail. The whole front is surmounted by a handsome balustrade, broken at convenient distances by the introduction of pedestals, between which the chimneys are placed, with due regard for regularity of line; and as these projections are finished with cornices and caps, they add to, rather than detract from, the effect of the building. The edifice, with the exception of the lower story, is constructed of white brick; the window-frames, mouldings, cornices, and the rusticated quoins on the edges of the walls being formed in Portland cement. The wings are only three stories high, and are, of course, less ornamented than the centre – the windows being all square-headed, and the cornices plainer; but the mouldings and string-courses are carried on so as to preserve uniformity, and the upper string-course of the centre runs into the principal cornice of the wings. The Hotel, which is entered by a fine stone porch, comprises the whole of the left wing, the centre (excepting the ground-floor), and the third story of the right wing. The remainder of the edifice is devoted to railway purposes exclusively. The portion of the building fronting the Station is 504 feet long and 92 feet high.

On Saturday last the new Hotel (the Queen's) was the scene of a well-merited recognition of eminent services; when Mr. E. Watkin was presented with a handsome candelabrum and a silver tea-pot and stand, by his brother officers of the London and North-Western Railway Company, on the occasion of his leaving

Front of the new Grand Central Railway Station, at Birmingham

The Queen's Hotel, Birmingham, remained unaltered in function and name until demolished in 1964 to make way for the shopping precinct that now covers the concourse of the new station. The reception for Edward Watkin is of particular interest, since his move to the Manchester, Sheffield & Lincolnshire Railway in 1854 was a major step in his career that was to lead to chairmanship of the South Eastern, the Metropolitan and the Great Central, and a knighthood. He also became a leading light in schemes to construct a Channel tunnel, which would give him control of railways from Manchester to the Continent. The last main line to London, the Great Central, was his most remarkable achievement.

that line to take the management of the Manchester, Sheffield, and Lincolnshire Railway. An elegant cold collation was provided by Mr. Scott, the manager of the establishment. Captain Huish presided; and amongst the gentlemen present were the Marquis of Chandos (the chairman), Mr. Benson (the deputy chairman), Mr. Glyn and Mr. Thomas Smith (directors), and Mr. C. E. Stewart (the secretary), of the London and North-Western Company; Mr. Denison, M.P. (the chairman), Mr. Packe (the deputy chairman) and Mr. Seymour Clarke (the general manager), of the Great Northern Company; Mr. Ellis (the chairman), Mr. Beale (the deputy chairman), and Mr. Carbutt and Mr. Hutchinson, of the Midland; and several other gentlemen. The cloth having been withdrawn, and several toasts given, the Chairman, in an appropriate address, presented the testimonial to Mr. Watkin, which was acknowledged by that gentleman in a suitable reply; after which the company retired.

[ILN JUNE 10 1854]

THE GRAND CENTRAL RAILWAY STATION AT BIRMINGHAM

The progressive extension of the railway system has led to the erection of several buildings for its general purpose; and these structures are entitled to rank amongst the most stupendous architectural works of the age. It is true that a certain critic of the day has sneered at the general taste displayed in our railway edifices, and the designs of engineers may not be sufficiently ornate for the architect's standard; nevertheless, the combined genius of both professions to meet our railway requirements have produced some striking results; and the London and North-Western Company, as the proprietors of the largest railway in the kingdom, have just added to their buildings a station of corresponding magnitude; erected for the accommodation of their own immense traffic and that of the Midland, Stour Valley, and North Staffordshire lines. The grand Central Station, which was opened on Thursday last June 1st, is situated in New Street, Birmingham. The entrance is at the bottom of Stephenson-place, where is a plain gateway leading to the main front of the station and hotel, which we shall

New Grand Central Railway Station, at Birmingham, opened on Thursday, June 1

---

describe more fully and illustrate next week. Entering the Station by an arcade, we arrive at the booking-offices for the respective railways; and, passing through these, emerge on a magnificent corridor or gallery, guarded by a light railing, and open to the Station (but enclosed by the immense glass and iron roof), from whence broad stone staircases, with bronze rails, afford access to the departure platform. We then stand on a level with a long series of offices, appropriated to the officials of the Companies; and a superb refreshment-room, about eighty feet long by forty broad, divided into three portions by rows of massive pillars.

We have now reached the interior of the Station, which our Artist (Mr. J. M. Williams) has so accurately and effectively represented upon the preceding page; and the details of which we abridge from *Aris's Birmingham Gazette*:—

We must ask the reader to imagine that he stands on a stone platform, a quarter of a mile long; that behind him is a range of forty-five massive pillars projecting from the Station wall; that in front of him are ten lines of rails, four platforms, and a broad carriage-way, bounded by another range of forty-five massive iron pillars; and that, above all this, there stretches, from pillar to pillar, a semi-circular roof, 1100 feet long, 205 feet wide, and 80 feet high, composed of iron and glass, without the slightest support except that afforded by the pillars on either side. Let him

add to this, that he stands on a stone platform a quarter of a mile long, amidst the noise of half a dozen trains arriving or departing, the trampling of crowds of passengers, the transport of luggage, the ringing of bells, and the noise of two or three hundred porters and workmen, and he will have a faint idea of the scene witnessed daily at the Birmingham Central Railway Station.

The roof merits more particular description. It consists of 36 principals or arches of iron, strongly framed together. The upper bar, which is called a rib, is curved in the segment of a circle; and each end rests upon a pillar; but between the rib and the pillar an ingenious system of rollers is introduced, so as to allow of either expansion or contraction by atmospheric changes. From each rib depend, at regular intervals, twelve "struts," which are laced together by diagonal bars. The lower ends of the struts are attached to a bar of iron, called the tie-rod; and which corresponds in curvature with the rib. Each of these principals weighs about 25 tons. They are placed at intervals of 24 feet from each other. Each rib is composed of five distinct pieces riveted together. These ponderous metal bars were raised by means of a travelling stage; and the last rib was fixed on the anniversary of the day when the first pillar was set up. The pillars weigh 3 tons 12 cwt. each. From rib to rib numerous "purlins" are stretched, and these serve to support the smaller divisions of the glazed roof. The roof is composed of glass and corrugated iron – the former bearing a proportion of three-fourths to the latter, which runs along in a broad strip on each side, and in two bands on the crown of the arches.

The ends of the station, both at Worcester-street and Navigation-street, are screened off down to the tie rods with glass. It is proposed, we understand, to continue the roof to Navigation-street-bridge, but the continuation will be ridge-and-furow, like the Great Exhibition of 1851. We must not omit to notice that ample provision is made for ventilation, by raising a lantern over the centre bay of the principals, and continuing it down the whole length of the roof. An elegant iron bridge crosses the station from the booking-offices' corridor, and affords passengers a safe and efficient means of reaching the further platforms by flights of steps descending from the bridge.

The Station-roof has been constructed by Messrs. Fox and Henderson; and the building contracted for by Messrs. Bremsen and Gwyther. The engineer is Mr. Baker, who has been assisted by Messrs. Livock and Son.

We shall complete our description and illustration of this fine Railway structure next week.

[ILN June 3 1854]

OPENING OF THE LIVERPOOL DOCKS OVERHEAD ELECTRIC RAILWAY

The opening of this railway on Saturday, Feb. 4, by Lord Salisbury, who turned on the electric current from the "generating station," at the Bramley-Moore Dock, is an interesting example of the application of one of the most wonderful forces of nature revealed by modern science to a mechanical agency of locomotion. The company of which Sir W. B. Forwood is chairman took over, in 1888, the powers obtained from Parliament by the Mersey Docks and Harbour Board for constructing such a railway on their own estate, running the whole length of the Liverpool Docks, a distance of six or seven miles, to which extensions, both at the north and at the south ends, were authorised by Parliament last Session, connecting the docks with the Lancashire and Yorkshire Railway in one direction, and with the Cheshire lines at the other end. The engineers were Sir Douglas Fox and Mr. J. H. Greathead, with Mr. S. B. Cottrell as resident engineer and general manager. The contractor, Mr. J. W. Williams, began his work in the winter of 1889. The railway, 16 ft. above the ground, is laid upon an iron floor, resting on plate-iron girders, supported by channel-iron columns, these columns standing at intervals of 50 ft., except when a greater span, 100 ft., strengthened by bowstring girders, is required to leave a passage for bulky goods to the docks, or where there is a swing bridge, at the entrance to the Stanley Dock, or a tilting bridge, near the Sandon Dock. The line has many curves in its length, but will be as safe as any railway laid on the ground; the rails are fixed directly to the iron floor, without any ballast. It is intended only for passenger traffic, with thirteen stations, and will be a great convenience to all persons having business or employment at any of the docks. A train will consist of two carriages, which can together carry fifty-six passengers, first class and second class. The fare is three-pence or twopence to or from any of the stations. Signals are made automatically by the train passing the stations. The locomotive power is an electric current generated by four Elwell-Parker dynamos, worked by four horizontal compound steam-engines; the current is sent along eight thick underground wires, capable of transmitting a force equal to 2000-horse power; it reaches the steel "conductors," placed on porcelain

The Pier Head Station

insulators between the rails all along the line; with these, by sliding hinged "collectors," the "motors" of the passing train form electrical contact, picking up the force by which the train is propelled at a speed which may be thirty-five miles an hour. The plant for generating electricity is supplied by the Electric Construction Company, of Wolverhampton. It can send a train every three minutes.

[ILN FEB 11 1893]

The generators for the Liverpool Overhead Railway were 'opened' on 4 February 1893, a month before service began on the first section between Alexandra and Herculaneum. The line was fully opened by the end of 1896 and a connection was made with the Lancashire & Yorkshire Railway at Seaforth in 1905. It was originally promoted by the Mersey Docks & Harbour Board in 1878 as a single-track line with passing places. The Board of Trade objected to this and it was eventually constructed by local businessmen as a double-track line with electric traction to obviate the risks of cinders in dockland.

It was a railway of 'firsts': the LOR was the first elevated electric line in the world and the only overhead urban railway in Britain; it had the first railway escalator, at Seaforth Sands between 1901–6; it was the first railway in Britain to adopt an automatic signalling system, using the intermittent-contact system and electrically operated semaphore signals; in 1921 it became the first railway to have track-circuited automatic colour-light signals, installed by Westinghouse. The frequency of train service fluctuated from one every two minutes to one every ten minutes. The line operated until 31 December 1956 when the cost of replacing the iron decking brought about its closure.

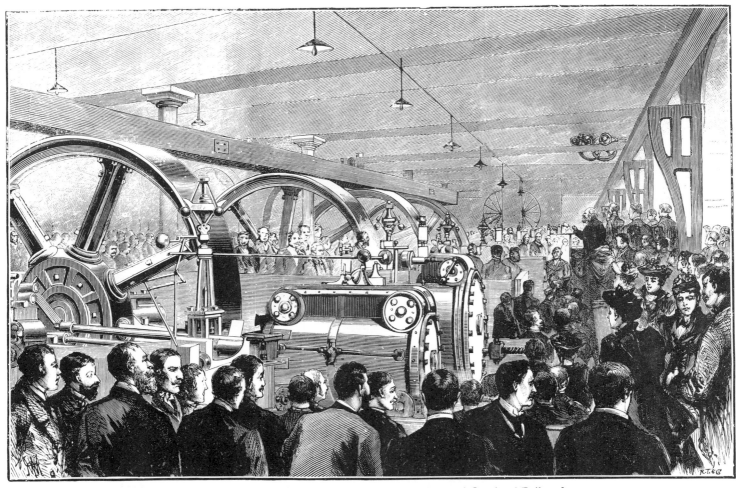

Lord Salisbury turning on the electric current [Liverpool Overhead Railway]

THE OXFORD AND BIRMINGHAM RAILWAY

The completed portion of this new line of railway was opened on the 30th ult., when the event was celebrated by a *déjeûner* at the Regent Hotel, Leamington.

The line from Oxford to Fenny Compton (31½ miles) is part of the Oxford and Rugby line, the portion of the latter lying between Fenny Compton and Rugby having long since been abandoned. From Oxford to Banbury the railway has been opened about two years; and the line just opened extends from Banbury to Birmingham (65 miles).

The "Battle of the Gauges," fought principally in reference to this line (and practically illustrated in our Journal), must be in the recollection of our readers. The Oxford and Birmingham line was projected in 1845: among the provisional directors were some members of the Grand Junction board; and, in fact, the Grand Junction, in the first instance,

promoted and gave every possible encouragement to the scheme, for the purpose of rendering themselves, by means of it and the Oxford and Rugby line, independent of the old London and Birmingham. The two Companies afterwards amalgamated, and offered the most determined opposition to the Bill for the construction of the line. The original estimated cost of the line was about £900,000, including the borrowing powers; but, according to the *Railway Times*, the actual outlay will amount to about £3,000,000, including the premium of £500,000, paid by the Great Western on the purchase of the line.

The Oxford and Birmingham line has been constructed by Messrs. Peto and Betts, under the superintendence of Mr. I. K. Brunel. The following are the most important engineering works on the line: – The Harbury cutting between Banbury and Fenny Compton, half a mile in length, and 110 feet deep, out of which there have been excavated about

3,000,000 cubic yards of marl and limestone; an embankment immediately beyond the cutting, and formed out of the earthwork thereof, four miles in length, and of the average height of 23 feet; this is stated to be the largest cutting in the world. (*See Illustration.*) The next important work on the line is the Whitmarsh cutting, out of which have been taken 350,000 cubic yards of red marl; a viaduct at Leamington, and bridge over the High-street, and later 130 feet span; an aqueduct at Myton, constructed so as not to impede the navigation of the Birmingham and Oxford Canal; a bridge over the Avon, 160 feet in length; viaduct at Warwick, of 30 arches, 25 feet span each; a bridge over the road and canal at Warwick, composed of iron girders, 150 feet span; the Hatton embankment, three miles in length, and 25 feet in height; the Hatton cutting, out of which 500,000 cubic feet of earthwork have been taken; the Finwood-bridge, 50 feet high and 140 feet long; an iron bridge over Stratford

Canal, 60 feet in length the Blythewood embankment, one mile long and 40 feet high; the Solihull viaduct, 500 feet long; an embankment at Haycock's-green, one mile long and 48 feet high; the Haycock's-green cutting, one mile long and 30 feet deep; a bridge under the Bristol and Gloucester Railway, constructed on an embankment, 50 feet high – the trains of the Bristol and Gloucester line having worked over it during the progress of the works; an iron bridge over the Warwick canal 150 feet long; and a bridge over the Coventry-road into Birmingham, 60 feet long. The whole of the works from Leamington and Warwick were constructed in 40 weeks. Some of the stations are of pleasing design, of which that at Leamington (*See the Illustration*) is a good specimen. They were designed by Mr. T. H. Bertram, the resident engineer, and erected by Mrssrs. Jay and Co., of London, under personal superintendence of Mr. T. Pearson, of that firm. They were commenced in May last, and are now nearly completed.

[ILN Oct 16 1852]

Cutting at Harbury

The Birmingham & Oxford Junction Railway was a subject of the gauge battle and, later, a cause of embarrassment for Mark Huish, who was compelled to do a volte face *when his circumstances changed with the formation of the LNWR; having supported the GWR against the London & Birmingham Railway over the Oxford & Rugby Railway while secretary of the Grand Junction Railway, he had to oppose the broad gauge once he became general manager of the LNWR. Huish went on to purchase four-fifths of shares in the B&O in circumstances that led to a Parliamentary Inquiry and the lease of the B&O by the GWR. The section of line between Fenny Compton and Rugby, which the* ILN *mentions as having been abandoned 'long since', was in fact only abandoned in 1849 and only ¼ mile of embankment from the junction with the B&O had been built; the earthworks may still be seen. The line from Oxford to Banbury was opened on 2 September 1850; the earthworks were for double track but only a single line had been laid. Work on the B&O began in 1847 but was delayed by financial stringency and protracted negotiations with the LNWR for a joint section of line at Leamington and a joint station in Birmingham. Hopes of the latter failed and work on the last section*

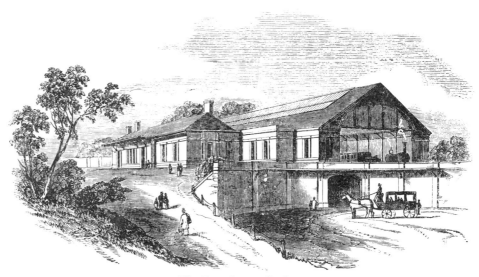

The Leamington Station

into Snow Hill station began in 1851; Snow Hill station itself was not begun until January 1852 because of the problems involved in the purchase and clearance of property. It is interesting to note that the section of line between Moor Street and Snow Hill station was largely built as an open cutting and then covered, the land on top being sold. The special train on 30 September was to run from Paddington to Birmingham and back to Leamington Spa for the banquet. The train consisted of ten carriages and was hauled by Lord of the Isles.

The ILN *discreetly draws a veil over the fact that this train was involved in an accident on the way to Birmingham, crashing into two waggons that a mixed train was trying to detach at Aynho. The* Lord of the Isles, *on which Gooch was travelling, was derailed, putting an end to ideas of reaching Birmingham. The mixed train engine eventually took the perturbed passengers to Leamington and an impromptu special was laid on for the guests from Birmingham. The* ILN *has managed to render Acock's Green as Haycock's-green.*

LONDON

THE CITY TERMINUS OF THE SOUTH-EASTERN RAILWAY, CANNON-STREET

In the Number of this Journal for Dec. 31, 1864, was a View of the space of ground between Dowgate-hill and Little Bush-lane, Cannon-street, which had been cleared for the site of the vast railway station and magnificent hotel to be erected by the South-Eastern Railway Company for the accommodation of their City traffic. Another of our Illustrations, published a few months before, showed the progress of construction of the railway bridge across the Thames, a little below Southwark Bridge, designed to connect the South-Eastern and Charing-cross lines with this proposed terminus in Cannon-street. The Engraving we now present, below, gives a view of the station and bridge, as seen from the river, in a state which approaches completion, as it is expected that they will be ready for opening in May.

The City Extension of the South-Eastern Railway branches off from the line between the London Bridge station and Charing-cross, in the vicinity of the Borough Market and St. Saviour's Church, Southwark; there is another junction about 300 yards farther on, towards the Charing-cross end of the line, the two branches meeting not far from the river, and thence running together upon the bridge. This has five lines of rails, which, by a fanlike extension of the bridge, open out on arrival at the station to eleven. The roadway of the bridge is level, except a camber of about 8 in. in the girders. The clear headway at Trinity high-water mark is 25 ft. 4 in. at the highest, and 24 ft. 8 in. at the lowest points between the water surface and the metal. The bridge has five openings – two of 125 ft. and three of 135 ft. 8 in. The line is supported by ranges of four columns for each opening sunk to the sub-strata of the London clay. The columns are iron cylinders, which, being sunk some 50 ft. or 60 ft. below high-water mark, until a satisfactory foundation had been reached, have been pumped

The destruction of Cannon Street's roof during World War II was a sad loss, for its position right on the bank of the Thames gave it a striking appeal. The station was designed by Sir John Hawkshaw, and was opened on 1 September 1866. The water tanks in the towers referred to in the article were to provide hydraulic power for the lifts down to the vaults and for carriage cleaning. The platform on the west side was used only by the 20-minute shuttle service with Charing Cross (it was later increased to every 10 minutes). During World War II the station was badly bombed and all the glass was removed for safety, never to be reinstated.

The new station of the South-Eastern Railway, Cannon-street, City

dry and filled up with concrete. At the base the cylinders are 18 ft. diameter, tapering to 12 ft. at or about low water; at this uniform diameter they are carried up to the girders. The columns are fluted and have moulded capitals; they support the roadway, borne on thirteen girders, 8 ft. 6 in. deep. The end of these girders rest upon transverse box girders placed on the tops of the columns. The width of the bridge is 80 ft., the same as that of Westminster Bridge. In addition to the five lines of railway, there will be a footway on each side of the bridge, projecting 8 ft. in width, supported by massive cantilevers placed at about 6 ft. 7 in. between centres. The girders on the outer sides of the bridge will be ornamented by raised moulded panels of ironwork, the whole depth of the panels and upper open rail being about 14 ft. 6 in. The footway will have an ornamental iron railing on the outer side. The quantity of cast and wrought iron used in this bridge, exceeds 12,000 tons.

The station, as well as the bridge, was designed and has been erected under the superintendence of the engineer, Mr. John Hawkshaw, F.R.S., assisted by Mr. J. W. Barry, Resident Engineer; the contractor for the station is Mr. George Wythes, his manager being Mr. Cannin; and the quantity of material employed in its construction is almost inconceivable. Twenty-seven millions of bricks have been used in the erection of the arches under the station – most of which are groined – and in the superstructure. These, laid end to end, would extend to 3835 miles; if laid closely side by side and end to end they would cover an area of 843,750 square yards, or 174 acres. The valuable cellarage under the station amounts to 139,380 superficial feet. The quantities of other materials employed in the works is no less great in proportion, including 2050 tons of wrought and cast iron. The length of the station is 685 ft., the width inside 189 ft., and the total height 106 ft. 6 in., the height of wall being 48 ft. 6 in. to the springing of the arched glass and iron roof. This roof is a segment of a circle, except the louvre which surmounts it, and has a rise of about 5 ft. from its base, and a side of 13 ft. 8 in. in depth. About two thirds of the arched roof is glazed. The portion between the louvre and the main light is covered with corrugated zinc, and the lower portion of the roof is slated. The side walls, which average 6 ft. 6 in. thick, are of solid brickwork, the extensive dead

surface being relieved, outside and inside, by ranges of arched bays. The river façade, when finished, will present an imposing appearance, with its ornamental towers at each corner, rising to above the ridge of the louvre; the front lattice girder being also dealt with tastefully by a boarded band round the circle, with diagonal panels; and a band of equal width extending between the springs of the arch, glazed in keeping. The towers (which are to be used for water-tanks) will have arched openings above a bold moulding, and be roofed partly with slate, partly with zinc. They, as well as the abutments on both sides of the river, with their rusticated quoins of stone, will add much to the architectural effect. A pilaster will be carried up over each of the ranges of river columns to 12 ft. above the roadway, and surmounted by an appropriate cornice.

The roof of the station, one of the greatest works of its kind, has been constructed by Messrs. Cochrane, Grove, and Co., of Woodside, Staffordshire, under an engagement to Mr. Wythes, the general contractor for the whole. It consists of nineteen principal, with as many intermediate, ribs, averaging about 34 ft. between centres, exclusive of the principal terminals. The tension rods of the principals are 5¾ in. diameter. The principals have struts from the rib to the tension-rod from 4 ft. to 30 ft, with diagonal bracing in addition. The roof has intermediate purlins of lattice bracing.

The station is laid with nine lines of rails, and contains five platforms for the arrival and departure of trains, with a road leading out of Upper Thames-street under the arches for cabs and carriages to enter the station to pick up passengers; the exit being under an archway connected with the hotel and booking-offices, which will cross the tunnel now being formed by the Metropolitan District Railway Company, under the fore court of that building, into Cannon-street. The platforms and roads are very nearly completed, and it is anticipated that the line will be opened for traffic about the 1st of May.

The city Terminus Hotel fronting Cannon-street is built by Messrs. Lucas, from the designs of Mr. E. M. Barry, architect of the Charing-cross Hotel; but we must reserve it for a future illustration.

[ILN Feb 24 1866]

NEW STATION OF THE GREAT WESTERN RAILWAY, AT PADDINGTON

The Station of this fine railway, as originally constructed, was intended as a temporary provision for business purposes, without any attempt at ornamentation. At the same time it was resolved by the Board of Management that, hereafter, a Station should be erected more in accordance with the magnificent railway itself; and this resolution has been carried out in a manner in every way worthy of its object, in the above Station, which was opened for business last month. A certain critic of the day has asserted that railway buildings are scarcely worthy of the genius of architecture being employed upon them (or words to that effect); and in the present Station, though without the fear of the above dictum, the constructors have met the question by producing a design, which realises one of the first conditions of fitness, that it should at once convey a correct idea of the purpose for which it has been erected, in this instance, as a Railway Station. It is the joint work of Mr. Brunel and Mr. M. D. Wyatt: the former having arranged the general plan, and the engineering and business portion; the latter the architectural details in every department. The principle adopted by them, was to avoid any recurrence to existing styles, and to make the experiment of designing everything in accordance with the structural purpose, or nature of the materials employed – iron and cement.

The Station, it will be seen by the following details, which we quote from the *Builder*, is very extensive.

The office buildings are 580 feet long, varying from thirty to forty feet in width. The departments for directing and managing the affairs of the company are carried on in the upper portion of the building, and those in connection with the traffic to and from the station in the lower part.

The space occupied by the platforms and lines of railway under the curved roofing is 700 feet long and 240 feet 6 inches wide, and contains four platforms and ten lines of railway. The two platforms on the departure side of the station are respectively 27 feet and 24 feet 6 inches wide; and the other two, on the arrival side, are 21 feet and 47 feet. The latter is of stone. The roofing over the above space is divided into three longitudinal openings, with two transepts, each 50 feet wide, at one-third and two-thirds of the length. The lengths of the openings are each 700 feet, and of the respective widths of 70 feet, 102 feet 6 inches, and 68 feet.

The roofing contains 189 wrought-iron ribs, or arches, of an elliptical form, and arranged in rows of three each, parallel to one other, with twelve diagonal ribs at the transepts. The height to the under side of the ribs in the central opening is 54 feet 7 inches from the line of rails; from the springing it is 33 feet 9 inches. The height in the side divisions is 46 feet. The ribs against the building are supported by sixty-three cast-iron pilasters, or square columns, and those to the other portion of the roofing rest on sixty longitudinal wrought-iron girders, each about 30 feet long, and supported by sixty-nine circular columns. The ribs over the central opening are 1 foot 8 inches high, formed of quarter-inch plate with flanges top and bottom, giving a width there of 6 inches. The ribs over the side openings are 1 foot 4 inches high, formed in the same manner. The central half of each of the curved roofs is glazed, and the other portion is covered with corrugated galvanised iron.

The execution of the design has been superintended by Mr. Brunel, principally through one of his chief assistants, Mr. Charles Gainsford. The work was done by Messrs. Fox, Henderson, and Co.

[ILN July 8 1854]

The GWR board originally tried to come to an agreement with the London & Birmingham Railway for use of its terminus at Euston Square; Brunel was not sorry to hear that the attempt had failed. The station that he and Digby Wyatt built befitted his vision of a line of communication from London to New York via Bristol; the PS Great Western carried her first passengers from Bristol to New York in April 1838, two months before the first section of the GWR opened, from Paddington to Maidenhead. The departure side was opened in January 1854 and the arrival side in the following May. The three aisles (a fourth was added in 1913–16) were broken by two transepts, one of which reached the West wall by the oriel window of the directors' balcony, and which were intended to accommodate traversers to move carriages from one track to another: they were never introduced. Brunel and Wyatt had both been involved with the Great Exhibition, and had naturally admired Paxton's industrialisation of the building process. Brunel accordingly employed Paxton glass roof lights in part of the roof. The decoration of the station was left to Digby Wyatt who devised a motif, based upon traditional Moorish designs, that was used on the columns, end screens and walls. The original circular cast-iron columns were replaced by hexagonal steel ones during and immediately after World War I.

The Great Western Railway new terminus, at Paddington

The new Victoria Railway Station at Pimlico [ILN MAY 4 1861]

*The line into Victoria from Stewarts Lane
was built by the Victoria Station & Pimlico
Railway, strongly backed by the London,
Brighton & South Coast Railway. The
Grosvenor Canal provided a suitable course
and the canal basin at the western end of
Victoria Street a convenient site for the
station. Construction began in 1859. The
LBSCR had subscribed two-thirds of the
VS&PR capital and therefore obtained its
own section of the terminus while arrange-
ments were made with the London,
Chatham & Dover Railway and the Great
Western Railway for their lease of the
eastern side. Naturally this entailed mixed
gauge track from Longhedge Junction,
Battersea, which the GWR would reach by
the West London Extension Railway.
Grosvenor bridge across the Thames was
the first railway bridge over the river in the
London area; it was designed by John
Fowler, engineer of the VS & PR, and took
exactly one year from the commencement of
construction to the passage of the first train,
on 9 June 1860. The Brighton side of the
station opened in October 1860 while the
LCDR and GWR side came into use in
August 1862. The influential inhabitants of
Belgravia had insisted upon the sleepers*

*being mounted upon rubber to reduce the
noise. The GWR ran trains to Victoria
from Southall, and later from Uxbridge,
Reading, Slough and Windsor, with a
number of other brief experiments. The
Great Northern was to run trains from
Barnet, the Midland from South Tottenham or Hendon both via the City Widened
Lines through Farringdon, and Lough-
borough Junction, and the LNWR from
Broad Street via the West London line.*

THE CHARING-CROSS BRIDGE

This bridge is for the purpose of
extending the South-Eastern Railway
from London-bridge to Charing-cross,
where a station will be erected upon the
site of the Hungerford Market. The
station will be on the same level as the
Strand. The bridge is to be erected upon
the site of the present Suspension-bridge,
which will be taken down to make room
for the new bridge. The Thames at this
point is 1350 feet in width, and is 30 feet
deep at high water. The bridge is to be
supported on cast-iron columns sunk
deep into the bed of the Thames. Upon

these columns the superstructure of the
bridge, which will be wholly of wrought
iron, is to rest. The bridge will have a
minimum width of 70 feet – sufficient for
four lines of way, with footpaths seven
feet in width on each side, on which the
passenger traffic across the Suspension-
bridge will be continued. The bridge will
be of eight spans, each 15½ feet; and the
height of the under side of the bridge
above Trinity high-water mark will be
nowhere less than 25 feet. The Act of
Parliament authorising its construction
was obtained last Session. The designs of
the bridge have received the sanction of
the Admiralty and of the Conservators of
the River Thames, and the works have
been commenced. Mr. Hawkshaw is the
engineer of the bridge and railway, and
Mr. George Wythes the contractor; but
the bridge, as well as the other iron
bridges along the line, are to be constructed and erected for the contractor by
Messrs. Cochrane and Co., who are
executing the iron-work for Westminster-
bridge.

[ILN MARCH 31 1860]

Charing-Cross Railway Bridge

King's Cross Terminus, Great Northern Railway (Mr. Lewis Cubitt, Architect) [*Builder*, 1851]

Regarded as the terminus that most conveniently serves the heart of London, Charing Cross was reached by a line from Cannon Street West Junction (later Metropolitan Junction) and crossed the Thames on the site of Brunel's 1845 suspension bridge, built to attract custom from Surrey to Hungerford Market. The chains and ironwork of Brunel's bridge were sold and used in the Clifton suspension bridge, although the new lattice girder bridge used Brunel's two red brick piers and abutments. Footways had to be provided on both sides of the new bridge to replace the suspension bridge. A halfpenny toll was charged until abolished in 1878 when the SER was paid the colossal sum of £98,000 by the Metropolitan Board of Works.

It seems probable that this was an artist's impression of what Cubitt's King's Cross station would look like, since the illustration appeared in the Builder *for 1851 and the station was opened on 14 October 1852. The view is looking north so no attempt has been made to include Cubitt's austere façade which still forms the south end. When opened, King's Cross was the largest station in London, erected for less than the cost of Euston's Portico and Great Hall. The 800ft long train shed spanned 16 lines – one departure and one arrival platform with 14 carriage roads between them. On the west side were offices, a boardroom and the station facilities; on the east side was the cab road covered by the flying buttresses to support the thrust of the laminated wood girders carrying the roof arches. The buttressing effect of the office block proved adequate but the timber trusses on the east side had to be replaced by wrought-iron girders in 1869–70. The departure side was dealt with 17 years later.*

THE HIGH-LEVEL CRYSTAL PALACE STATION

The South London and Crystal Palace Railway, from Brixton to Camberwell, through Peckham, Nunhead, and Sydenham, issuing by a tunnel beneath the road in front of the Crystal Palace on its western side, has now been open several weeks; and though, from the unfinished state of the intermediate stations, there has not yet been sufficient opportunity to develop the local traffic, the superior convenience of the new Crystal Palace station is already felt by many visitors who take their passage either from the Victoria or Ludgate-hill stations of the London, Chatham, and Dover Railway, in order to avoid the tedious walk up half a mile of corridors and staircases imposed on those arriving by the Brighton Company's line. We give a View of the high-level station, which is situated on the slope of the Upper Norwood-hill, over-looking the remains of Dulwich Wood and may be approached on that side, by the Farquhar-road and the Palace-road, from Gipsy-hill. The platform of the station being on a level with the lower floor (in the machinery department) of the Crystal Palace, railway passengers will have easy access by a handsome and well-lighted subway, 40 ft. wide (of which also we present an illustration), ascending to the main floor, either in the centre transept or behind the concert-room by a broad flight of steps. This subway is not yet finished, so that they have to walk across the public road and go in at the doors behind the Handel orchestra; but the distance from the station to the central transept is only thirty yards. The station has four platforms, of which two are set apart for the use of first-class passengers only, and these will communicate by a separate passage with the first-class entrance in the centre transept; the entrances for second and third class passengers being nearer the south transept, and all the arrangements for them being distinct from those for first-class passengers. The traffic to the Crystal Palace will be separate from the residential traffic of the district. There will be room in the station and sidings for engines and carriages enough to carry away 7000 or 8000 passengers in an hour; and there is ample accommodation for goods traffic. As the traffic during the present month will consist exclusively of Crystal Palace passengers, the trains will not run on Sundays: at present nineteen trains run daily each way. The length of the line, from the Lyndhurst-road station, Peckham, is six miles and a quarter. The capital, consisting of £675,000, has been raised on preferred and deferred half shares, and the company has borrowing powers to the extent of £225,000. It is to be worked by the London, Chatham, and Dover at fifty per cent on the gross receipts. When all the authorised lines of the Chatham and Dover Railway are complete the new station will communicate directly with the stations at Victoria, Farringdon-street, Charing-cross, Cannon-street, London-bridge, King's-cross, Paddington, all stations on the Metropolitan and Great Northern Railways, and with Clapham, Brixton, Camberwell, Deptford, New-cross, Greenwich, Woolwich, and all stations on the South-Eastern Railway and London and South-Western Railways. The line has been constructed by Messrs. Peto and Betts; the engineer is Mr. Turner; Mr. Shelford is the resident engineer, and Mr. Edward Barry has been the architect of the Crystal Palace station, which was built by Messrs. Lucas, at a cost of about £100,000. The South London portion, between Peckham and Brixton, was constructed by Mr. Firbank, of Newport, Mr. Jacomb being the resident engineer.

[ILN Sept 30 1865]

The Great Exhibition in Hyde Park attracted just over 6m visitors between May and October 1851. In August 1852, the rebuilding of the Crystal Palace began on a site at Sydenham Hill by a company set up by its builder, Joseph Paxton. The intention was to create a Winter Park and Garden, providing the finest display of rare plants and trees, and to display copies of the world's finest statuary. Queen Victoria opened it in June 1854 in the presence of 40,000 people. The LBSCR line to the low-level station necessitated a walk along a 720ft glass-covered colonnade so the station of the Crystal Palace & South London Junction Railway, which deposited its passengers alongside the Palace, was preferred. The new line, from Peckham Rye, was opened on 1 August 1865. Services were suspended during both wars and the line beyond the junction at Nunhead was closed on 20 September 1954.

The new High-level Station at the Crystal Palace

Works at the Midland Railway Terminus, Euston Road

It was during the construction of the approaches to St Pancras through the burial ground of the church that a body in a coffin was exposed, causing a great scandal. Proper reburial was arranged and a young assistant named Thomas Hardy was sent to supervise; two poems resulted from the experience. Before the Midland Railway ran into St Pancras, it had shared King's Cross with the GNR, obviously not a satisfactory position for a company with the Midland's aspirations. Sanction for the 50 mile extension from Bedford to St Pancras was granted in 1863 and work began on the new terminus in 1866. Barlow's original plan for a double or triple roof span was changed by the suggestion of James Allport, the Midland's general manager, that the space below the station could be used as cellerage. A barrel of Burton beer became the unit of Barlow's calculations; the harmful effect of intruding columns, which a roof of two or more spans would require, encouraged the decision to produce a single span. Regular goods trains ran to Agar Town goods station from September 1867 and St

Pancras itself was opened without ceremony on 1 October 1868. Only the foundations of the hotel were complete.

THE MIDLAND RAILWAY WORKS, EUSTON-ROAD

The vast works now going on at King's-cross, on the north side of Euston-road, in Old St. Pancras-road, and throughout Somers Town and Agar Town, for the construction of the new terminus of the Midland Railway, have been repeatedly noticed in this Journal. Their magnitude far exceeds anything else of this kind. Half Somers Town was demolished to make room for the new station and hotel, which will occupy, including the station yard, about ten acres, or the space inclosed between Euston-road, Old St. Pancras-road, Skinner-street, and Brill-row, as far north as the gasworks. Beyond that locality the Midland lines pass through St. Pancras church-yard to Agar Town, crossing beneath the North London Railway to St.

Paul's-road, near Camden-square. One peculiarity in the approaches of the Midland Railway has greatly increased the difficulty and cost of their construction. Besides the high-level line, carried from Camden-square to Euston-road upon a viaduct of moderate elevation, which will lead to the platform of the proposed terminus, there is a tunnel line from Camden-square to the Metropolitan Railway station at King's-cross. In the account we published, last week, of the new works of the Metropolitan Railway Company, this tunnel was particularly mentioned; and we gave an Illustration of the appearance of its entrance, between that of the Great Northern tunnel and the entrance to the underground portion of the Metropolitan tunnel of the Midland Railway will be a most important means of traffic, as it will bring passengers arriving from Derby or Manchester directly into the heart of the City, to Aldersgate and Moorgate street; or else, by the Farringdon-street junction, to Ludgate-hill, and the London,

Chatham, and Dover line; or, by the Metropolitan Extension, round Brixton, Clapham, and Wandsworth, to the Victoria station at Pimlico. This will probably give the Midland for a time some advantage over its chief competitor, the London and North-Western, which brings passengers no nearer to the City than Euston-square. Notwithstanding the late discussions respecting the expenditure of the Midland Company, the works at King's-cross are still carried on with the greatest activity; and the Illustration engraved on page 160, showing their appearance a week or two since, does not quite represent the forward state, at this moment, of the brickwork covering the tunnel in the foreground of our view. The sketch was taken, it may be explained, from the south side of the proposed site, next to Euston-road, having King's-cross to the right hand, and the Brill, in Somers Town, to the left, with the church spire of Oakley-square in the distance. The enormous span of the iron arches to form the roof of the station, which will be far larger than those of Charing-cross or Cannon-street, fills half the breadth of this view. It is 240 ft. in width, and the height from the railway level to the crown of the arch is 105 ft. The arch is not semi-circular, but obtusely pointed, being designed on the radii of four different centres. It will be covered partly with glass, and partly with slate. It is really wonderful to see the manner in which this huge fabric is put together, piece by piece, rising in the boldest curves from the massive iron "springers" on each side, and meeting at the ridge of the roof. Every successive portion, whilst being constructed, rests upon a timber centering, or scaffolding, a substantial framework of beams, with platforms and ladders, by which the workmen have access to all parts of the arch. The fires kindled for heating rivets, and for other processes belonging to the ironwork, may be seen burning on these lofty platforms at different stages. The timber framework, in several divisions of width, moves forward upon wheels as the work goes on, serving to aid the construction of one iron arch after another. The prodigious masonry and earthwork of the basement are scarcely less worthy of admiration. Here will be the great store-cellars of Burton ale, and other depositories of the Midland goods traffic. The floor of the station itself, which consists of convex plates of wrought iron, "Mallet's buckle-plates," fixed between longitudinal and cross girders of the same material, resting upon cast-iron supports, is a marvel of strength attained by mechanical invention. The building of the hotel, for which Mr. Gilbert Scott prepared a superb design, has not yet been commenced. The underground works, besides the tunnel, which crosses the upper line of railway twice, have involved some alterations of the Fleet sewer, and other troublesome tasks of that nature. The chief engineer is Mr. W. H. Barlow, F.R.S.; and the assistant engineers are Mr. Campion (resident engineer) and Mr. W. M. Grier. The contractors for the earthworks and masonry, including the tunnel, are Messrs. Waring Brothers; the contractors for the ironwork are the Butterley Company, of Derbyshire. It is expected that the station and its approaches will be finished by the end of this year. We shall take a future opportunity of giving a more complete and precise description of their plan.

[ILN Feb 15 1868]

THE METROPOLITAN RAILWAY

This remarkable undertaking – which had been so long in abeyance that the public had well-nigh despaired of its ultimate accomplishment – has now been commenced in earnest, and the contractors are proceeding vigorously with the works at various points. We have, therefore, collected a few details which we think will be of interest to our readers. The need of railways communication between the City and the great series of railway on the north of the Thames, both for passengers and goods, had been long grievously felt, but the difficulties in the way of carrying a railway into the City appeared to be almost insuperable. To have a railway, after the American fashion, passing through a densely-populous district, and crossing on the level our overcrowded streets and thoroughfares, was utterly out of the question; and scarcely less so to carry an unsightly viaduct through the heart of the metropolis. The only alternative was that adopted by the Metropolitan Company – namely, that of an underground communication, by which the most densely-crowded districts could be traversed without the slightest annoyance or obstruction to the existing traffic. A reference to the map will show that the railway starts from opposite the Great Western Railway Hotel at Paddington, with a fork up the South Wharf-road to join the Great Western Railway on the level, near the site of the old passenger station. The line then crosses the Edgware-road, and enters the New-road, which it follows to King's-cross, it being one of the peculiarities of this railway that it occupies, throughout the greater part of its course, the under surface of the existing roadways, thus avoiding the enormous expenditure which would otherwise have been necessary for the purchase of valuable house property.

From King's cross the line, avoiding the House of Correction at Coldbath-fields, and passing for some distance under the Bagnigge Wells-road, takes an almost straight course to Farringdon-street; and this part of the railway, except when passing under roadways, will be in open cutting.

In addition to the principal terminal stations at Paddington and Holborn-hill, commodious passenger stations will be erected at the Edgware-road, Baker-street, in the triangular plot of ground opposite Trinity Church, Regent's park, Hampstead-road, Euston-square, and King's-cross. The terminal stations, and the Edgware-road, Regent's-park, and King's-cross stations, will be open, or covered with a glass roof; the others, as that at Baker-street (vide engraving), will be commodious, airy, and well lighted with gas . . .

It is intended to run light trains at short intervals, and calling at perhaps alternate stations, and all risk of collision will be avoided by telegraphing the arrival and departure of each train from station to station, so that there will always be an interval of at least one station between the trains. The traffic is to be worked by locomotive engines of a novel and ingenious construction. In order to obviate the annoyance in the tunnel arising from smoke and the products of combustion, the locomotives will have no firebox, but will be charged with hot water and steam at a certain pressure to be supplied by fixed boilers at the termini, and will be furnished with a large heater to assist in maintaining the temperature. It is estimated that each locomotive will thus carry with it sufficient power to enable it to effect the double journey. In order to test the efficiency of locomotives constructed on this principle the directors have instructed Messrs. Stephenson and Co. to build a broad-gauge engine, which will be employed in the construction of the works.

[ILN Supplement April 7 1860]

Proposed station at Baker Street

The mixed gauge Metropolitan Railway from Bishop's Road, Paddington, where a physical connection was made with the GWR, to Farringdon Street was opened on 10 January 1863. It was worked by the GWR and carried 29,000 passengers in the first three weeks. A train of gas-lit rigid eight wheelers operated every fifteen minutes. As the article states, the intention was for the Metropolitan to be worked by a new form of steam locomotive using hot firebricks instead of a live fire, but 'Fowler's Ghost', named after the railway's engineer, proved a failure. The small firebox failed to generate enough heat in the long cylinder of firebricks to produce enough steam. Instead Gooch provided tank engines with surface condensers to consume the smoke and exhaust steam. Relations between the companies had not been good for some years, and in August the GWR withdrew its stock, compelling the Metropolitan to borrow GNR engines and carriages until its own were delivered. The new design by Beyer Peacock provided the Metropolitan with the 4-4-0T engine that would meet its needs until electrification in 1905. The railway was a great success; in 1865 15m ordinary tickets were sold; in 1875 the figure was 43.6m. The effect of daylight descending through shafts, as seen here, has been recaptured in the 1983-4 renovations.

NEW STATION OF THE LONDON AND NORTH-WESTERN RAILWAY, EUSTON-SQUARE

The gigantic works which have been for some time past in the course of erection at the metropolitan terminus of the North-Western Railway being now completed, we have, this week, to chronicle their opening to the public, and to present our readers with some of the Illustrations which we have prepared of the buildings. Our views comprise the great Hall, and one of the Pay-offices, and some of the bas-reliefs which decorate the great Hall.

Passing under the magnificent Doric entrance, which has always formed so grand a feature to the entrance of this line of railway, the huge pile of building recently erected at once arrests the eye. This building, which has been designed by Philip Charles Hardwick, Esq., and erected by Messrs. William Cubitt and Co., at a cost of about £150,000, will now form the grand entrance to the London and North-Western Railway.

The structure, on the exterior, is of plain Roman style of architecture, and is 220 feet long by 168 feet in width. At the southern front there are five entrances, over which extends, for a considerable distance from the face of the building, a capacious awning, under which carriages may draw up and passengers alight without being exposed to wet or any other inclemency of the weather. The outer-doors just mentioned lead into what is called the "outer vestibule," which is 22 feet in depth and 64 feet in width, having a beautifully designed mosaic pavement, constructed of patent metallic lava, within a border of Craigleith stone. On the northern side of the "outer vestibule" are again five other entrances, leading into the Grand Hall, or Vestibule; and this hall, for size and grandeur, is probably unique: in dimensions it is truly gigantic, being 125 feet 6 inches in length, 61 feet 4 inches in width, and 60 feet in height. At the northern end is a noble flight of steps, leading to a vestibule, in which are doors opening into the general meeting room, the board room, and the conference room, and the gallery which runs round the hall – thus giving facility of communication to an infinity of offices connected with the railway traffic, &c.

The style of architecture adopted is Roman Ionic, and it has been treated with the utmost skill. The ceiling is formed of panels, deeply coffered, the bands forming the panels being enriched with a double guilloche pattern on them. The hall is lighted by attic windows above the entablature, between which are massive

The Great Hall, Euston-square Station

Euston, London's first main-line terminus, was opened on 20 July 1837, and was renowned for, and is still associated with, the magnificent portico designed by Philip Hardwick which sadly has been lost to us. This article describes the Great Hall which had been opened on 27 May 1849. Its grandeur did not stifle criticism of deficiencies in the layout and other facilities which became more obvious as traffic grew. In 1852 a Carrara marble statue of George Stephenson by E. H. Baily was placed at the foot of the stairs leading up to the Shareholders' Room, which had seating for 400. Lord Stamp, the president of the LMS, made the first noises about a complete reconstruction in 1933, but slow progress with the plans and the intervention of Hitler postponed the day. British Railways did not tackle the project for some years, spending £½m on titivating the elderly station and even being sufficiently enlightened to redecorate the Great Hall and Shareholders' Room according to Hardwick's original designs – quite a contrast to the philistinism that characterised the management's response to efforts to save or re-erect the Doric Arch in 1961.

consoles to support the ceiling; these consoles are as peculiarly effective and striking in character, as admirable in workmanship. The pillars at the head of the stairs, and corresponding ones at the southern end of the room, are painted in imitation of dark red granite, the capitals and bases to represent white marble. The vestibule at the head of the stairs is lighted from above; and, over the very handsome doorway leading to the general meeting-room, is a noble bas-relief, of which we have given an Illustration, and shall presently describe, as we shall also do of the panels in the attic at the corners of the room, in which are bas-reliefs, some of which we have represented. The general meeting-room we shall describe and illustrate in a future Number; as also the directors' boardroom, an exquisite apartment. The area of the hall and the staircase is formed of the best Craigleith stone. The walls, which are rendered with grey Martin's cement, are painted to simulate granite. The hall is warmed by hot-water pipes, on Perkins's system; and, to promote ventilation, some of the panels

in the ceiling are perforated, and behind them are coils of hot-water pipes; and in the general meeting-room a similar arrangement has been followed. At the southern end of the hall an illuminated clock is to be placed.

As this hall will, in fact, be a great ante-room to those departments in which the passenger traffic is carried on, the luggage will be brought here from the outer vestibule, and a large counter for refreshments will be one of the conveniences of the place.

The bas-reliefs which adorn the panels in the corners of the hall are eight in number, and typify the chief cities and boroughs with which the North-Western Railway communicates. They are London, Liverpool, Manchester, Birmingham, Carlisle, Chester, Lancaster, and Northampton. Of these, we have selected London, Liverpool, and Manchester, as affording good specimens of the general character of the bas-reliefs. London is typified by a female figure, murally crowned, and bearing in her hands the sceptre of Royalty, and the

rudder, emblem of maritime power; below her sits an old man with a long beard, symbolical of Father Thames, and by her knees a genius, his arm resting on a globe; and at his feet emblems of music, painting, and the drama, indicate the universality of the art knowledge of the great metropolis of the world. The background is filled with St. Paul's and a group of shipping. Liverpool is a sitting female figure, resting on a rudder, with a genius by her side holding a quadrant. An aged man, having shells and corals in his hair, symbolises the Mersey: in his right hand he holds a trident, and his left rests upon a well filled cornucopia. A portion of the Exchange, and a group of shipping, fills up this characteristic group. Manchester is individualized by a laurel-crowned female, sitting and holding a distaff her hand resting on a bolt of cotton; a genius by her knees holding the shuttle, indicative of the cotton-spinning notoriety of Manchester. Mercury, emblem of commerce, sits in the foreground, busy drawing plans on a piece of paper; and the background is composed of piles of cotton

Bas-relief of London, in the Great Hall

goods, a huge factory, and the tower of the cathedral. Birmingham has the symbols of the iron trade – Vulcan, with his hammer and anvil, being in the foreground: a beautiful vase, showing the variety and perfection of the iron-works, and the portico of the new Town-Hall, fill up the group. Chester, with its far-famed dairy produce, its cheeses, its walls, and its venerable cathedral, is well characterised. Carlisle shows its cattle market, its manufactures, and its maritime symbols, with its cathedral tower; Lancaster its furniture and other manufactures; and Northampton has in its emblems the shoemaker, as well as its agricultural symbols, and a horse to typify its celebrated horse fair.

The large group in alto-relievo over the door leading into the general meeting-room, is an extremely picturesque and effective composition. We have accordingly selected it for illustration. It represents Britannia supported by Science and Industry. The whole of these bas-reliefs and the massive consoles reflect great credit on the gifted artist, Mr. John Thomas, whose talents have so often been noticed in our Journal, by whom they were designed and carried out, and through his courtesy we were enabled to make our drawings from the bas-reliefs when they were in his studio.

Leading from the grand hall on the basement, on the eastern and western sides, are several glass doors connecting it with the newly constructed booking-offices. That on the eastern side, through which the general passenger traffic of the line will pass, is the largest, being 60 feet by 40 feet; whilst that on the western side, which is to be appropriated to the London and York, the traffic of the branch lines, and special purposes, is 56 feet by 33 feet. The architecture of these booking-offices is in keeping with that of the main building. They have each light and elegant galleries passing round them on a level with the gallery of the great hall, and connected therewith, as well as with all the offices. The roof of each is a splendid cupola springing from the four corners, where it is apparently supported upon brackets resting upon lions' heads, the whole being surmounted by a stupendous and exceedingly light and elegant dome of glass. The arrangement of this department reflects the highest credit on those who have designed it.

We have mentioned that the whole is erected from the designs of Philip Hardwick, Esq.; and we must not forget to name his able Clerk of the Works, Mr. Bavin.

We have to tender our thanks to Mr. Hardwick for his ready acquiescence to our request to illustrate this noble building, and the facilities he has afforded our artist.

[ILN Jun 2 1849]

Arrival of cattle at the Railway Terminus, Euston-square [ILN Dec 15 1849]

The idea of unloading cattle at Euston station inevitably seems incongruous to the modern traveller who has long been accustomed to the separation of goods and people. In the early years of railways, facilities had not been sufficiently developed to permit segregation, so passengers would doubtless have had to suffer the inconveniences of sharing the platforms with cows on more than one occasion. The dramatic improvement in the quality of food in towns and cities must have been one of the most evident and universal benefits to be derived from the new form of transport. It certainly transformed the routine of livestock farmers who no longer had to worry about the problems of escorting their animals to markets, sometimes entailing treks of a hundred miles or more, with all the worry about their weight and condition on arrival. In time many of the old drove roads returned to nature.

Inauguration of the Albert Viaduct at Saltash by the Prince Consort

VIADUCTS AND BRIDGES

OPENING OF THE CORNWALL RAILWAY

As there are sharp curves at both ends of the bridge, which causes the line to assume a horseshoe form, of which the bridge is the arch, an excellent view of it can be obtained on approaching it from either the Cornwall or Devon side. The train, therefore, after reaching the Saltash station, continued on for about a quarter of a mile, to give the Royal party an opportunity of inspecting the bridge from one of the best points of view. The train having returned to the Saltash station, the Prince Consort alighted, and, accompanied by Mr. Woolcombe, walked across the bridge and minutely examined the works. His Royal Highness then proceeded to examine the works underneath the bridge; and, having partaken of a collation, he embarked on board the *Vivid*, and proceeded down the Hamoaze amidst a Royal salute from the battery on the hill. The Royal party again shortly afterwards disembarked at Tor Point, on the Cornish side of the harbour, whence

they rode over to Tregantle, on the western side of Mount Edgecumbe, where some considerable defensive fortifications are in course of erection. His Royal Highness, after a short stay, again embarked on board the *Vivid*, in which he was conveyed to Mill Bay, whence he proceeded to the railway station, where he partook of a substantial luncheon before taking his departure for London. The Royal train started from Plymouth shortly before seven o'clock, and arrived at Windsor a few minutes after one a.m.

The Cornwall Railway was formally opened on the following day throughout its entire length to Truro . . . and was thrown open for public traffic on Wednesday.

[ILN MAY 14 1859]

The construction of the Royal Albert Bridge was a lengthy process, partly due to the impoverished state of the Cornwall Railway. Preliminary work on the site began in 1848, but nothing was done between 1849 and 1852; when work resumed the bridge was to accommodate only a single track – two had originally been planned. Brunel's experience with the bridge at Chepstow proved useful, since the form which took its designer's name, 'Brunel', was again adopted, although the tubes were oval rather than circular. Having witnessed the floating of the tubes of the Menai bridge, Brunel was in a more favourable position than had been Stephenson, and the operations went without a hitch. Brunel's chief assistant, Brereton, supervised the second span's installation, while his employer wrestled with the almost intractible problems of the SS Great Eastern. Sadly Brunel was not present for the opening by Prince Albert. The accident referred to at the end of the article (see page 42) occurred on 6 May 1859 when the locomotive Elk *and two coaches of the down evening train from Plymouth derailed on the approach to Grove Viaduct near St Germans and plunged into the mud of the creek. The poor quality of some of the details in the engraving is surprising – one would have expected a more competent artist to be assigned a royal subject.*

Departure of H.R.H. Prince Albert in the "Vivid" Steamer

The Royal Albert Viaduct at Saltash -

ACCIDENT ON CORNWALL RAILWAY

An accident involving the loss of three lives occurred on this line, about three miles west of the Albert Bridge, on the night of Friday (last week). An engine and some portion of the train following it were precipitated from a viaduct twenty-eight feet high into the mud and water below. The driver, the fireman, and one of the guards were killed. After some delay all the passengers were removed from their perilous situation, very few having received any material injury.

[ILN JUN 4 1859]

SUSPENSION RAILWAY TUNNEL

The Chester and Holyhead railway on leaving Chester will keep near the banks of the river Dee to Flint, and will then proceed near St. Asaph and Denbigh to Avergelly, from whence following the coast of the Irish Sea, it will proceed by Conway and Bangor to the Menai Strait, which it will cross by means of a suspended tunnel, and so enter the Isle of Anglesea. Its course will then lie near Llangefui and Llanerchymedd, and having entered Holy Island by crossing the straits, will proceed at once to its destination, Holyhead. The tunnel proposed by Mr. Robert Stevenson to cross the Menai Straits is intended to be formed of iron, and to be suspended from massive stone piers, as shown in the engraving. It will simply consist of a strong iron beam of about one hundred and fifty yards in length and fifteen feet in depth, which will be hollow to allow the free transit of the trains, and so supported as to prevent vibration. Gigantic piers will be built on either coast, in which the ends of the tunnel will be firmly imbedded.

This stupendous undertaking originated with Mr. Robert Stephenson, and is the first of the kind ever proposed.

[PICTORIAL TIMES MARCH 12 1846]

OPENING OF THE BRITANNIA BRIDGE FOR TRAFFIC

In our Journal of March 9, we recorded the passing of the first train through this magnificent structure, on March 5; and then gave the details of the experiments made by Mr. Stephenson and his staff of engineers, to test the capabilities of the tube to sustain the equilibrium of forces.

During the trial of the dead-weights, a very interesting episodical proceeding took place in the interior of the Carnarvonshire land tube – that of putting the last rivet into plates, making exactly the 2,000,000th that have been used. The rivet having been put in by Mr. Mare, was driven home and fastened by Mr. Stephenson, by successive strokes with a huge hammer. This ceremony was followed by the waving of hats and the deafening acclamations of the workpeople.

Mr. Stephenson, in a brief address, eulogised the industry of these men, and their devotion to their work; adding that he could never forget the ingenuity and the labour exhibited in the humbler sphere of the great operation, nor the masterly manner in which the work had been carried out under the superintendence of Mr. T. Fleet, who had distinguished himself as a sterling and honest workman.

This picture is of great interest for, if it accurately reflects Robert Stephenson's thinking at the time, it depicts an intermediate design of the Britannia Bridge which an unusual event was to modify. Selecting a site about a mile to the west of Telford's suspension bridge, where Britannia Rock would make a good foundation for a pier, Stephenson first proposed a bridge of two cast-iron arches of 305ft span with the trackbed 105ft above high water. The Admiralty rejected the design so Stephenson turned to the idea of suspending wrought-iron channels between piers. A trellis work of members was replaced by vertical wrought-iron plates, and a channel became a tunnel to gain extra strength. The final development of the design was prompted by the launching of an iron steamship in the Thames; the Prince of Wales *stuck after a failure of the launching gear, causing her hull to remain unsupported for 110ft. The total absence of damage determined Stephenson's decision to omit the chains.*

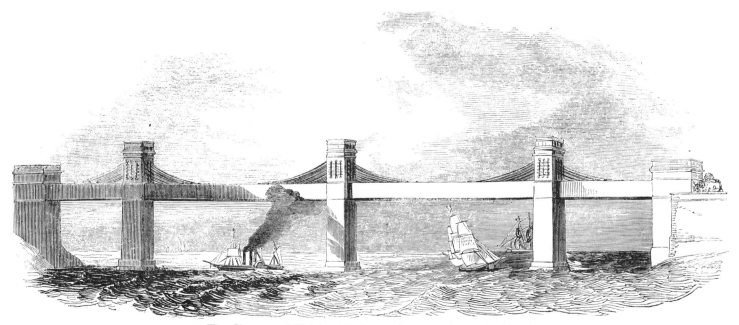

The Chester and Holyhead Railway – iron tunnel over the Menai

On Friday and Saturday last (March 15 and 16), Capt. Simmons, the Government Inspector for the Railway Commissioners, made his official inspection of the vast tube, accompanied by Mr. E. Clark (the resident engineer) and Mr. Hedworth Lee (the engineering manager of the Chester and Holyhead line); when a series of important experiments took place to ascertain the law of deflexion and the absolute structural strength of the fabric. The experiments consisted in observing the deflexions under successive loads, the passing of three locomotives, with a train sufficient to cover each of the tubes, through the bridge at various speeds; and the running of locomotives and tenders, without trains, at variable rates of progress. The last experimental Government train was a heavily laden one of coal-waggons, weighing 240 tons, with three locomotive engines. This was run through the tube at the ordinary rate at which such trains travel, from ten to twelve miles an hour; and the deflection, as taken by a deflectometer fixed in the centre tower, was scarcely perceptible. This train was then drawn completely over one of the tubes, and there left as a dead weight, while Captain Simmons descended, and made a minute inspection of the masonry, the riveting, plate-work, cellular top and bottom of the tubes, riveting, and other arrangements, which occupied a considerable time. On returning to the tube, the deflection caused by the load was found to be about three-fourths of an inch. Similar experiments made in the other tubes exemplified the perfect success that has attended the continuity of the beam, the most remarkable feature in the structure, caused by the junction of each of the before isolated tubes, for, as the engines entered upon the small land tube, the motion due to their progressive weight was ascertainable in every tube, even over to the further extremity of 1560 feet in length. Locomotives in steam were then passed through as fast as practicable, but only at twenty miles an hour, owing to the curves at either end. The deflection was the fraction of an inch, and the vibration scarcely perceptible – the tonnage weight of the tube itself acting, in reality, as a counterpoise or preventive to vibration. Captain Simmons was understood to be extremely interested with the bold design and immense strength of the remarkable high-road, which is now described by its engineers as strong enough to support a line-of-battle ship suspended,

The Britannia Tubular Bridge – Entrance from the Bangor side

or a load of locomotives piled one on the top of the other over its whole surface. The experiments were considered satisfactory, as tending to show that all parts of the stupendous work obeyed the calculated requirements, and to a certain extent determined the conjectural questions of duration and stability to arise under the test of every day usage.

On Monday, the 18th, the Britannia Bridge was opened for traffic. The first passenger train that passed over was the Express from Holyhead, at three o'clock, P.M.; it was crowded with passengers, anxious to be among the first to pass through the tube. The train arrived at Euston-square exactly at eleven o'clock; thus effecting a saving of an hour over the usual transit.

The full benefit of the change will not, however, be experienced until the forms of Government routine have had time to come into operation. In the meantime, the mail bags will continue to be taken out of the train at Bangor, and conveyed round in a cart to Llanfair, where the train will await their arrival.

We understand that an invitation was

forwarded to Prince Albert, requesting the honour of his Royal Highness' presence at the opening of the Bridge; and that a courteous reply has been returned, stating that the Prince Consort's engagements prevented his attendance on Monday, that the Prince of Wales was too young to undertake the journey alone, and that it was her Majesty's intention to pay a personal visit to the line at an early opportunity.

The opening of the line on Monday was celebrated by a dinner at the Royal Hotel, in Holyhead, given by the Hon. W. A. Stanley, M.P. There were about 40 or 50 guests present, comprising the officers of the Government and Chester and Holyhead steam-boats, the officers of the Chester and Holyhead Railway, and the principal inhabitants of Holyhead. The healths of Mr. R. Stephenson and others were drunk after the usual loyal toasts, and the party broke late hour.

The inauguration was to have taken place on the 17th, St. Patrick's Day, out of compliment to the natives of the sister isle; but that day happening to fall on a Sunday, this could not be accomplished.

The Britannia Tubular Bridge across the Menai Straits – sketched from the Anglesey Shore

The design of the tubes on the Britannia Bridge was worked out during a series of detailed experiments on a 75ft model of a tube at William Fairbairn's shipyard at Millwall. The bridge was to push back the known limits of building techniques and engineering skills to a remarkable degree for a single structure. Work began on the masonry in spring 1846 and on the tubes with the first delivery of wrought iron in June 1847. Before the iron plates could be punched for rivets and erected, they had to be flattened or straightened with 40lb

hammers. At night arcs of light could be seen showering sparks over the proceedings as white-hot rivets were thrown 40ft up to those working on the top of the tubes; 900 tons of rivet iron was used. The extraordinary achievement which the bridge represented was symbolised by the four couchant lions placed at the bridge approaches; they were carved by the sculptor John Thomas who did work on the Houses of Parliament and at Somerleyton Hall, church, village and school for Sir Moreton Peto, the famous railway contractor.

The floating of the tubes into position and the gradual lifting by hydraulic presses were fraught with tension and difficulties. The scale of operations was unprecedented: each of the main tubes weighed over 1,500 tons; the chains on Telford's bridge, which had also been floated out, weighted 23½ tons. The last rivet was driven in by Robert Stephenson on 5 March 1850, after which a train of 700 people hauled by three locomotives crossed the bridge. On 18 March, the bridge opened for traffic, completing the final link in the LNWR main lines.

Our Artist has depicted the train entering the tube from the Bangor side; showing two of the four colossal statues of lions – "we must not," says Sir F. Head, "compare them to sentinels, for they are couchant – which in pairs terminate the land ends of the abutments that on each side of the Straits laterally support its approaching embankment." They are composed of the same grey Anglesey marble as the towers. "These noble animals, which are of the antique, knocker-nosed, pimple-faced Egyptian, instead of the real Numidian form, although sitting, are each twelve feet high, twenty-five feet long, and weigh thirty tons. Their appearance is grand, grave, and imposing – the position they occupy being 180 feet in advance of the entrances into the two tubes, which so closely resemble that over the drawbridge into a fortress, that one looks up almost involuntarily for the portcullis."

In the larger View we have the stupendous Bridge seen from the Anglesey shore. Beneath are the deep Menai Straits, in length about 12 miles, through which, imprisoned between precipitous shores, the waters of the Irish Sea and of St. George's Channel are not only everlastingly vibrating backwards and forwards, but at the same time, and from the same causes, are progressively rising or falling from 20 to 25 feet with each successive tide, which, varying its period of high water every day, forms altogether an endless succession of aqueous changes.

The first thing that strikes the spectator on approaching the Cyclopean piles of masonry is the vast masses of stone of which they are constructed. The limestone is in such immense blocks, that to the eye of the uninitiated it seems almost impossible to move them; yet they *were* moved with perfect ease; for such is the ingenuity, simplicity, and strength of the tackle used, that it appeared to be a matter of small moment whether a block of stone weighed one ton or twelve tons.

When the tubes are riveted together into two continuous hollow beams, each 1513 feet in length, as stated by Sir F. Head, it will far surpass in size any piece of wrought-iron work ever before put together, its weight, 5000 tons, being nearly equal to that of two 120-gun ships, having on board, ready for sea, guns, powder, shot, provisions, crew, flags, captains, chaplain, admiral, and all! The cost of this stupendous bridge to the Chester and Holyhead Railway Company, to the 30th of June last, had been

half a million of money; and the entire expense has been estimated at from £600,000 to £700,000.

The great work has now been four years in hand, and is nearly complete, while Telford's suspension-bridge took eight years. The floating and actual transference of the tubes has occupied since June last.

[ILN MARCH 23 1850]

RAILWAYS IN THE SCOTTISH HIGHLANDS

It was only last Session that the Government grant in aid of the maintenance of "Highland Roads and Bridges" was discontinued. It is now more than a hundred years since the Government of the day saw that the only way of making the Scottish Highlands amenable to law and loyal to the Crown was to construct roads through all the disaffected districts. This was done, and, afterwards, Parliament voted £5000 a year for the proper maintenance of these roads, attaching, however, to the grant conditions which secured from the proprietors of land a very ample contribution to the same object. The money was well spent. There are, probably, no finer roads in the world than those which for nearly forty years have been under the management of the Government; and by their means the country has greatly prospered. Last year Parliament came to the conclusion that the Highlands should pay for their own roads; and not without reason, for property had increased immensely in value, and not only roads but railways flourished, yielding a higher dividend than many great lines in the heart of England.

Greater roads, however, than those which first subjugated the Highland clans are rapidly in progress, and promise to benefit the country even more largely. A continuous line of railway now connects the county of Ross; and railway schemes are ripe for execution which will bring the rivers, moors, and forests of Sutherland within twenty-four hours of London. On the 23rd ult. an extension of thirty-five miles beyond Inverness was successfully completed and opened for traffic. The country through which it passes will pleasingly surprise those whose notion of the region beyond the Grampians is the traditionary idea, imbibed by Gibbon, of gloomy hills assailed by the winter tempests, lakes concealed in a blue mist, and cold and lonely heaths over which the

deer of the forest are chased by a troop of half-naked barbarians. The line of the Ross-shire railway is, in fact, as sunny, as pleasant, and as fertile as almost any district in the kingdom. It is rich in wheatland, highly cultivated, and studded with townships and villages in which frugal men have realised fortunes. Three large navigable rivers flow through it, and at the mouth of each there is a wide area of champaign country, yielding a rent which is not exceeded except in the best parts of England and the Lothians. The extent of arable land is not, however, great; within some miles of most of the stations the tourist will find Highland scenery of the wildest and most romantic character. At every point the landscape is bounded by a noble panorama of hills on one side, and on the other, except for a few miles, by the sea.

Leaving Inverness, the railway crosses the river at the harbour of the town. The bridge, which we have engraved, is a very handsome structure of almost white stone, designed by Mr. Mitchell, the engineer of this and the other Highland railways. Owing to the loose nature of the soil, it was very difficult to get a good foundation – a difficulty experienced in a still greater degree at the construction of a suspension-bridge a little higher up the river, erected at the expense of Government. The latter, designed by the late Mr. Rendall, cost £30,000, besides the expense of purchasing some buildings and compensating persons who were injured by the progress of the works. The railway viaduct, a much more attractive structure, cost only £11,000. A few hundred yards further on, the line crosses the Great Caledonian Canal on an iron swing-bridge of 74 ft. span, and passes by a rocky promontory on the confines of the Fraser country, which was once the scene of a desperate clan fight. For nearly fourteen miles from this point almost all the land is in the possession of gentlemen bearing the name of Fraser, and of the head of the clan, Lord Lovat, whose seat is about three miles distant from the station at Beauly, or Beau-lieu, a pretty village on the banks of the river of the same name, which is crossed by a timber viaduct of 450 ft. long. Entering the county of Ross, we enter also the country of the Mackenzies, one of the most powerful of the Highland clans, and which played a distinguished part in the history of the North. The view from above Sir Kenneth Mackenzie's house, looking upon the great valley of the

The Inverness and Ross-shire Railway: Viaduct over the river Ness

Relatively few articles or illustrations appeared in the ILN *on Scottish railways, and the choice of subject was often idiosyncratic, as has been noted elsewhere. It was not long after the opening of the Inverness & Nairn Railway in 1855 that thoughts turned to the possibility of a line to the north. The likely expense of bridging the River Ness, the Caledonian Canal and the rivers Beauly and Conon led to a suggestion that a steamer might run from Nairn to the north side of Cromarty Firth; a railway would be built to Tain and Invergordon, and perhaps Dingwall. The Inverness & Ross-shire Railway dismissed such ideas and began building a line from Inverness to Invergordon in 1860; Joseph Mitchell, whose name is synonymous with railway construction in the Highlands, was engineer. As a road inspector and engineer he had previously been responsible for spending much of the £5,000 per annum referred to at the beginning of the* ILN *article. The Inverness – Dingwall section opened in June 1862 while the remainder to Invergordon opened in March 1863.*

Conon, and the wooded slopes and rocky ridges which form a background for Braham Castle, the residence of Lord Seaforth, is one of the finest in Scotland. The distant hills are peculiarly picturesque in outline and rich in colour, while the foreground is varied by woods and water, the former including some very handsome specimens of the old Scotch fir, gnarled like oaks, and of a glowing ruddy colour in the bark. Another great river has to be crossed, the Conon, famous in Celtic lore for the number of dread tales of second-sight, witches, and warlocks with which it is associated. The bridge is of stone, five arches of 77 ft. span, with a skew of 45° to the river. We understand that it was an engineering work of some delicacy to obtain the requisite angle by a series of ribs of stone. Iron girders might have been adopted here, but, owing to the splendid stone adjacent, Mr. Mitchell, the engineer, adopted the principle of making each rib of each arch, in a manner, an independent bridge. The effect is very bold and graceful: the bridge is one of the finest stone structures in the North. A couple of miles further on is Dingwall, the country town of Ross-shire; it stands on a rich plain of considerable extent at

the mouth of the Peffer or Peffney, which gives its name to a spa of considerable reputation a few miles distant. Beyond this we enter the country of the Munroes and Rosses, both great names in Highland story. The railway skirts the shore nearly the whole way to Invergordon, a distance of nine miles and a half. The country is in high cultivation, and abounds in thriving villages. The terminus is the principal shipping-port of the county, and much traffic is expected in agricultural produce of all kinds. Comfortable inns exist in all parts of the country, and sport of every kind is abundant. A point nearly opposite Invergordon, on the coast of Moray, is supposed to have been the limit to which the Romans, under Severus, penetrated in Scotland. Looking across the sea, it is said, the country appeared so wild, so stormy and desolate, that they resolved to penetrate no further, and there they planted their terminus. With the Romans, Terminus was a god, usually represented without arms and legs, to show that he was immovable. The railway terminus is not so "stationary." It has already proceeded further north than the Roman eagles ever flew, and extensive preparations are now in progress to penetrate to the heart of Sutherland, to the village of Bonar Bridge. Nor is it likely to stop till it reaches the utmost limit of the kingdom, for already the people of Caithness are bestirring themselves to know the cost of an extension to the town of Thurso, on the shores of the Pentland Firth.

[ILN May 16 1863]

THE ALBERT EDWARD BRIDGE OVER THE SEVERN ON THE COALBROOKDALE RAILWAY

One of the most remarkable of those great engineering works that attend the construction of railways throughout this country is the new bridge represented in our Illustration. It is, we believe, the largest cast-iron arch carrying a double line of railway that has yet been erected anywhere in the world, the span being 200 ft., with a rise of one tenth, and the height 60 ft. at the centre. A similar arch, from the designs of the same engineer, Mr. Fowler, was recently erected to carry the Severn Valley Railway over the same river lower down, and is known as "the great bridge at Arley," but as yet only one line of rails has been laid over it, and in height, as well as in its ornamental features, the Albert Edward bridge of the Coalbrookdale line has decidedly the advantage. Being situated, too, in a commanding position, with a magnificent landscape in the background, it will be sure to attract much of the attention of all travellers and visitors to the neighbourhood. This bridge is designed to connect most of the Great Western system of railways with an important portion of that system at Coalbrookdale, being close to the Buildnas Junction of the Wenlock and Severn Valley Railways, whence, by works of considerable magnitude, the joint line, known as the Coalbrookdale Railway, which traverses that picturesque valley, is carried to its junction with the Wellington and Shiffnal branches at Lightmoor. The Albert Edward Bridge is composed of four cast-iron ribs, of an average depth of 4 ft., and of a width of

This is another early instance of a photograph acknowledged as the source of inspiration for the engraving; railway photographs from the early 1860s are rare. John Fowler was a highly regarded engineer, having been trained partly on the London & Brighton under John Raistrick; he was later to work on the Forth Bridge with his former pupil, Benjamin Baker. The line over the Albert Edward Bridge was opened as part of the Wenlock Railway, the short section from Buildwas Junction to Coalbrookdale opening on 1 November 1864; the almost identical Victoria Bridge at Arley on the Severn Valley Railway had been opened two years earlier.

The Albert Edward Bridge of the Coalbrookdale Railway over the Severn

15 in., stiffened and connected with struts and ties of cast and wrought iron. These, at the springing of the arch, rest in hollow shoes, which are sunk into large blocks of Derby stone, and are bolted downwards through the masonry; thus forming an immovable abutment, on which the stability of the structure mainly depends, whilst, at the same time, the arch is free to rise and fall under the effect of change of temperature or load. When recently tested by the Government inspector, Captain Tyler, the deflection under a load of 400 tons was only half an inch; and on the removal of the weight the bridge resumed its original level. After long and repeated experiments with severe rolling loads, which showed that no perceptible vibration existed, Captain Tyler expressed himself fully satisfied with the structure in all respects. We are informed that about 450 tons of cast and wrought iron were used in the arch and super-structure, which seems a remarkably small quantity of material for a bridge of so large a span; but it is by an examination of the arch from beneath that we are enabled to perceive the careful and studied arrangement by which this amount of iron has been made to produce one of the strongest structures of its kind with an appearance of traceried lightness and beauty. The bridge was cast and erected by the well-known ironmasters the Coalbrookdale Company, for the contractors for the line, Messrs. Brassey and Field. The designs were supplied by Mr. John Fowler, of 2 Queen-square-place, Westminster, consulting engineer to the Great Western Railway and to the Metropolitan Railway. They were executed under the immediate superintendence of Mr. Joseph Fogerty, member of the Institute of Civil Engineers, in whose charge, as resident engineer, the works both of this line and of the Severn Valley and Wenlock Railways have been carried on during the past five years. It may be remarked in general that the viaducts and bridges of these lines bear much evidence of bold design and skilful execution; but in the section traversing the Coalbrookdale Valley there is an unusual amount of difficult engineering work. Sweeping suddenly round a sharp curve into the beautiful valley which once formed the favourite hunting-ground of the monks of Buildnas, [sic] before the ironworks and railways had been invented to disturb its quiet, we see that quite a mountain of earth has been thrown up to make a platform from whence numerous branches

and sidings run at various levels amidst the foundries of the Coalbrookdale Company. Passing through a pretty station, with long white platforms, perched on an embankment 60 ft. above the turnpike road, we then skirt the edge of a steep wooded cliff by a series of sharp curves trenched out of the hillside, and we are carried over a portion of the ironworks and the great reservoir of the same company on a fine curved viaduct of twenty-six arches, which has been three years under construction. Further on the railway passes through another reservoir confined by massive walls on each side of the line; till, emerging from deep cuttings, in which is exhibited a section of the great coal-field of Shropshire, we ascend to the summit level and junction-station at Lightmoor by a gradient of 1 in 50, which extends over a greater part of the line. Such is the Coalbrookdale Railway, which was opened to public traffic on Tuesday.

It is singular that the bridge which forms the subject of our Illustration – the most recent and one of the most enterprising works of its class – is within sight of the first iron bridge that was constructed in England – one which was constructed by the same ironmasters in 1779, and which has given a name to the rising and important town of Ironbridge, on the banks of the Severn.

Our Engraving is executed from an excellent photograph taken by Mr. W. Fall, photographer, of Market-square, Ironbridge, Salop.

[ILN Nov 1864]

THE TAY BRIDGE

We give one Illustration of this important structure, which has recently been completed. The project of building a bridge over the Tay, so as to shorten the way from Dundee and the North-East of Scotland to the South, was conceived very early in railway history. A meeting of the shareholders of the Edinburgh and Northern Railway (afterwards the Edinburgh, Perth, and Dundee, and now merged into the North British), held in September, 1845, empowered the Board to take all the necessary steps to construct a bridge at or near Newburgh, or to agree with any other company to assist in constructing the bridge. The intention at that time took the form of a high-level bridge, which the Dundee and Perth and Edinburgh and Northern Companies agreed to construct at an estimated cost of between

£100,000 and £150,000. This agreement was never carried into effect. Previously, proposals had been made for a low-level bridge near the same spot, making use of Mugdrum island in the Tay, and, in consequence of opposition to this scheme, another project was to construct a swing bridge, so as to accommodate the river traffic. The question rested in abeyance till 1865, when the initiatory steps for the promotion of a bridge were taken by an independent company; but this also came to nothing. In 1866 the North British Company promoted a bill for a bridge and railway connection at Dundee, substantially coinciding with the bridge now built; but this also fell aside owing to the financial circumstances of the line. It was not till the Session of 1870 that an Act for the bridge was obtained, the project being promoted as a separate undertaking, but warmly supported by the North British Company. From the end of 1871 till now the bridge works made progress but various causes helped to retard operations in earlier years.

Among these causes were the death of the contractor, Mr. De Bergue, and the alterations in the form of the bridge, as well as in the methods employed in constructing it, owing to the bed of the river not having answered the original expectations. After fourteen piers, being those nearest the south end, on the original plan of engaged pillars of solid brickwork resting on a submerged base, had been completed, and a good deal of work at the other and shallower side had been done, the plan of using brick above high water was discarded in favour of iron, and in the case of the larger piers the method of laying the foundations was also changed.

Starting from Dundee on a wide radius, to change the direction from the shore line to the straight flight over the river, the bridge raises by a gradient of 1 in 73 to the summit level, at the north end of the large spans, where the roadway is 88ft. above high water, and about 100ft. above the mean tide level. The descent to the south side is 1 in 363, or to the eye nearly level. The thirteen spans of 245ft. each, placed in the centre of the river, and filling up nearly one third of the length of the bridge, form of themselves a great work, the size and importance of which can hardly be judged either by the view from the river below or by the passenger who will only see the work from the train. Approaching from either side, there is a distance of about 3500ft., where the line is laid on the top of the girder, and the train will travel in the open. When the wide spans are reached the rails run on the bottom of the 27ft. high girder, and the long straight lines of the structure give the roadway the appearance of a tube or tunnel, as this part of the bridge is approached. Far beneath, the passenger will see the hurrying ebb or flow of the strong tide of the Tay, sometimes in rough weather lashed into fury by the tempests that sweep down from the hills. Excepting the unfastened girders that fell, no part of the structure has shown a sign of failure, although the storms since the highest and most exposed parts of the structure were built have been of unsurpassed severity. A walk across the bridge gives a sense of enormous strength in the structure, and although the lines of the structure are wholly straight, or diagonal, its extent, its lightness, and its ever-shifting lines give it a picturesque effect. The view of country, of sea and river, fertile land and distant mountain, obtained from the higher piers is superb. The rails are laid double throughout— that is to say, a service rail with a guard rail within, keyed into a double chair, and laid upon a continuous sleeper of pitch pine. The roadway presents a sound, serviceable line, the excellent finish of every part being noticeable. The weight of the steel rails and chairs is given at 1 cwt. per foot, the rails themselves being 75lb. to the yard.

[ILN DEC 1 1877]

THE NEW TAY BRIDGE AT DUNDEE

The terrible disaster on the night of Sunday, Dec. 28, 1879, when the iron railway-bridge over the Tay estuary, while a passenger-train was crossing, amidst a violent hurricane of wind, suddenly fell in the raging waters below, and ninety lives were lost, cannot yet have been forgotten. The bridge which had been constructed in six years, at a total cost of £350,000, from the designs of the late Sir Thomas Bouch, C.E., was opened for traffic on May 30, 1878. It was 3450 yards long, consisting of eighty-five spans, eleven of which, with lattice girders, measured 225ft., others 227ft., 166ft., 145ft., and 129ft., on piers formed of six cast-iron columns resting upon masonry and concrete. These iron columns, two in each pier, were connected laterally with each other by cross-bracings of wrought iron; and the loosening of the tie-bars, which were insufficiently fastened, made the bridge unable to resist the tremendous force of the wind. The foundations of the piers themselves had not actually given way. The North British Railway Company lost no time in applying to Parliament for powers to construct a new bridge, on the old foundations, for which plans were prepared by Mr. James Brunlees, C.E.; but the Bill was rejected in the Session of 1880. The directors then called in Mr. W. H. Barlow, C.E., who made an accurate examination, applying various tests and experiments to the existing piers. He reported in favour of making entirely new foundations; and in 1881 a Bill was introduced for the construction of a new Tay Bridge, which would cost £670,000 sixty feet westward of the one that fell. It was stipulated with the Perth Town Council, in the interest of the river navigation, that four of the openings between the piers should be 215ft. wide, with a clear height of 77ft. above high water at ordinary spring tides; and vessels were to be towed through at the expense of the railway company. The Board of Trade also required the removal of the ruins of the old bridge. The Bill having passed, the contract for the works was taken by Messrs. William Arrol and Co., of Glasgow, and operations were commenced early in 1882, which are now successfully completed.

We give some Illustrations of the new Tay Bridge. The entire length of the viaduct is 10,780ft., the width of the river being 9580ft. There are eighty-five spans, of which eleven are 245ft. in length, two of 227ft., one 162ft., thirteen 145ft., twenty-one 129ft., one 113ft., one 108ft., twenty-four 71ft., four 66ft., one 56ft., two iron arches 81ft. (approach on the Dundee side), and four brick arches 50ft. (approach on the Fife side). The height above the water to the under side of the girders is 65ft. on the south side, 77ft. in the centre, and 16ft. on the north side of

The Tay Bridge, near Dundee, from the south

The Tay Bridge Disaster: Diving operations in search of the wreck of the railway train.

the river. The foundations of the piers consist of solid brick and concrete cylinders, arranged in pairs, encased in strong wrought-iron caissons, up to low-water mark, and continued upwards, faced with Staffordshire brick impervious to water. Above high-water mark, each pair of cylinders is united by a massive connecting piece of masonry, on the top of which are laid the iron plates forming the base of the iron superstructure. This is of singularly graceful design; two iron octagonal columns, each firmly braced inside and plated outside, rise above the pair of piers, and the inner portions meet above in an arch, while the outer parts extend to support a platform 40ft. wide, upon which the girders of the span rest, the lattice-girder form of construction being employed. The effect of using these iron columns, instead of raising the piers of solid masonry to the girder level, is greatly to reduce the weight put upon the foundations, while obtaining strength enough to bear any strain on the bridge. The flooring of the bridge is of steel, in deep furrows, coated with asphalt and ballasted. The sides are protected by lattice-work, which will break the force of the wind on trains passing over the bridge. The structure will bear a lateral wind-pressure of 56lb. to the square foot. All the materials were severely tested. The quantity of wrought iron used, including many girders from the old bridge, is 19,000 tons; of steel, 3500 tons; and of cast-iron, for the piers, 2500 tons; with three million rivets, averaging five inches in length; ten million bricks, weighing 37,500 tons; and 70,000 tons of concrete. The cost has not greatly exceeded the estimate, being about £282,000 for the foundations, £268,000 for the piers, and £268,000 for the girders and parapets. Adding, however, the cost of the bridge that was destroyed, the North British Railway Company has spent more than a million sterling in bridging the Tay. The public advantage gained is that of shortening the journey from Dundee to Edinburgh by one hour, and from Aberdeen to Edinburgh by two hours, while the traffic between Dundee and the east of Fife is doubled. The new bridge was first used for ordinary passenger traffic on the Queen's Jubilee day, instead of the ferry at Tayport.

The eminent engineer, Mr. William Henry Barlow, of London, is a son of the late Professor Barlow, of the Royal Military Academy, Woolwich. He was born in 1812, studied under his father, and was a pupil in the machinery department of Woolwich Dockyard, and with the engineer of the London Docks. He went, in 1832, to Constantinople, for Messrs. Maudslay and Field, to erect machinery at the Turkish Ordnance Factory, and was also employed about the light-houses on the Bosphorus. In 1838 he became assistant-engineer of the Manchester and Birmingham (London and North-Western) Railway, and was subsequently engineer to the Midland Railway in the construction of several branch lines, and in designing the St. Pancras Station, with its great roof of 240ft. span. He was joint engineer with Sir John Hawkshaw in completing the Clifton Suspension Bridge. In 1850, Mr. Barlow, who is the author of valuable scientific researches in mechanics and electricity, was elected a Fellow of the Royal Society, and he is one of its vice-presidents.

Mr. William Arrol, born at Houston, near Paisley, and now about forty-seven years of age, was a working man; first employed in the establishment of Messrs. Coats, of that town, he was afterwards apprenticed to Mr. Reid, a well-known blacksmith, engineer, and yachtsman; he laboured in the shipbuilding yards of the Clyde, and became foreman of the girder department at Messrs. Laidlaw and Sons' Barrowfield Iron Works. But he set up in business on his own account in Glasgow at the age of twenty-six, and in time became proprietor of the great Dalmarnock Iron Works. He now employs four or five thousand men, and has the character of being one of the best of masters; all his assistants are of his own training. Among his important works have been the bridges on the Glasgow, Hamilton, and Bothwell Railway; the South Esk railway bridge at Montrose; the Broomielaw viaduct of the Caledonian Railway, and several bridges in Brazil; he took the contract for the Forth Bridge at Queensferry, as originally designed by Sir T. Bouch, and is contractor for the bridge that is now being constructed to cross the Forth at the isle of Inchgarvie. Mr. Arrol has invented and applied various useful devices, such as the patent drilling and riveting machine, for the more economic execution of heavy ironwork.

[ILN Aug 6 1887]

Entire books (by John Thomas and John Prebble) and even a novel (Hatter's Castle by A. J. Cronin) have been devoted to the tragedy of the first Tay Bridge and its designer, Thomas Bouch. It was a story of continual changes and errors of design, margins cut down to the limit (for which Bouch was known), appalling negligence and sheer bad workmanship. The inquiry took the view that the defects with the bridge were so numerous that it would sooner or later have come down. Opened on 31 May 1878, when Bouch was knighted after Queen Victoria had crossed the structure, the bridge was in use for only 18 months. On the night of the collapse, which took the lives of 75 people, an exceptionally severe storm blew down the firth; the reading on the Beaufort scale was 10 to 11, taken by officers aboard HMS Mars which was anchored near the bridge. The train which went down was the 5.20pm Burntisland to Dundee hauled by 4-4-0 No 224; the booked locomotive was normally a tank locomotive but a breakdown necessitated its replacement by the spare engine at Dundee, whence the local had started at 1.30pm. A number of people watched the train crossing the bridge and saw streaks of fire fall into the raging water. The disaster naturally shocked the nation and broke Sir Thomas Bouch, who died within a year of the storm.

Work on the bridge which still carries traffic across the Tay at Dundee was begun after some delay over the design and site of the new viaduct, and over what to do with the remains of the first bridge. The Board of Trade wanted all the girders taking down and every pier uprooted. In the end it was agreed that the piers should remain, and they may still be seen today. Some of the girders from the first bridge were incorporated in the new design. The new bridge was opened to passenger traffic on 20 June 1887.

COMPLETION OF THE NEW TAY BRIDGE AT DUNDEE

1. The New Tay Bridge, View from the South-east.
2. Inside the Bridge.
3. The New Tay Bridge, from East Tayport, Two Miles distant.
4. General View of the Bridge from the North End.
5. Floating out the last Span.
6. The New Tay Bridge, View from South-west.
7. Looking through the Piers, from South End.

THE WORKS AT THE FORTH BRIDGE RAILWAY, N.B. [THE GRAPHIC AUGUST 30 1884]

1 Machinery for drilling the Steel Tubes of which the Bridge is to be Constructed   3 A Caisson on Launchway, at Low Water

2 View from the North Shore, Looking South   4 Launch of a Caisson

5 View from the South Shore, Looking North

Fife Main Pier

PROGRESS OF THE
FORTH BRIDGE, QUEENSFERRY

The construction of the great railway bridge to cross the Firth of Forth, at Queensferry, just beyond Dalmeny Park, where the opposite shores of Fifeshire and Linlithgowshire nearly approach each other, with the rocky islet of Inchgarvie between them, is one of the grandest works of modern engineering. It was designed, for the North British Railway Company, by Sir John Fowler and Mr. Benjamin Baker, has been four or five years in actual progress, and will be completed in the autumn of next year. The width of the estuary in this part is reduced by the peninsula of North Queensferry to a mile and a half; and on the south shore, the water shoals rapidly, with a bed of boulder clay and a very deep stratum of mud; but the Fife shore is an almost perpendicular cliff, and the intervening islet is a rock in the centre of the deep channel, with 200ft. depth of water on each side, and with a strong tide-current sweeping up and down on each side. It was impossible to erect piers anywhere but on this islet; hence the bridge must rest on three main piers, one at

South Queensferry, one at Inchgarvie, and one on the Fife shore, besides two supplementary piers which serve to relieve the balance arms of the "cantilever" girders, and to connect the bridge with a long approach viaduct.

A cantilever is a girder supported only at one point, its overhanging extended part being balanced by its weight at the other end; this engineering device is the most novel feature of the Forth Bridge. The main spans of the bridge are to be upheld over the deep-water channels by the projecting ends of cantilever girders, with connecting central girders over about one-sixth of the span.

[ILN Dec 15 1888]

It was originally intended that Sir Thomas Bouch would be the designer of the Forth Bridge, and he had planned a suspension bridge with two spans separated by a central tower on a small island in the middle of the firth. Work had actually begun, and the solitary pier on the island of Inch Garvie

may still be seen. The Tay tragedy prompted a re-examination of his scheme. In the event John Fowler and Benjamin Baker produced the successful design in the form of three enormous diamond-trusses linked by 'floating' girders. Work was resumed with the new design in 1883 so this illustration shows work at an early stage; it took seven years to construct, opening taking place on 4 March 1890. It was the first major British structure to be built of mild steel. The undertaking was so colossal that a separate Forth Bridge Railway Co was formed by the Great Northern, Midland, North British and North Eastern companies; curiously the Midland was the largest subscriber.

When the Forth Bridge was opened in 1890, it was said that the prototype of the cantilever bridge across the firth was that built at Wandipore in the Himalayas in about 1670. The choice of tubes and lattice work was determined by Baker's conviction that members under compression should be tubular, preferably of circular section, while those under tension should be open lattice girders. The total length of the bridge is just over 1½ miles, and just under 51,000 tons of steel were used in the main spans.

POLITICS AND ECONOMICS

In the spirit of laissez-faire that character-ised the Victorian economy, Parliament was reluctant to intervene with the railways. However, fares and rates was one area which it did not prefer to ignore. When this article appeared in February 1844, passenger receipts far outstripped revenue from the conveyance of goods; not until 1852 did the income from freight charges exceed passenger revenue. Nonetheless the competition between railways, which Parliament encouraged by sanctioning rival schemes and rarely granting amalgamations, led to the need for a central body to administer the proportions of charges for goods traffic passing over more than one company's tracks. Accordingly the Railway Clearing House was set up in 1842 with a staff of six; it eventually had 2,500 clerks. By 1875 112 general Acts had been passed concerning the control and regulation of railways, but the determination to preserve a competitive spirit was not the only contribution Parliament made to mitigating the complaints of the writer. Later in the year the Railway Regulation Act of 1844 was passed, stating that if at any time after 21 years the dividend of any railway should exceed 10 per cent, the Treasury might revise the rates to ensure that not more than 10 per cent should be earned. The 1873 Regulation of Railways Act created the Railway and Canal Commission which, amongst other duties, was to hear and determine questions of through rates. An important extension of the Act's powers was authorised in 1888 when companies were ordered to prepare a revised schedule of Maximum Rates for submission to the Board of Trade which was to hear objections against them. It was some years before the new rates were ratified and one consequence of them was to reduce the flexibility that had previously been the case; rates were seldom reduced because of the difficulty of increasing them again. So the Act was not an unmitigated blessing for the consumer and complaints about the level of rates seem to be an endemic aspect of pre-grouping history. It must be said that it is surprising for the writer to be complaining that shareholders were benefitting at the public's expense; in the early 1840s trade was depressed and dividends so low that few companies were paying dividends of more than 4 per cent.

RAILWAY MONOPOLY

ATERIAL as is the Railway System, generally to the interests of the community, it has of late acquired a peculiar interest, in consequence of the appointment of a Select Committee of the House of Commons to inquire into the mode in which Railways are managed. The present is, therefore, a fit opportunity for returning to the subject, to which we lately directed the attention of our readers.

When the various leading Railway Companies were first formed, the public hailed their formation, because they were led to believe, that the principal object which their originators had in view, was the accommodation and benefit of the community. The proprietors disclaimed all intention of seeking to obtain anything more than the ordinary rate of interest for the capital invested in these undertakings. And they assured the public, times without number, that they would, by a reduction of fares, give them the benefit of whatever success should attend their enterprise.

In this, the public have been grossly deceived. The Railway Proprietors, instead of reducing their fares, have kept them up at the rates which had been fixed on, before it could be ascertained what would be the result of the new experiment. The leading lines have proved more successful than the most sanguine had ventured to anticipate. But the benefit is exclusively enjoyed by the shareholders. The public have derived no advantage from the success of these undertakings. Instead of lowering the fares, as the country had been led to expect, the Railway Directors have proposed dividing the unexpectedly large revenue derived from their respective line among the shareholders.

Hence, instead of the fares being reduced, as they might have been, and ought to have been, to the extent of from one-third to one-half, they have thought proper to keep up the fares at the rate originally fixed, when all was uncertainty as to the success or otherwise of the new experiment, and to divide the profits among themselves. The Railway share-holders are consequently, on the leading lines, dividing among themselves from six to ten per cent on the price of the original shares. And hence the fact that the original £100 shares are, in some instances, at from £130 to £140 premium; while other shares on which £50 only have been paid, are at present at a premium of from £78 to £80.

These are stubborn facts; they are facts that speak for themselves. They disclose a state of matters constituting a monopoly of the very worst kind. The Directors of the leading Railway Companies having secured a monopoly of conveyance, act towards the public as they think proper. They make their own terms because they know the public have no remedy. They know that the public, having no other means of conveyance between the places through which their lines pass (the coaches being knocked off the road), are completely at their mercy. And hence, the exorbitance of their charges – charges so exorbitant as to prove that their own pecuniary advantage, and not the accommodation of the public, has been the leading object the shareholders have had in view in the formation of the various railroads which now intersect all parts of the kingdom.

The public are grossly and grievously wronged in this matter. And they have a right to look to the Legislature for redress. The Railway Companies having broken faith with the public, it is the duty of Parliament to interfere, and see that the public be righted. Passengers ought to be travelling in the leading lines at from 50 to 75 per cent cheaper than they are at present. Extravagant prices, as the result of monopolies in corn, and in all other commodities, are now everywhere denounced; and why not the exorbitant prices consequent on the monopoly in the conveyance from one part of the country to another, which is enjoyed by most of the railroad companies? The country has a right to raise its voice against the deception which is thus being practised upon it. And as Parliament has the power to apply the remedy, as it is within its province to redress the wrong, we trust the country will not raise its voice in vain. The committee lately appointed to inquire into the state of matters connected with Railway Companies have had large powers conferred upon them by Parliament. The monopolist-character and exorbitant charges, of several of these companies are clearly legitimate subjects of inquiry for this committee. The public look to the gentlemen composing that committee to do their duty in the matter. We trust the country will not be disappointed, but that one of the results of the appointment of the committee will be the extinction of railway monopolies, by fixing a moderate scale of charges.

[ILN FEB 24 1844]

Although railway company dividends were low in the early 1840s, they were not as poor a return as some government stocks, and with the rise in railway share prices after 1841 and a growth in traffic and dividends, railways became relatively attractive to investors. A major cause of what became known as the railway mania was the small amount of money needed to purchase the title to a security; consequently scrip and even letters of allotment quickly changed hands, thereby increasing prices. This mania to get rich quick with railway stocks reached its height in 1844–5, with 1845 seeing the highest prices and 1846 the largest number of miles authorised. The highest call on capital was in 1847; inflation has rendered absolute figures meaningless, but the figure for that year accounted for 8–10 per cent of national income and the entire nation's capital investment. Many of the schemes authorised never came to fruition; some were ploys to thwart the plans of competitors while others were ill-conceived lines for which the capital was never subscribed. It was not uncommon for prospectuses to list a provisional committee of distinguished names without even consulting the gentlemen concerned.

RAILWAY MANIA
WRITTEN AND ILLUSTRATED
BY ALFRED CROWQUILL

"GIVE him plenty of *Line* and he is sure to hook himself effectually," says Izaak Walton, when speaking of catching a Jack. Alas for poor John Bull, this system has proved upon him most effectual indeed, when just as he was swallowing the delightful bait in the shape of unlimited scrip, and going on, to all appearance, most swimmingly, a sudden and an unexpected stop is put to his meanderings, and he finds a most tremendous hook in his gills. Now comes on, as *Long Tom Coffin* has it, "his flurry," all wild, terrified, dashing, and foam. Beware of his struggles, for in his alarm he tries to bolt with a quantity of *Line*, but it is no go! He is fast! He must come to the surface and yield his fat. It is a terrible thing to be hooked in any sense of the word, but to be hooked by remorseless scrip is the worst of all. A sudden fright has fallen on the Market, for everybody, panic-struck, is rushing to sell, and the Market becomes glutted. The enthusiasm cools down, and eyes become disenchanted, and the imaginary lump of gold turn into their real shapes, of worse than waste paper. The intoxication is over, and now ensues the *delirium tremens*. The Stag draws in his horns, for holding is no part of his business. The small speculator trembles with despair in the possession of a hundred shares, upon the obtaining of which he has so much congratulated himself. The aforesaid shares, at £25 each, amounting to more than he ever even hoped to possess; he only intended to turn a pound or two. They now hang like a loadstone round his neck, and must eventually sink him, by slow and torturing degrees, in the shape of frequent calls; for those who can pay must. A most

beggarly account will it be when the muster takes place, for the deserters will leave the troops of the *Line* in a pitiable condition. The awful traffic by Railway Committee-men and others will soon be most frightfully apparent. Disappointed men have whispered a few of the "secrets of the prison house," and shown the world that it has been but a *melée* of interested men to clutch as much gold as possible, and "the devil take the hindmost." This has been a very simple process; for the fairy-like tales spread abroad to catch the ear of the unwary, of men going to bed worth nothing but a letter of allotment, and getting up in the morning possessing thousands, by the magic of Railway speculations were sure baits. Directors have advertised a number of shares at £2 or £2 10s. per share first instalment, then alloted only a certain number to the public, that a price might be made, which, of course, was done to a certainty, during the height of the fever; directly the sound of premium reached their ears, they thrust the whole quantity into the Market, which bore a very large proportion to the allotted one, and thus sold and divided the profit equally amongst their right honourable Board, careless to whom they sold, as the instantly realising was the only object. Who bought them? Why, men who were of equally honourable dealings – who never intended to hold, but who sold at a profit, and so on to the end. The present holders – who never intended to be so – are not worth a dump – not one in a thousand; nor could they face another instalment or call. Then where is the capital to come from? since the partners or shareholders are men without means, and merely unlucky devils who have, at an unfortunate moment, popped their necks into a hank, from which they have not the power to extricate themselves.

The neglect of all business has been unprecedented; for many months no tradesman has been found at his counter, or merchant at his office, east, west, north and south. If you called upon business, you were sure to be answered with "Gone to the City;" and the straightforward, honourable, and particular man of business, who formerly asked for your account, now troubles you to ask him for it many times before you get it, or pleads, as an excuse, the scarcity of money, and his heavy Railway calls. This is done now by most reputable houses, without a blush, as everybody is in the same boat, and it is looked upon more leniently than it otherwise would be. All rule and order are upset by the general epidemic, as in the Plague of London, where all ties of blood, honour, or friendship, were cast away; and man grew callous to the suffering of his fellow man, and only looked to his own welfare and safety in the calamity, and as to how far he could best secure himself from the general ruin.

The fallacy of the Railways only *provisionally registered* became the object of immense competition, and men paying to each other large sums upon imaginary security, must be apparent to all men of business; and so it has been, but the desire of gain has become so strong, that a Railway to the Moon would have found speculators, if part of the *Line* could have been surveyed, with the strong recommendation of some Railway King or other potential person: to such an extent had this gullibility gone, that people who had written soft letters to Boards of Directors for a few shares, begin to turn their minds to having Railways of their own; many cases of which have been successful. Chairmen and Directors were very easily procured; but, in case of any hurry as to the sending the prospectus to the printers before the afore-said gentlemen could be consulted as to their willingness to join the design of the line, a reference to any prospectuses lying now upon every man's desk would furnish a respectable Board, taking them at random. This is a known fact. Many respectable and influential men have read their names printed as Provisional Committee-men without the slightest knowledge of the Railway or the parties connected with it. Very often, from this helter-skelter way of doing business, the same name would be found upon two opposition lines; but it did not matter – nobody cared; the involuntary Director found a sop was preparing for him to stifle his growl, so he let the swindle go on. Engineers have been placed in the same predicament, and have feathered their nests most delightfully, for the demand has increased the price tremendously of the articles, and their minutes have become guineas, and their patronage to surveyors, &c., immense. The surveyors have been paid in the same ratio, and many a young man with a swallowing of surveying has left a good permanent situation under the temptation of four or five guineas a day, which must soon slip between his fingers, and he becomes nothing, as the present slight vibration of the panic, for it is hardly as

yet a shock, has electrified the most heedless, and shown them that the storm is not so far off as has been supposed by sanguine speculators.

Deposits paid to provisional registered railways, which failing passing through the house, return almost pitiful dividends to the holders of promissory share letters, the money being swallowed up by the whole tribe of Directors, Chairmen, Surveyors, Engineers, and other locusts given life to by this mania.

Bankers begin to screw up their money *tight*, as it is called amidst money dealers, refusing even to look at shares as deposits or security. Yet, according to the Railway advertisements, wherein their names figure to a great extent, and the immense amount supposed to be deposited by the Railway Companies, they ought to be as free as a spendthrift's. But, is the money there? Go and inquire, you fond holders of scrip; you are partners, and have an undoubted right to know the amount placed in their hands to the credit of your Company; this, legally done, they have no power to refuse, and they will inform you "that the enormous amount is only in the prospectus," and that you are bound to pay for the future proceedings of the aforesaid *Line* to the full amount of your liabilities or shares. Thus many a speculator, who has been doing pretty well heretofore, will find in such events that the other leaf of his gambling or account book has to be put in black to mourn for the loss he has made.

Shrewd men with money have most ingeniously put other men's fingers in the

fire, keeping themselves out of harm's way, by thrusting some needy man before them, for whom they find the necessary capital and give a handsome commission. Want of money and the belief of ultimate success, with a very faint knowledge of their liabilities, and the example of high and low around them, have led many men of apparently respectable condition to become cover as it were to the head gambler, who rejoices securely in the profit, and, in case of failure, leaves the poor and tempted victim to shut up his shop – bolt – or go over the Bridge if he pleases. Such cases are not imaginary – they are facts!

Noble Lords, who are certainly liable for their right honourable gambling ribs, will find their names no protection from the forthcoming storm; their own personal peril is no trifle, since we see names of great odour in the polite City of Westminster crowded together as dividers of the Railway sops. Provisional Committees must now provide for the crash, and Directors direct their attention to their accounts, and see how their daily increasing expenses are to be met, and that they don't get hung up in their own Lines.

The constant succession of Railways proposed and carried, would, it was supposed, keep up the ball for a year or two more – the public, therefore, have neglected due precaution in speculation.

All Companies have shared in the great folly! – Railway Mania! – seized apparently at the same moment all over the world, upon great capitalists and speculators.

The sudden cloud that has overspread them has been startling and unexpected, therefore unprovided for; and victims stand aghast at their perilous situation.

The magnitude of the error will meet its equal magnitude of punishment: and many families will have to mourn the year Forty-five as they have before mourned over the fatal speculations of the years '25 and '35, when Mines and Bonds worked almost the same ruin, and caused the same delirium. It seems that every tenth year brings its bubble; upon looking back this will be found to be the case.

They have planned and drawn a Grand Terminus for all Railways – to be placed somewhere near Charterhouse Square. We should advise them not to lay out their money in this grand and picturesque idea, for we plainly perceive one already formed in St. George's Fields, which to a certainty will be the Grand Terminus – it is now called the Queen's Bench.

[ILN Nov 18 1845]

This article, full of interesting facts and comparisons, provides an interesting contrast to the editorial on the railway mania. It serves to remind that the press was just as, if not more, purposefully critical than today. The writer seems able to assume that the reader will be aware of the 'cases of gross, and even corrupt, mismanagement'. General accusations of poor management may be made today but they are rarely accompanied by much evidence or any of the invective used in Victorian times. It is interesting that the railway system had not even reached the size of today's network, notwithstanding the depradations of Beeching (1855, 7,157 route miles; 1979, 11,020 miles). The statistics on traffic receipts also indicate the growing importance of goods traffic relative to passenger receipts. The accident figures were remarkably low: only nine deaths in accidents caused by circumstances beyond the victim's control was very commendable for a railway system that had only the most rudimentary signalling and safety systems in comparison even with those of 1900. The statistic for 1854 of 104m passengers journeys on a network of 7,157 miles compares interestingly with 736m journeys in 1979 on a network of 11,020 miles. It is surprising to note that in 1854 the railways employed only 11.59 individuals per mile against 16.51 per mile in 1979, although clearly the much higher traffic reflects dramatic improvements in productivity and efficiency.

RAILWAY STATISTICS

SOME years have elapsed since men of sagacity and foresight predicted the speedy advent of a railway heptarchy, and it is now proposed to amalgamate all the lines under a single directory. Rival companies, each desirous of monopoly, have so stimulated competition that, in spite of an annually-growing traffic, dividends have fallen to an unrenumerating scale, while, to execute extension lines, a pernicious system of preference shares has been generally introduced. Cases of gross, and even corrupt, mismanagement have been proved; and, in some instances, truth has been concealed from shareholders by the payment of profits out of capital. When it is considered that the total amount of money authorised to be raised by railway companies, by shares and on loan, to the end of the year 1854, amounted to £368,106,336, of which £286,068,794 had been raised, and that the balance of £82,037,542 is nearly all absorbed at the present date, except where new projects have been abandoned, the gigantic magnitude of these undertakings must forcibly strike the most cursory observer. At the end of 1854 the total length of lines authorised by Parliament amounted to 13,983 miles; but of this 1177 miles were abandoned by subsequent Acts, or by warrant under the authority of the Commissioners of Railways, and, consequently, there remain 12,806 miles for which the Parliamentary powers which were obtained have not been repealed. Of these, 8054 miles were open at the end of 1854; and 4752, which have received the authority of Parliament, remained to be opened since that date. These figures exhibit the actual dimensions of this comparatively modern system of transit and locomotion.

The benefits arising to the whole community from the substitution of iron for earth roads are too palpable to require comment, for you may now travel for less per mile in a first-class carriage than you paid a postboy in the times that are past, and fly over forty miles where you crawled over eight. It might have been presumed that an enlightened Government would never have thrown any impediment in the way of such truly national undertakings, or permitted the projectors to be mulcted in enormous sums of money before they placed a brick or dug a turf; yet it appears from the Return to the Order of the House of Commons, moved for by Mr. Hadfield

(Paper 460), and printed 6th August, 1855, that the preliminary expenses paid by 160 companies amounted to £14,086,110 14s. 5½d.; while 45 companies have not given in any return.

The details of railway statistics are very curious and interesting, and as the following figures are taken from the Parliamentary Report every dependence may be placed on their fidelity. Of the 8054 miles open for traffic at the close of last year, there were in England 6114 miles; in Scotland, 1043; in Ireland, 897. In England 5261 miles were constructed on the principle of the narrow gauge, 647 on that of the broad gauge, and 206 on the mixed; in Scotland the narrow gauge alone exists; in Ireland, with the exception of eight miles, the Irish gauge is used.

In the three kingdoms there are 114 companies having single lines, extending over 1962 miles, but several of these may be expected to become double in due season.

In 1854 on the lines opened for traffic, 90,409 persons were employed, being an average of 11.59 individuals per mile; and there were 2410 persons. [sic].

The total number of passengers conveyed on railways, in 1854, amounted to 111,206,707, and the total receipts from all sources of traffic amounted to £20,215,724. The number of passengers conveyed per mile, was 14,160. This refers to the three kingdoms.

The passenger traffic on the English lines alone is put down at 92,346,149, or at the rate of 15,487 persons per mile; and receipts from them yielded £7,896,402, or £1324 per mile. The proportion of each class is thus distinguished: – first, 13.3 per cent; second, 36 per cent; third, 50.7 per cent.

In Scotland the passengers numbered in 1854, 11,949,388, or 11,725 persons per mile, and the receipts were £742 per mile. In Scotland, first class, 11.3 per cent; second, 15.9; third, 72.8; a very different scale of proportion from that which obtains in England.

In Ireland the number of passengers amounted to 6,911,170, the ratio per mile being 7983 individuals. Of these 13.3 per cent were first class; 39.8 per cent, second; and 46.8, third: a small number wee not apportioned.

"As regard the returns of Great Britain and Ireland, of the 111,206,707 conveyed, it appears that 14,517,461 were first-class passengers, 37,930,655, second-class, and 58,732,048 third-class, there being 26,543 not apportioned into classes; and of the £9,174,945 received from passengers £2,738,458 was derived from first-class passengers, £3,264,545 from second-class, and £2,999,466 from third-class passengers; a sum of £172,478 not being apportioned into classes. Although the relative proportions of each class of traffic has not varied much, yet a slight increase may be observed in the proportionate receipts for third-class traffic, and a slight decrease in the proportionate receipts for second-class traffic."

The Goods traffic is an important item in railway receipts, not only as a source of income to the several companies, but as indicating, in this channel of transit, the progress or decline of internal trade. The whole amount received through this department in 1854 was £11,040,779. Comparing the years 1853 and 1854, the increase of the latter over the former was 16 per cent; the same results appear in Scotland, while the increase has been 20 per cent. In 1849 the revenue from the goods traffic was only £5,528,606; and it is gratifying to remark that while railway lines have increased in length since that date 40.6 per cent, the goods traffic has increased 99.67 per cent – the receipts per mile having been £2115 in 1849, and £2576 in 1854. Another point is worthy of note. In 1849 the passenger traffic yielded 53.17, and the goods traffic 46.83, in each £100 received, but these relative proportions were reversed in the year 1854, for the receipts from passengers declined to 45.34 per cent, while those from goods rose 54.66 per cent.

The working expenses on railways average 45 per cent on the gross receipts, the proportion being in England 45 per cent, 43 per cent in Scotland, and 46 per cent in Ireland. This expenditure is subdivided under the following heads:

Maintenance of Way in
England and Ireland 14.5%
Scotland 15.9%
Ireland 14.6%
Cost of Locomotive Power including expense of rolling stock in
England and Wales 39.7%
Scotland 42.9%
Ireland 44.3%
Traffic charges in
England and Wales 26.1%
Scotland 20.5%
Ireland 23.4%
Miscellaneous expenses, police, watchmen, &c. in
England 11.6%

Scotland 16.0%
Ireland 14.6%
The rates and Government duty in
England 8.1%
Scotland 4.7%
Ireland 2.6%
(There is no passenger traffic in Ireland)
Expenditure per mile by trains run in
England ... ... 31.28d.
Scotland ... ... 28.42d.
Ireland ... ... 29.18d.
Receipts per mile in
England ... ... 68.82d.
Scotland ... ... 59.33d.
Ireland ... ... 61.19d.

One of the most important points in these statistics in the rate of profit which results from railway enterprise as a whole; and here must be distinguished the dividends on the whole of the ordinary share capital from those on preference shares and loans. The former stand thus in the subjoined years:

1849	... ... 1.88	1852 ...	... 2.40
1850	... ... 1.83	1853 ...	... 3.05
1851	... ... 2.44	1854 ...	... 3.39

The preference shares yield an average dividend of five per cent. The money loaned has produced 4.27 per cent.

[ILN 1856]

It would have been surprising if a nation that viewed the economic principles of Adam Smith as almost sacrosanct had entrusted the creation of the railway system to the government. The idea was certainly discussed, for the ills of the laissez-faire approach were as evident as its benefits, and governments on the Continent were assuming greater responsibility for the development of their systems: competition was not held to be the key to the welfare of the traveller, and very different methods were used to safeguard the public interest. In France, for example, the government looked for a partnership with the railway companies, with the right of the government to plan the network and to impose whatever conditions regarding rates, safety and representation on boards it though fit. In 1844 a Select Committee was set up under Gladstone, then president of the Board of Trade, to review the development of the railway system. Gladstone's proposal to increase the government's voice in planning procedures was rejected but he did succeed in creating an option for the government to purchase any railway after 20 years. Gladstone's committee heard evidence that

advocated nationalisation of the entire railway system, but it would have been too radical a departure for most parliamentarians. Gladstone's purchase clauses were reconsidered by the 1866–7 Royal Commission with the results seen in the ILN *article for 18 May 1867. It is worth noting that in due course the government was to give assistance to certain lines in Scotland as well as Ireland; for example the Treasury contributed over a third of the subscribed capital for the Wick & Lybster Light Railway.*

THE ROYAL COMMISSION ON RAILWAYS

THE Royal Commissioners on Railways have at length made their report. The document sums up in great detail the results arrived at from the mass of evidence adduced before the Commission, and gives judgment against the proposition that the railway system should be taken under the control of the State. The general conclusion of the Commissioners is, in short, that no comprehensive plan shall be undertaken, and that the dealing with the railway system shall be confined to modification in private bill legislation, and in the management by the companies. The reports says:–

We are of opinion that it is inexpedient at present to subvert the policy which has hitherto been adopted of leaving the construction and management of railways to the free enterprise of the people, under such conditions as Parliament may think fit to impose for the general welfare of the public.

We consider that there is not sufficient reason for excepting Ireland from this general conclusion; but, as it has been the established policy to assist railways and other public works in Ireland, we recommend that, when Parliament thinks fit to make advances to Irish railway companies, the money should be lent for a fixed period of considerable length, so as to enable the company to develop its resources before it is called on for repayment. We are, however, of opinion that advances should not be made to the Irish railway companies as a condition of reducing their rates and fares; but that, as the railway companies have the best opportunities of judging whether rates can be reduced so as to be recuperative within a reasonable time, they should be left to carry out such experiments at their own risk.

We recommend that Parliament should relieve itself from all interference with the incorporation and the financial affairs of railway companies, leaving such matters to be dealt with under the Joint-Stock Companies' Act, and should limit its own action to regulating the construction of the line, and the relations between the public and joint-stock companies so incorporated, requiring such guarantees as may be necessary for the purpose of securing the due performance of the condition upon the faith of which the Parliamentary powers of the company have been granted.

We do not consider that it would be expedient, even if it were practicable, to adopt any legislation which would abolish the freedom railway companies enjoy of charging what sum they deem expedient within their maximum rates, when properly defined, limited as that freedom is by the conditions of the Traffic Act; but we are of opinion that railway companies should be required to give a reasonable notice of their intention to raise their rates of charge.

We are unable to see any method of ensuring punctuality in passenger trains by means of legislative enactments, except that proposed by the Committee of the House of Commons in 1858 – viz., that punctuality should be guaranteed, and that passengers injured by delay should be enabled to recover summarily a fixed sum; but we have already referred to the objections to this proposal.

We are of opinion the railway companies should be bound, under adequate penalties, to give at least a week's notice of any alterations of time of their regular passenger trains.

We do not consider that any direct legislative enactments would cause greater economy in the working of railways; but we are of opinion that, with the object of affording a more accurate view of the operations of the railway companies and of making any undue extravagance apparent, and thus stimulating economy, it is desirable that the several railway companies should render their accounts to the Board of Trade, showing receipts from traffic and the detailed cost of working the line, upon a uniform plan; and that, after consultation with the railway companies, the Board of Trade should not only prescribe the form of such returns and accounts, but lay down the basis on which they are to be computed.

Parliament has relied for the safe working of railways upon the efficiency of the common law and of Lord Campbell's Act, which give persons injured and near relatives of persons killed a right to compensation. We consider that this course has been more conducive to the protection of the public than if the Board of Trade had been empowered to interfere in the detailed arrangements for working the traffic.

[ILN MAY 18 1867]

This editorial is a good example of some ILN *journalism at that time – low on analysis, high on rhetoric. For example, the reader is not given a single reason why the railway mania came to a fairly abrupt end with the repeal of the Corn Laws and the Irish potato famine. These two events caused a sharp rise in imported food, a reduction of the Bank of England's reserves and fears that further advances might be refused. The article implies that sanity returned in the wake of the mania, resulting in amalgamations becoming the order of the day. This overlooks the fact that one of the most important railways of the pre-grouping era, the Midland, was created in 1844 at the beginning of the mania. It is also easy to forget the positive results of investment on an almost unprecedented scale; in 1847 ¼m men were employed on construction which represented about 4 per cent of the working male population. George Hudson, known as the 'Railway King' and the epitome of aggressive railway management and manipulation, must have flinched at the reference to high dividends being paid out of capital; his nemesis had yet to come. Six months after this editorial, he was undone at a meeting of the Eastern Counties Railway from which it became evident that high dividends had been paid partly out of capital to keep the prices of shares in his empire artificially high. It was the end of his career.*

THE RAILWAY QUESTION

The spectacle offered by Great Britain in the memorable year 1845 was by no means creditable to our character as a nation. The speculation of the period passed the limits of folly and bordered upon those of crime. Under the influence of cupidity, men who perfectly well knew that the Railways then projected could not be constructed, and that even if they could be constructed, they could not remunerate the *bona fide* shareholders, rushed into the market for premiums, and fostered the frenzy which they did not share. As in the Mississippi madness which afflicted the French, and the South Sea delusion which made lunatics of the English, at the commencement of the eighteenth century, wise and foolish, great and little, rich and poor, were smitten with the lust of gain; all ranks and classes of men scrambled for wealth, not caring who was ruined if they could gain a portion of the spoil – not condescending even to look at remote but inevitable consequences, if, in the meantime, they could clutch premiums; and, in many instances, loading with abuse the few sage and cool-headed men who in that time of frenzy were courageous enough to tell the truth. The madness was so contagious, that not only that simple and credulous portion of the speculators who in good faith considered Railway stock as the most stable and the most profitable of all forms of investment; but the wiser minority, who were perfectly aware that "it was not and could not come to good," yielded to the irresistible attraction of the new and fierce excitement of the time.

Though in earlier periods of our commercial history we had been guilty of astounding folly, all previous follies were cast into the shade by the superior magnificence of this. Too serious to be laughed at, too violent to be arrested, too obstinate to be reasoned down, too attractive to be despised, too natural to be wondered at – all that sensible men could do was to watch the course of the mania, and predict a day of reckoning and a return to reason. As they predicted, the day of the reaction arrived. The rush out of railway speculation was as violent and unreasonable as the rush in. The madness of cupidity was succeeded by the madness of fear, and dupers and duped floundered together into one large quagmire of perplexity, alarm, and bankruptcy. So true is that error invariably carries its own punishment along with it; and that the rule of right is never violated with inpunity, either by small offenders or by great ones, by individuals or by nations.

But the great panic blew over, the first unreasonable terror and distrust subsided, and men looked somewhat more dispassionately upon the true state of the undertakings to which they were pledged. Attempts were made by those whose sole business was Railway management, and who were interested professionally, either as engineers or law agents, in the stability and prosperity of these undertakings, to put the best face upon the matter, and to depict the various projects in the most flattering light. These attempts were far from unsuccessful, and something like confidence in the great lines of Railway succeeded the panic of 1846. Amalgamations and extensions became the order of the day. Competing companies were bought up, branch lines were undertaken, and previously established short lines were drawn into the "system" of the great ones.

The cost at which all these operations was effected was startling. Six, and eight, and even ten per cent was continually guaranteed to the shareholders of such lines as were necessary for the extension of the great leviathans; but though people wondered, they did not distrust. Shares continued at a premium; tempting dividends were declared, and the Railway world continued to wag almost as merrily as before. This comfortable state of things did not, however, last long. It was found that, although dividends of eight and ten per cent were declared, the calls were far more onerous than the dividends were remunerative; and that the man who received a dividend of ten pounds on a share, had not unfrequently to pay twenty or thirty as a call, to carry on the work either of construction or of amalgamation. Railway affairs underwent another change in popular estimation. A new form of mistrust arose – a mistrust that these glittering and too beautiful dividends were declared out of capital, not out of revenue; and that the expenses of Railway management were too enormous to allow even moderate dividends, without a total change of system. We are in the midst of this new perplexity at the present moment; and the stock of the Great London and North-Western line – the triton among the minnows of railways – which, in the palmy days of confidence, was considered cheap at 250, is down at par, or a shade under, with a tendency to a still further depreciation.

Other lines, both great and small, are in a similar predicament; and thousands and tens of thousands of persons, who have invested their savings in these great national and pre-eminently useful undertakings, see their property gradually melting before their eyes, without power to avert the ruin, or even to stop it at the point to which it has arrived. They would, in many instances, be content to surrender their shares, to be secured from further liability. But, even upon these terms, they cannot free themselves. Calls continue to be made, and must be met – not under the simple penalty of loss of interest in the concern – but under the aggravated penalty of the liability of the whole fortune of shareholders, if the demand be disregarded. Thirty-one millions of pounds sterling were called up last year; nearly twenty-six millions have been called up this year; and the Directors of the various Companies are empowered by their acts of Parliament to make further calls for the completion of their lines.

[ILN OCT 28 1848]

STATIONS

THE GREAT NORTHERN RAILWAY

Few persons who have inspected the buildings of the Great Northern line of Railway can fail to have been struck with their vast extent and completeness; of which the pair of views upon the next page present interesting specimens. In the whole the buildings Mr. Lewis Cubitt, the architect, has sought to combine with the greatest strength and cheapness of construction the utmost facilities for the transit and stowage of goods. The entire station as it stands, with coal-stores, goods offices; arrival, departure, waggon, and carriage-sheds; granary, canal-docks, and temporary passenger-station, covers a space of about forty-five acres. We have engraved the Granary and Goods'-shed of the London terminus at Battle-bridge.

The Granary, which fronts the canal dock, and has water ways for barges, is 70 feet high, in six stories, 180 feet by 100 feet, and will hold 60,000 sacks of corn. On the last story [*sic*] are immense wrought-iron water-tanks, holding 150,000 gallons; and from the highest floor to the ground inclines, down which the full sacks slide, without a touch, from top to bottom. From floor to floor the grain is hoisted by hydraulic apparatus, invented by Mr. Armstrong, by which contrivance the cranes in the goods-shed are also worked.

The railway is brought into direct communication with the river at Limehouse by the Regent's Canal, water ways from which, commanded by the cranes, pass under the centre of the goods-shed platform; so that timber brough in floats, hogsheads of sugar, and all articles of heavy merchandise for the use of inland towns along the line, can be carried from the shipping direct.

The Goods-shed, the largest of its kind in the kingdom, is of brick, 600 feet in length, 80 feet wide, and 25 feet high, with timber roof, glazed with the cast glass windows, 8 feet by 2 feet 6 inches. Our Engraving shows very distinctly the platforms, railway trucks, waggons, cranes, canal; and, without further explanation, will enable our readers to understand with what ease and rapidity goods can be laden or unladen, lifted from the canal, or shipped in barges.

The only part of the shed that our Engraving does not show is the stables, 300 feet by 30 feet, under each side of the goods platform, light, perfectly ventilated, and affording room for 300 horses to be employed in the delivery of coals, vegetables, meat, grain, and all goods and parcels carried by the rail.

Nearly half the tonnage of the line is in grain, consisting of corn, chiefly from Lincolnshire. Until the opening of the Great Northern line, this corn was almost entirely conveyed coastwise, at great delay and risk of loss and damage. Now, within twenty-four hours it reaches its most distant market with the most perfect punctuality and safety by rail; and for the accommodation of this traffic the Company keep a stock of 100,000 sacks. The carriage of potatoes has reached 300 tons a week; hay, from 30 to 40 tons; carrots, as much as 20 tons a week; and on a single market-day, from the neighbourhood of Biggleswade and

Leeds from Holbeck Junction

The Granary

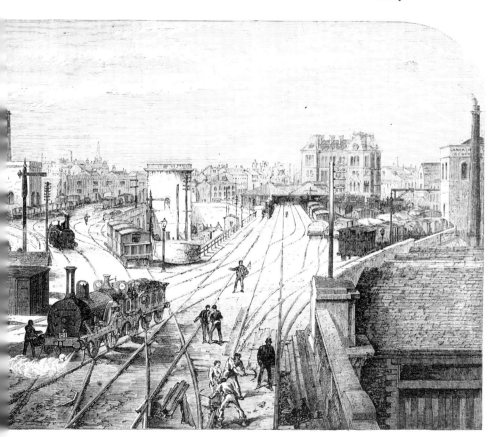

This view of 1868 shows Leeds Central Station (London & North Western, Great Northern, Lancashire & Yorkshire and North Eastern Joint) with Central goods station (L&NW and L&Y Joint) beyond the engine blocking the crossover. The history of Leeds Central has not been fully unravelled, largely because the secretary of the station's management committee, Samuel Smiles (of Self-Help fame), left many events unrecorded. Agreement between the predecessors of the aforementioned companies to construct the station was reached in 1846. A temporary station opened in 1848, and thereafter a confusing series of new agreements and withdrawals followed, much to the annoyance of travellers. It was finally completed in 1857. The goods station at a lower level was built by the Leeds & Thirsk (later part of the North Eastern Railway) and later added to by the Great Northern which shared the running line to Wellington Street Goods as it was known. Central Station closed in 1967.

[ILN May 30 1868]

The Goods Shed

Sandy, no less than 30 tons of cucumbers have arrived at the London stations. Vegetables can now be brought by rail from fifty to sixty miles off in as short a time, and as fresh condition, as by market cart from Barnet, Finchley, Greenwich, Hampton, or any place within eight to twelve miles of London. The rails, in short, give a radius of full fifty miles for metropolitan market, gardens; and, however great may be the present consumption of fruit and vegetables, there can be no doubt that it is infinitely below the wishes of the population. But the scarcity of such articles of food, in consequence of the narrow limits and high rent of the land on which they are grown, so raises the price as to place them out of the reach of the great majority of the population. And, for such extension of gardens, the railway affords still further facilities by carrying down in the returning coal-trucks, at a very low rate, the fresh stable manure from London – an item of traffic as yet in its infancy, but which is rapidly gaining ground.

Our Engraving of the Goods-shed shows at one end the canal under the centre of the platform: the boats can thus come into the shed and have goods of all kinds passed to or from the railway trucks as the case may be. The canal enters the Thames at Limehouse, and a branch line of rail is in course of construction to join the East and West India Dock line, so as, without any transhipment, to carry goods coming by rail direct to the ships.

[ILN MAY 28 1853]

The text accompanying these illustrations of the Great Northern Railway's granary and goods shed near King's Cross provides a vivid illustration of one of the prime benefits bestowed by the coming of railways: the improvement in, and reduction of cost of, people's diet in urban areas. The much-increased areas surrounding conurbations that could provide fresh vegetables, fruit and fish inevitably lowered prices; equally the shorter journey times and greater care with which the goods were handled, compared with the generally poor conditions of the roads and slowness of canals, raised the standard of food in the market place. The reference to the 'terminus at Battle-bridge' refers to the road which crosses the railway immediately north of the station. It is curious that the writer does not give the station its proper name since it had been in use since 1850 when the temporary station between Gas Works and Copenhagen tunnels was given this name. The permanent King's Cross was opened on 14 October 1852.

LOCOMOTIVES AND PROPULSION SYSTEMS

PROSSER'S RAILWAY GUIDE AND SAFETY WHEELS

NOW IN USE ON AN EXPERIMENTAL RAILWAY ON WIMBLEDON COMMON

The objections in the way of a more perfect development of the railway system are found in the great cost, and in the extreme danger of the iron rail and its attendant locomotive apparatus. The atmospheric mode of traction has done much to remedy these evils; but although a safe and relatively a cheap system, it is still a costly one. In the view of such circumstances we may say with a late railway writer, "How many small towns and villages will sooner or later be blotted from the map of England, unless a more economical system be introduced." The villages, hamlets, and farms of the rural districts require railway accommodation, and the poorer countries of Europe need to be united by the iron road; but the

cost, at the present time, shuts them entirely from the civilising privilege. Happily, however, it holds goods in this case, that "the will has found a way," and that a means of meeting the difficulty has been devised. Wooden railways are to supply the poor with locomotive power; and Mr. Prosser's "guide and safety wheels" are to obviate all the practical difficulties attending the use of them. This statement is founded not merely on experiments or paper conjectures, the ordinary modes of introducing new inventions to public notice, but it is made from the actual daily working, ever since the 18th of June, of a fully appointed train, travelling at from twenty to twenty-five miles an hour over gradients of the third class, and round curves of ten chains radius and less. All this may be seen: go when you will, to Wimbledon Common, between the hours of one and

six daily, you may command the use of the train, to make any experiments that may suggest themselves to your mind. Many experienced engineers have gone down to Wimbledon, with minds prejudiced against the system, and have, after their visits, been constrained to allow, not only that there is something, "but *much* in it." It is of course the interest of some parties to cry out against wood, but can they cry out against safety? Who that reads the almost daily accounts of fearful railway accidents, chiefly owing to trains running off the way, but would not, if he has a spark of humanity remaining in his composition, do all in his power to mitigate, if not entirely to prevent, so great and crying an evil? Safety is a great point in Prosser's system: the guide wheels are so admirably suspended from the carriages, that if the train inclines to one side or the other, it is

View of a train of Prosser's patent guide wheel carriages traversing a curve and descending an inclined plane on a wooden railway

entirely prevented from getting off, even though a piece of wood or other substance be placed across one of the rails; while the cylindrical bearing wheels keep their even course on the top surface of the wooden rails, instead of grinding down the edge of the rails, as in the case of the conical flange wheel on the iron rails: moreover, the bearing wheels revolve on their axles; each wheel therefore, in rounding a curve, observes its natural course; thus grinding and destruction are prevented. Indeed, from experience, it is found that the rails on Wimbledon Common are not worn at all by the constant passing of the train over them.

With these introductory remarks we proceed to describe, in detail, Mr. Prosser's invention.

Many improvements have been made in the construction of railways since their first introduction, and experience daily suggests some mode of overcoming difficulties and impediments that still exist. The chief attention of engineers has been directed to improve the mode of locomotion, and accelerate the speed of trains of carriages. Very little attention was paid to the advantages of improving the mode of guiding carriages along the rails, and diminishing the friction and wear and tear of machinery, until Mr. Prosser's patent for guide wheels came out. The first idea of the patentee was certainly to invent such a mode of guiding carriages along the rails as should enable him to construct cheap lines by the substitution of a cheaper material for rails than iron; but the advantages derived from the substitution of a guide wheel for the flange on the bearing wheels is equally applicable to iron rails as to any other material. The invention being simple, a short description of the guide will suffice to give the public some idea of their construction.

The four principal wheels which support the carriage are without flanges, and present a perfectly flat surface to the rail. It is evident that, upon encountering the slightest curve in the rails, these wheels would be quite inadequate to keep the carriage upon its destined route. The remedy provided is in four extra or antifriction wheels; these are placed two in front and two behind the carriage, upon axles at an angle of forty-five degrees; a deep groove, formed by two flanges, is made in their circumference, exactly corresponding to the inner and upper angle of the rail, and thus they serve as the guiding wheels to the whole machine.

When the railway is in the direction of a right line, only one of each pair of bevel wheels can be in action at the same time, according to the tendency which the carriage may have to move on either side from the centre of the rail. On a curve, the difference is simply that the outside bevel wheel of the front pair, and the inside one of the back pair, come into play, and counteract the disposition there is in the carriage to fly off at a tangent with the curve.

Another very important function performed by the bevel wheels is, that in case of an accident occurring to the running wheels, they would act as supporters to the carriage, and carry it on in safety.

The truth of this assertion has been clearly demonstrated by experiments made on the trial line at Wimbledon Common. When the forewheels of the steam carriage were removed, it ran without them at full speed, throwing the whole weight of the front portion of the carriage and its passengers on the bevel or guide wheels.

The speed attainable on so short a line is of course limited; but the power given to the engineer on the wood (for this line was laid with wooden rails) enables him to drive it at the rate of twenty-six miles an hour, and to stop the carriage in a distance of twenty-four yards.

A curve of 600 feet radius may be traversed with safety at a speed of twenty-five to thirty miles per hour by means of the bevel wheels.

By the adoption of these guide wheels the annual expense of working a line will, it is said, be materially diminished; the wear and tear of engines and carriages resulting from the continual abrasion and oscillation, which is caused by the flange wheel, will be obviated. In using the flange wheel a great loss of power is sustained consequent on the continual friction produced by the flanges against the edge of the rail. An experiment to test the difference in power required to propel a carriage fitted with the guide wheels, and one with the usual flange wheel, was made last autumn on the Hayle railway, in Cornwall. A loaded truck fitted with the guide wheels, and divested of the flanges on the bearing wheels, was found

Side elevation of a railway carriage fitted with Prosser's guide wheels

In retrospect it would seem that Victorian editors and journalists were rather gullible when it came to giving time and space to inventions that were at best eccentric and at worst hopelessly impractical. The coverage given to the demonstration of Prosser's patent guide wheels and wooden track on Wimbledon Common is a case in point. The ILN was far more interested in examining bizarre proposals for a new form of propulsion than it was in commenting upon or recording the development of conventional locomotives

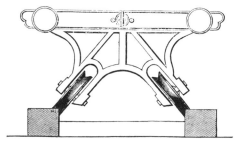

End view of a railway carriage fitted with Prosser's guide wheels

to be propelled with *one fourth* less power than a similar truck equally laden, but with the usual flange wheel, thus clearly demonstrating the advantages of the guide wheel in saving of power. The only obstruction to running carriages with the guide wheel upon the railways already constructed, are the form of the chairs, which coming within an inch and a half of the top of the rail, do not give sufficient depth for the groove of the guide wheel. In railways about to be made, the substitution of a chair, with the inner cheek lower, will enable the managers to run their trains with either the guide wheels or the flange, so that it would not prevent trains from other railways unprovided with the guide wheels from travelling over their line, although they for economy may themselves adopt the guide wheel.

In traversing curves the advantage is still more apparent. In the present arrangement the flanges of the wheels grind with great force against the edge of the outer rail, and produce an increased strain on the axles and other portions of the carriage, and each concussion acts with more or less injury on the machinery of the engine, the flange wheels being of necessity connected with it. Here, by the substitution of the bevel wheels, the line of direction is altered with greater ease, and without affecting the driving or running wheels of the engines or carriages.

Another great advantage by the adoption of the patent guide wheel, is their enabling carriages to travel over a line of railway with rails of less cost than iron – such as wood; also to reduce the expenses of making the line.

The cost which has hitherto attended the formation of railroads averages 25,000*l.* per mile, being 2600 miles, at a cost of 63,500,000*l.* A few of these (where the traffic is great) work at a profit; there are others that pay common interest; while there are some that make no return whatever to the shareholders. Under these circumstances it is obvious that branch or shorter lines of railways cannot be laid down on the present system without, in many instances, a great sacrifice of capital. It follows, therefore, that the introduction of an economical plan would enable all provincial towns to have an expeditious means of access to the metropolis, or to the existing lines of railway, and thus place them on an equality with other rival districts.

The rails may be made of beech, or other hard English timber, six to eight inches square, let into wooden sleepers, and secured by wooden wedges, forming one great frame or wooden grating of longitudinal and cross-sleepers.

The bite of the wheel upon an iron rail depends much on the weight of the engine. It is generally made to weigh from sixteen to eighteen tons, which, on moderate gradients, and at a speed of twenty or thirty miles per hour, enables it to draw from eighty to a hundred tons. The carriages are built to weigh about three tons: this strength is found necessary to withstand the concussion, abrasion, and oscillation.

An engine weighing ten tons, running on wood, will have more tractive power than one weighing eighteen tons running on iron; and as the concussion and abrasion on wood is so trifling, carriages built to weigh one and a half tons will be as strong as those having to run on iron weighing three tons.

An important question connected with this subject is the durability of the material of which the rails are composed.

The engine on the Wimbledon experimental line weighs about six tons; it passes over the rails upwards of fifty times every day in every variety of weather, which is equal to the traffic of any railway. The rails consist of Scotch fir; they exhibit no appearance of wear from the friction of the wheels on the upper surface, the saw marks not even being effaced; nor have the bevel wheels exercised any abrasing effect on the edges, which remain as sharp and well defined as they were when first laid down.

The capability of wood to sustain the strain to which it must necessarily be exposed, especially when moving over it at high velocities, has been satisfactorily proved by the experience of the Great Western and other railways, where continuous longitudinal sleepers of wood have been employed, and experience has shown that the solidity of the road is much greater than when the iron rails were attached either to stone blocks or transverse wooden sleepers. In proof that wooden rails cut from beech will bear the wear and tear of trains passing over it, it is well known that beech cogs have been known to last eighteen to twenty years when working in gear with an iron wheel.

The rails in the Vauxhall line are metallised by Sir W. Burnett's process for preventing dry-rot and decay of timber. Scotch fir, if subjected to pressure, will crush at ten tons; while beech (the wood recommended for railways) will bear a pressure of eighty-two tons before it begins to yield.

Some of the impediments with which railroads have to contend are, the undulations of the country, and the necessity of diverging from a right line in order to obtain the traffic of important towns.

These obstacles can only be overcome by an enormous outlay of capital in making the required excavations and embankments, or by the oftentimes ruinous system of tunnelling; and, after all, inclines of greater or less gradients are unavoidable, and prevent the line being worked economically. Curves on iron railroads are highly prejudicial, especially if the radius be small, as the wear and tear becomes proportionably increased.

Now, by the introduction of Prosser's plan, the evils arising from the obstacles alluded to would be very materially diminished; for, in the first place, the surface resistance obtained by the elastic character of wooden rails, enables a train to be propelled up inclines, with much greater facility and ease than on rails constructed of iron; and the peculiar construction and arrangement of these patent guide wheels give a train the power to traverse curves with comparative ease, which would not be attempted on the present system.

The cost of making railroads depends much on the quantity of ground to be removed: it is obvious that if embankments to any extent can be avoided, a great saving would be effected; the subsequent expense of keeping them in repair reduced, delays in the traffic from slips and from sinking of sleepers avoided, and the danger to passengers lessened, as, from the latter cause, many lives have been sacrificed.

The advantages of wooden railways thus constructed, in point of economy, durability, and as feeders to the great and central lines already formed, must be apparent to every one who has given the subject any consideration.

Thus long lines of railways may be laid down with iron rails, whilst the feeders from different towns within their reach may be accommodated with railway communication at an expense that their more limited traffic will warrant the proprietors to incur.

These branch railways will pour into the main lines a great accession of traffic, and yield to the enterprising promoters of them a large and certain profit on the money expended in their formation; it is therefore to the interest of railway proprietors to be among the great supporters of the plan.

The result of a series of experiments made to ascertain the proportionate power of the bite of wood over iron, has fully borne out the assertion of the patentee, that the bite of the driving wheel on wood is nearly double that on iron.

On the surface of an iron wheel four feet diameter, a lever eight feet long was placed, with a weight of seven pounds attached to the lever three feet from the centre of the axis of the wheel; the surface of the lever being iron at the tangent of the wheel, it required a weight of twenty-eight pounds attached to the crank to make it revolve. On substituting a wood surface for the iron one it required a weight of forty-two pounds.

Another experiment confirmed the result with the iron surface; a weight of twenty-eight pounds attached to the spoke of the wheel at a distance of six and three quarter inches from the centre, made it revolve; whilst, with a wood surface, it required the same weight, to be attached to the spoke at a distance of eleven and a half inches from its centre; thus clearly demonstrating that the power obtained by the bite of the wood is nearly double the bite of iron.

William Cubitt, one of the first railway authorities, is quite in favour of wooden rails for particular purposes, and under particular circumstances: "when the price of iron is high," says this eminent engineer, "I would certainly use wooden rails; and for atmospheric railways, the wooden rails are especially applicable."

"Mr. Sims, engineer to the Indian Government, inspected the Wimbledon wooden way just before his departure to the East, in company with a railway engineer of long standing, to whom he communicated in a letter his opinion on this important subject. He was much pleased with the results of his examination and experiments, one of which was to stop the train suddenly, first on the iron, then on the wood, when going at the rate of twenty miles an hour: the result was, that, on the iron, the complete stoppage of the train was effected in eleven seconds; while on the wood it was effected in eight seconds. This experiment was repeated, and precisely the same result was produced the second trial."

[PICTORIAL TIMES OCT 4 1845]

THE "FAIR-FIELD" RAILWAY STEAM-CARRIAGE

About a year since (Oct. 30, 1847) we gave in our columns an Engraving of a Lilliputian Locomotive, constructed by Messrs. Adams and Co., of Fair-Field Works, for Mr. Samuel, the engineer of the Eastern Counties Railway. This carriage engine was constructed for the supervision of the line, to save the expense of the large machines. Another engine, intended to work branch lines of the Bristol and Exeter broad gauge, was last week making some experimental trips on the West London, which line is laid for both gauges, or what is called the "Mixed;" and the results were highly satisfactory, putting beyond all doubt the soundness of the principle.

The order for this Steam-Carriage was given to Messrs. Adams and Co., by Mr. Charles Hutton Gregory, the engineer of the Bristol and Exeter line, under the sanction of his directors, after a single trial of the Lilliputian Locomotive of Mr. Samuel, which is christened the "Express." The conviction was conclusive in the mind of Mr. Gregory, that light steam-carriages were not only practical, but economical, and that by their agency profits might be made on branch lines which previously had yielded only losses.

Still, though the "Express" was a little "fact," the passenger-carriage had yet to become a greater fact, and doubts in abundance were circulated. But united purpose grew from the conviction of mechanical truth; for it was not regarded as a problematic scheme, but as a well-ascertained plan.

The design and plan of the "Fair-Field" is by the patentee. It was approved by Charles Hutton Gregory, who gave the carriage its name. The engine is peculiar, as will be seen by the View we have given. The frame is, for convenience, made to bolt to the carriage firmly, in a separate length, so as to remove with facility, in case of repairs. The boiler is tubular and vertical, 3 feet in diameter, and 6 feet high – 100 tubes, 4 feet in length, 1½ inches diameter. Fire box, 2 feet high, 2 feet 6 inches diameter. This will give 20 square feet of heating surface in the fire-box, 150 feet tube surface in the water, at 50 feet in the steam, which has great effect in drying it before it leaves the boiler. The vertical tubes are found to generate steam very naturally. The cylinders are 8 inches in diameter, and of 12 inches stroke. The pistons communicate by their connecting ends with a separate crank-shaft, on which are placed the excentrics, and the driving-wheels (4 feet 6 inches in diameter), the axle of which is in front of the boiler, and put in motion by side rods or crank pins. Thus, when the side rods are removed, the whole becomes an ordinary wheel carriage. The tank is in front of the boiler, and will contain 220 gallons of water. The coke-box is attached to the carriage end. The fuel and water would be sufficient for a journey of about 40 miles. The first-class compartment is fitted for 16 passengers, but 6 extras could find room. The second class will carry 32, but on occasions, 48 – total, 60. The running wheels are 3 feet 6 inches in diameter, and run independently on their axles, as well as the usual movement of the axles in the journals. The frame is within nine inches of the rails, and no steps are required. The total weight is estimated at ten tons; and the consumption of coke will be under 10lbs. per mile.

The Steam-Carriage was delivered on to the West London before she was in through working condition, in order to test her powers. The result has been that she has exceeded a speed of 35 miles an hour *up* a 3 mile incline of 1 in 100; and 41 miles *down* the same incline, with the disadvantages of a very sharp curve and no run at starting, very loose rails, and one of them deeply rusted from disuse, grinding in the flanges with great friction. There is little doubt that, when in order, she will make 60 miles per hour on good rails on a level. We understand that, when completed, it is the intention to run her for several days on the West London, to give directors and engineers an opportunity of trying her.

We should mention that in the trimmings of the carriages, is worked the monogram of the Railway Company – a tasteful novelty, introduced by Payne and Son, of Great Queen street, Lincoln's-inn-fields.

[ILN DEC 2 1849]

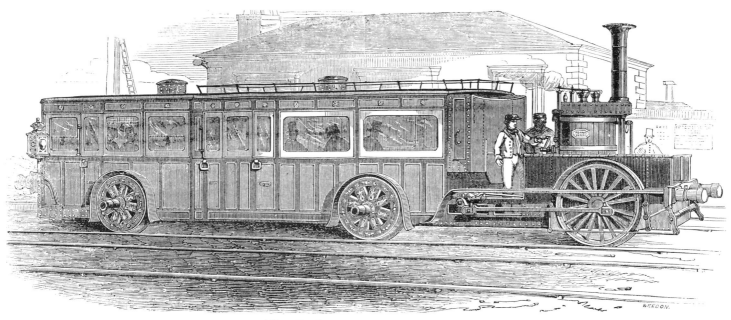

The "Fairfield" Railway Steam-Carriage

Charles Hutton Gregory was Brunel's successor as chief engineer of the Bristol & Exeter Railway and had the distinction of designing and erecting the first railway semaphore signal while engineer of the London & Croydon Railway. Of this contraption for the Bristol & Exeter Railway, nothing has been found to indicate on which B&E lines the steam carriage operated, or indeed whether it left the West London Railway for the West Country.

NEW EXPRESS ENGINES ON THE LONDON AND NORTH-WESTERN RAILWAY

The magnificent new Engines now worked on the London and North-Western Railway for the express trains are of the largest class of passenger engines yet introduced upon the narrow gauge. They combine several important improvements, which have recently been patented by Mr. McConnell, the locomotive engineer of the company.

From the admirable proportions of all the parts, both of engines and tenders, they retain a beautiful and symmetrical appearance, notwithstanding the great power and strength of the working portion. The cylinders, which are compactly arranged inside the framing, are 15 inches in diameter, with a 24-inch stroke. The pistons, which are of wrought iron, forged solid with the rod, are, with increased strength, at least one-third lighter than when constructed on the ordinary principle; while the very rapid

reciprocating motion of this part of the machine makes any reduction of weight a matter of importance. This will be better understood when it is known that it makes a difference in this instance of not less than 40 on [sic] per minute on each piston when travelling at the rate of 60 miles per hour. The driving-wheels are 7 feet 6 inches diameter, and the axles are hollow – a mode of construction which ensures greater soundness in the manufacture, with the advantage of increased strength, and a reduction of fully one-third of the weight. The bearing-springs and buffers are of india-rubber, prepared by an improved process, rendering its elasticity uniform, and remaining unaffected by any changes of temperature.

The more peculiar improvement introduced into the construction of these engines, however, consists in the arrangement of the boiler and tubes: thus, a portion of the fire-box is continued, or rather projected, into the barrel or circular part of the boiler, and forms a recess or chamber for the more perfect combustion of the gases evolved from the fuel in the fire-box, into which a further supply of air is admitted through hollow stays employed for the support of the combustion chamber, and communicating with the external atmosphere. Owing to this projection, the tubes traversing the boiler are much shorter than usual; but, although the gases pass off at a higher temperature, a more intense heat is generated by the same quantity of fuel; thus, effecting great

economy in the use of coke. Experiments have been made with anthracite coal, which has been found to answer perfectly, making this improvement of great importance where coke cannot be procured, unless at an extravagant price. The application of a surcharging vessel, which has been introduced into the smoke-box for the purpose of heating and drying the steam, adds a vast amount of force to its action, and greatly reduces the consumption of fuel. Not less than 50 per cent of elastic force being obtained by this application. Small steam pumping-engines are fixed upon the foot plates to keep up the supply of water in the boilers at all times. By this means the necessity of running out on the line, for the supplying water in the boiler, is obviated.

Bourdon's pressure gauge is an appendage of great convenience to the driver, by its indicating the actual pressure of steam in the boilers.

Altogether, these engines may be considered an important step in the progress of locomotion upon railways.

[ILN Dec 18 1852]

New Express Engine for the London and North-Western Railway

The 'McConnell Patent' or 300 class 2-2-2s were built between 1852–4, two by E. B. Wilson & Co and 10 by W. Fairbairn & Sons of Manchester. No 300 became No 39 in 1856 and No 639 in the combined list of the former locomotive divisions which were amalgamated after the retirement of J. E. McConnell in 1862. No 639 is thought to have been scrapped in August 1863 after only 11 years' service, a reflection of the rapidity of locomotive development. It is interesting to note that the buffers were made of 'india-rubber'; some broad gauge buffers were made of leather stuffed with horse hair and made ideal music stools when the engines were withdrawn.

FAIRLIE'S STEAM-CARRIAGE

On several occasions the principles of the double-bogie engines and light carriages for railways, advocated and developed with so much perseverance by Mr. Fairlie, have been favourably criticised; and recently there was a successful public exhibition of a light steam-carriage for branch lines and lines of small traffic. The length of the carriage is 43 ft., including a compartment for the guard; the engine, carriage, and framing complete weighs, exclusive of passengers, 13½ tons; and including its load of sixty-six passengers (sixteen first-class and fifty second), only 18½ tons. When entirely completed it will have a broad step or platform on each side, extending its entire length, and protected by a hand-rail, to enable the guard to pass completely round the train. Passengers can also pass along it to the guard, affording thus an easy means of intercommunication. The engine, running on two pairs of small wheels close together, so as to give the smallest amount of wheel base, forms one bogie, or platform, upon which the front part of the passenger-carriage is

supported and pivoted, this carriage having another bogie or platform, to which it is also pivoted, supporting its rear end. There is thus a large freedom of motion, and it was astonishing to witness the speed and grace with which this long body was swung at more than eighteen miles an hour round curves of only 40 ft. upon an oval line of rails under 200 yards in circumference, laid down in a garden attached to the Hatcham Ironworks. Mr. Samuel – the pioneer of light engines and rolling-stock – had many years ago a small engine-carriage running with great success upon the Great Eastern Railway; and numbers will remember the Express. Mr. Fairlie himself has built an engine for the narrowest gauge passenger railway in existence worked by locomotives, which, under the title of the "Little Wonder," has earned a notoriety for itself upon the Festiniog Railway; but never before has the world seen a railway carriage of such large dimensions with sixty-six passengers spun round at railway pace in a metropolitan plot of ground of less than three quarters of an acre. From accidental circumstances the present carriage is not of the standard dimensions proposed by that engineer – namely, a carriage with two first-class compartments to seat sixteen persons, three second-class for thirty, and four and a half third-class compartments to seat fifty-four – in all one hundred passengers. The standard machine complete would weigh about 14 tons, and with the passengers from 20 to 21 tons, and could be driven forty miles an hour up gradients of 1 in 100, passing round curves of 50 ft. radius at half that speed with perfect safety, as was recently done upon a temporary line of rails. In fact, as to the safety of running these carriages, there is no question whatever. The weight per wheel of the Fairlie steam-carriage is only about 2½ tons, and it follows, therefore, that very light rails may be used, and everything light in proportion; whilst the capability of passing such sharp curves would also be a very important element in the construction of cheap lines. Indeed, as roads are now the first consideration in opening estates for building, agriculture, or

mining, such light railways may hereafter advantageously take their place; and there is no reason why light village lines should not be made profitable feeders to the branches and main trunks of railways. On the diminution of working expenses by light rolling stock no remarks can be required.

[ILN AUG 14 1869]

Robert Fairlie was born in Scotland in 1831 and received his training as a locomotive engineer at Crewe and Swindon. After a time on the Londonderry & Coleraine and Bombay & Baroda railways, he set up as a consultant in London. In 1863 he patented his articulated locomotive concept, which differed from previous double boiler and bogie engines in a number of ways, and two years later the first Fairlie locomotive entered service on the Neath & Brecon Railway. This design for a steam-carriage, or rail motor as they would later be called, was about 35 years ahead of its time, although the method of attachment of the

two components in the steam rail motors of the 1900s was rather different from that envisaged by Fairlie. The London & South Western Railway introduced two steam railcars on the East Southsea branch in mid-1903. The Great Western Railway introduced 'a motor car service, a combined car which will carry about fifty-two passengers . . . working by steam' between Stonehouse and Chalford in Gloucestershire on 12 October 1903. The LNWR introduced its first railcar on the Dyserth branch in 1905, the year in which the Great North of Scotland Railway had two built by Andrew Barclay. The Lancashire & Yorkshire Railway followed suit in 1907 with a railcar service between Halifax and Stainland.

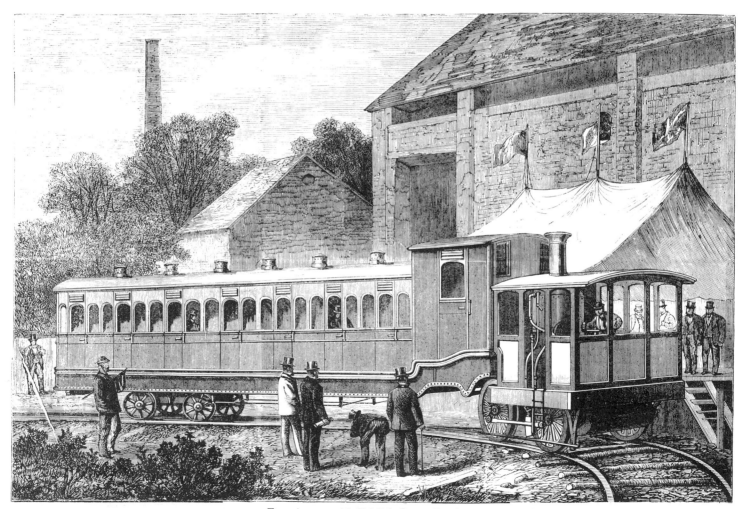

Experiments with Fairlie's Steam-Carriage

LOCOMOTIVE ENGINE FOR THE PARIS UNIVERSAL EXHIBITION

An Express Engine, destined for the Paris Exhibition, and appropriately entitled the Eugénie, has been constructed by Messrs. Fairbairn and Sons, of Manchester, upon the design of Mr. M'Connell, of Wolverton, combining all the latest improvements of that gentleman – viz., prolonged firebox, combustion-chamber, solid wrought-iron piston, hollow axle, &c. The general contour of this engine is symmetrical, suggesting the idea of stability and lightness. It has been running express and mixed passenger trains on the southern division of the London and North-Western Railway, and has amply realised all expectations as to its performance. Sub-joined is an account of the experiments, which show very good results, the engine consuming a moderate quantity of fuel per mile, with a corresponding good evaporation.

In a journey of 280 miles, with express and other passenger trains, with an average load of 41.5 tons, the consumption of coke was 19.6lb. per mile, evaporating 8.9lb. of water per 1lb. of coke.

The following are the principal dimensions of this Engine: – Diameter of cylinder, 15 in.; length of stroke, 22 in.; diameter of driving-wheel, 7 ft.; ditto of boiler, 4 ft.; length of boiler, 10 ft. 6 in.; ditto of firebox proper, 3 ft. 9½ in.; ditto of combustion-chamber, 4 ft. 7½ in.; heating surface in combustion-chamber and firebox, 159 sq. ft.; ditto in tube, 731 sq. ft.; total heating surface, 890 sq. ft. The boiler contains 414 tubes, 6 ft. long, 1¼ in. outside diameter. Area of firegrate, 13 sq. ft. Weight of engine in working order, 21.18 tons.

[ILN June 30 1855]

This engine appears never to have become part of the LNWR stock list. From the wording of the article it seems that it remained in the ownership of the builders, Messrs. Fairbairn, and that the LNWR granted permission for trials to be run over the Southern Division.

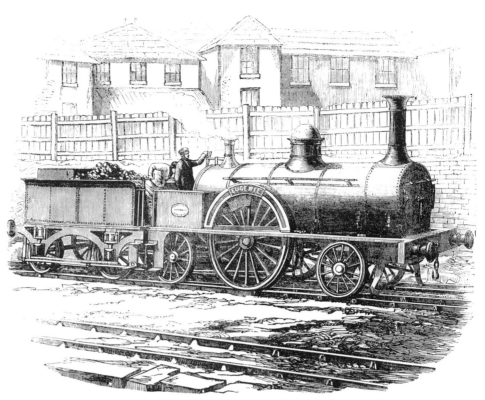

M'Connell's Express Locomotive Engine for the Paris Universal Exhibition

THE PNEUMATIC RAILWAY IN THE GROUNDS OF THE CRYSTAL PALACE

We give an Illustration of the Pneumatic Railway, invented by Mr. T. W. Rammell, C.E., a working model of which has, during the last two weeks, been exhibited in the grounds of the Crystal Palace. It extends from the Sydenham entrance to the armoury, near the Penge gate, a distance of nearly six hundred yards. A brickwork tunnel, about 10 ft. high by 9 ft. wide, and capable of admitting the largest carriages used on the Great Western Railway, has been laid with a single line of rails, fitted with opening and closing valves at each extremity, and supplied with all other apparatus for propelling passenger-trains on this principle, by a strong draught of air behind the train when it travels in one direction, and pumping away the air in front of it when it travels the other way. The motive power is supplied by this contrivance: – At the departure-station a large fan-wheel, with an iron disc, concave in surface and 22 ft. in diameter, is made to revolve, by the aid of a small stationary engine, at such speed as may be required, the pressure of the air increasing, of course, according to the rapidity of the revolutions, and thus

generating the force necessary to send the heavy carriage up a steeper incline than is to be found upon any existing railway. The disc gyrates in an iron case resembling that of a huge paddlewheel; and from its broad periphery the particles of air stream off in strong currents. When driving the air into the upper end of the tunnel to propel the down-train fresh quantities rush to the surface of the disc to supply the partial vacuum thus created; and, on the other hand, when the disc is exhausting the air in the tunnel with the view of drawing back the up-train, the air rushes out in a perfect hurricane from the escape valves of the disc case. When the down journey is to be performed the breaks [*sic*] are taken off the wheels, and the carriage moves by its own momentum into the mouth of the tube, passing in its course over a deep air-well in the floor, covered with an iron grating. Up this opening a gust of wind is sent by the disc, when a valve, formed by a pair of iron doors, hung like lock-gates, immediately closes firmly over the entrance of the tunnel, confining the increasing atmospheric pressure between the valve and the rear of the carriage. The force being thus brought to bear upon the end of the train, the latter, shut up within the tube, glides smoothly along towards

Pneumatic Railway for Passengers at the Crystal Palace

its destination, the revolving disc keeping up the motive power until it reaches the steep incline, whence its own momentum again suffices to carry it the rest of the distance. The return journey, on the contrary, is effected by the aid of the exhausting process. At a given signal a valve is opened, and the disc-wheel set to work in withdrawing the air from the tube. Near the upper end of the tube there is a large aperture, or side-vault, which forms the throat through which the air is exhaled, the iron doors at the upper terminus still being kept shut. In a second or two the train posted at the lower terminus, yielding to the exhausting process going on in its front, and urged by the ordinary pressure of the atmosphere from behind, moves off on its upward journey, and, rapidly ascending the incline, approaches the iron gates, which fly open to receive it, and it emerges at once into daylight. Instead of a train being used at Sydenham, there is one very long, roomy, and comfortable carriage, resembling an elongated omnibus, and capable of accommodating some thirty or thirty-five passengers.

Passengers enter this carriage at each end, and the entrances are closed with sliding glass-doors. Fixed behind the carriage, there is a framework of the same form, and nearly the same dimensions, as the sectional area of the tunnel, and attached to the outer edge of this frame is a fringe of bristles forming a thick brush. As the carriage moves along through the tunnel the brush comes into close contact with the arched brickwork, so as to prevent the escape of the air. With this elastic collar round it, the carriage forms a close-fitting piston, against which the propulsive force is directed. Although the curve in the tunnel is unusually sharp, being of eight chains radius, and the gradients are as high as one in fifteen (those of Holborn-hill being only one in eighteen), it is surprising that the motion is much steadier and pleasanter than ordinary railway travelling. The journey of 600 yards is performed either way in about fifty seconds, with an atmospheric pressure of only two ounces and a half to the square inch; but a higher rate of speed, if desirable, can easily be obtained.

[ILN Sept 10 1864]

This experiment was based upon the pneumatic system devised by T. W. Rammell who addressed himself to the problems of urban transport. In August 1864 this carriage began operations in the grounds of the Crystal Palace, which had been rebuilt at Sydenham and reopened ten years before by Queen Victoria. Between 1.00pm and 6.00pm, passengers could travel in the broad gauge carriage for 6d return. It was as a result of this demonstration of the system that a company was formed to construct what would have been London's first tube railway, from Great Scotland Yard, near Whitehall, to York Road for Waterloo station. Work on the ½ mile Waterloo & Whitehall Railway began in October 1865 on the tunnel between Whitehall and the edge of the Thames, but the financial crisis of 1866 ended work and the scheme. The abandoned tunnel still remains.

LOCOMOTIVE WORKS AND ENGINE SHEDS

GREAT CIRCULAR ENGINE-HOUSE, NORTH-WESTERN RAILWAY

At the north-east corner of the Camden Town Depôt of the North-Western Railway, by the Hampstead-road, has lately been erected this vast accommodation for the engines and tenders used in the luggage department of the line.

The building presents some striking peculiarities of construction, which our Artist has represented in his Illustration, and which we find thus detailed in our active contemporary, the *Builder*:

"The building is of circular form, 160 feet in diameter in the clear of walls. The roof is supported on twenty-four columns at equal distances, and forms a circle 40 feet in diameter from the centre of the building. The columns are 21 feet 9 inches high. On the top of these columns are twenty-four cast-iron girders, running in a right line between each column, and connected at each column with bolts. These girders are formed into an arch, being 2 feet 9 inches deep; the top flange is moulded, and the spandrils perforated, directly over the columns; and connected with them are an equal number of standards, 30 feet 3 inches in height, from the top of girders; at the top they are flanged each way, to receive the purlins and principal rafters, twenty-four of which run up to the lantern-light, and twelve finish on the purlins, at the top of standards. The lantern-light stands 4 feet 3 inches from the roof, and is formed at the same inclination with the roof, with wood louvres at the sides, and cast-iron sash-bars at the top, and covered with rough plate glass; at the top is a piece of cast iron, 2 feet 6 inches in diameter, into which the tops of the sash-bars are fastened; at the apex is a large wooden ball, covered with 10lbs. lead. The height from the line of rails to the tension-rod is 25 feet. The principal rafters drop on a cast-iron shoe, resting on stone templates. The tension-rods pass through the shoes and standards, and are secured with nuts and screws. The top part of the principals and lantern-light are supported by cast-iron brackets, springing from the bottom of standards, and secured to the principals within 9 feet of the curb of

---

The London & North Western Railway roundhouse at Camden was not the first; that distinction goes to the North Midland's roundhouse at Derby, erected in 1840. But for some reason, perhaps because it was in the capital, Robert Stephenson's structure for the LNWR attracted all the attention. The influence of Crampton is evident in the two 4-2-0s. The roundhouse ceased to be an engine shed in the early 1870s when Willesden was opened. The old building became a bonded warehouse until imaginatively restored to become the well-known theatre, opened in 1960.

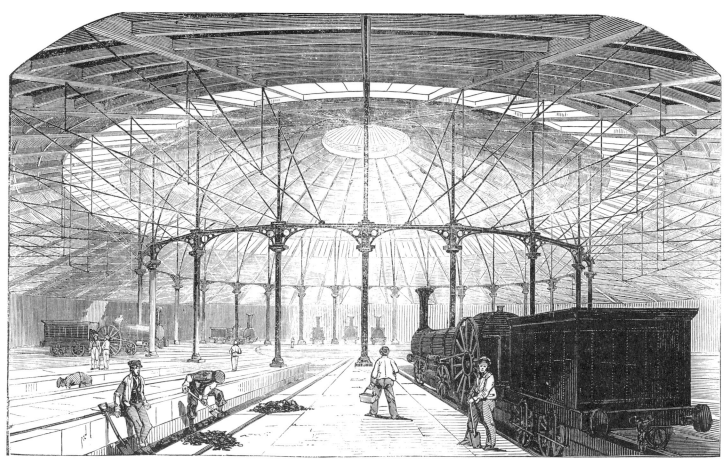

Interior of the New Great Circular Engine-House, at the Camden-Town Depot of the North Western Railway

lantern. From the line of rails to the top of the ball is 69 feet 6 inches. From the line of rails to the top of concrete is 21 feet 6 inches, with a bed of concrete 2 feet 6 inches deep, making a total height from the bottom of concrete to the top of ball of 93 feet 6 inches. The foundation of the building is immensely strong, having 24 transverse walls, 2½ bricks thick. These walls run in pairs, at parallel widths, form the outside wall to within 25 feet 9 inches of the centre, which from the bed for the rails to lay on to receive the engines; and the walls are connected by an invert at the bottom, and a semi-arch at the top, which forms the bottom of ash-pits." The building has one entrance for the engines, which is at a point on the west side; and two smaller doorways for ordinary purposes.

Not far from the principal entrance is a large oven-formed fire-place for the purpose of supplying the engine with firing. At the opposite point is a substantial framework of wood, with buffers, to break any collision with the wall. In the centre is a large turn-table, 36 feet in diameter, where all the engines are run, to be turned into their respective *berths*, which are 23 in number, leaving the entrance clear.

[ILN DEC 4 1847]

LONDON AND NORTH-WESTERN RAILWAY

THE ENGINE-WORKS AT CREWE

If an exemplification be needed of the magnitude of the arrangements necessary for the maintenance of an arterial railway – such as the London and North-Western line – it may be found at Crewe, the third community in the kingdom, that – like Swindon on the Great Western, and Wolverton on the London and Birmingham lines – owes its origin to the enterprise of the railway system. It has been established entirely from the necessity of fixing the Company's laboratories of their locomotive operations, and the *dépôts* of their mechanical power, where constant accumulations of labour have formed communities of handicraftsmen and mechanics. Crewe was an unmarked spot upon the map until the railway converted it into the most important station on the line, constituted it a school-house for engineers and mechanics, and laid out for a section of the population of the north new fields for honourable industry.

Of the present thriving condition of this vast railway township, we find a very

striking picture in the paper by Sir Francis Head, in a late Number of the *Quarterly Review*; and which Mr. Murray has very judiciously reprinted under the grotesque title of "Stokers and Pokers", in his *Home and Colonial Library*. The object of this paper is to detail the practical working of a railway, and, for this purpose, he made a short inspection of one of our largest lines. This he describes in his most felicitous vein – such as none but the Old Man of the Brunnens of Nassau could do; and not the least interesting is the review of the scene he witnessed at

CREWE

"The Company's workshops at Crewe consist of a Locomotive and of a Coach department. In the manufactories of the former are constructed as well as repaired the whole of the engines and tenders required for the Northern Division, namely, from Birmingham to Liverpool; Rugby to Stafford; Crewe to Holyhead; Liverpool to Manchester; Liverpool, Manchester, and Warrington to Preston; Preston to Carlisle. The establishment also 'works,' as it is termed, the Lancaster and Carlisle and Chester and Holyhead Lines. The total number of miles is at present 360, but the distance, of course, increases with the completion of every new branch line. In this division there are 220 engines and tenders (each averaging in value nearly £2000), of which at least 100 are at work every day. Besides repairing all these, the establishment has turned out a new engine and tender on every Monday morning since the 1st of January, 1848. The number of workmen employed in the above department, is 1600, their wages averaging £3800 a fortnight.

"Without attempting to detail the various establishments, we will briefly describe a few of their most interesting features.

"Close to the entrance of the Locomotive Department stands, as its *primum mobile*, the tall chimney of a steam-pump, which, besides supplying the engine that propels the machinery of the workshops, gives an abundance of water to the locomotives at the station, as also to the new railway town of Crewe, containing at present about 8000 inhabitants. This pump lifts about eighty or ninety thousand gallons of water per day from a brook below into filtering-beds, whence it is again raised about forty feet into a large cistern, where it is a second time filtered through charcoal for

the supply of the town. On entering the great gate of the department, the office of which is up a small staircase on the left hand, the first object of attention is the great engine-stable, into which the hot dusty locomotives are conducted after their journeys to be cleaned, examined, repaired, or, if sound, to be greased and otherwise prepared for their departure – the last operation being to get up their steam, which is here effected by coal, instead of coke, in about two hours.

"After passing through a workshop containing thirty-four planing and slotting-machines in busy but almost silent operation, we entered a smith's shop, 260 feet long, containing forty forges all at work. At several of the anvils there were three and sometimes four strikers, and the quantity of sparks that more or less were exploding from each – the number of sledge-hammers revolving in the air, with the sinewy frames, bare throats and arms of the fine pale men who wielded them, formed altogether a scene well worthy of a few moments' contemplation. As the heavy work of the department is principally executed in this shop, in which iron is first enlisted and then rather roughly drilled into the service of the company, it might be conceived that the music of the forty anvils at work would altogether be rather noisy in concert. The grave itself, however, could scarcely be more more silent than this workshop, in comparison with the one that adjoins it, in which the boilers of the locomotives are constructed. As for asking questions of, or receiving explanations from, the guide, who with motionless lips conducts the stranger through this chamber, such an effort would be utterly hopeless, for the deafening noise proceeding from the riveting of the bolts and plates of so many boilers is distracting beyond description. We almost fancied that the workmen must be aware of this effect upon a stranger, and that on seeing us enter they therefore welcomed our visit by a charivari sufficient to awaken the dead. As we hurried through the din, we could not, however, help pausing for a moment before a boiler of copper inside and iron outside, within which there sat crouched up – like a negro between the decks of a slave-ship – an intelligent-looking workman, holding with both hands a hammer against a bolt, on the upper end of which, within a few inches of his ears, two lusty comrades on the outside were hammering with surprising strength and

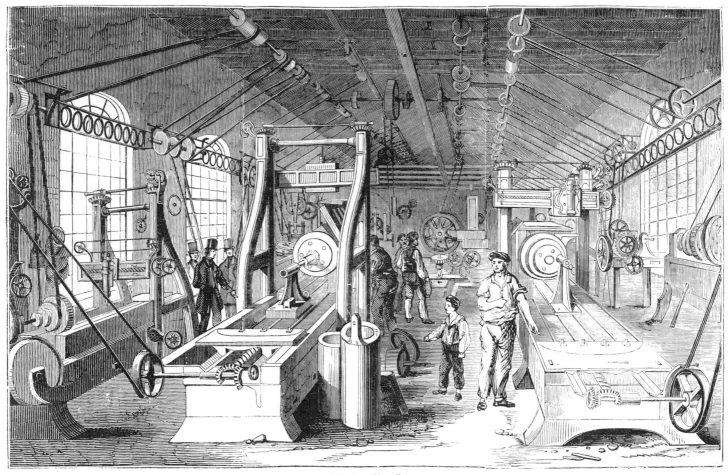

"Fitting Shop"

quickness. The noise which reverberated within this boiler, in addition to that which was resounding without, formed altogether a dose which it is astonishing the tympanum of the human ear can receive uninjured; at all events we could not help thinking that, if there should happen to exist on earth any man ungallant enough to complain of the occasional admonition of a female tongue, if he will only go by rail to Crewe, and sit in that boiler for half an hour, he will most surely never again complain of the chirping of that 'cricket on his hearth' – the whispering curtain lectures of his *dulce domum*.

"The adjoining shop contains a brass and also an iron foundry, in which were at work seven brass-moulders and five iron-moulders. In the corner of this room we stood for a few moments, looking over the head and shoulders of a fine little boy, who was practically exemplifying the properties of the most wonderful of the mineral productions of nature – the loadstone. Among the mass brought into this workshop to be recast are occasionally a quantity of brass shavings and other

sweepings, among which there is a small proportion of iron filings, &c. The little boy's occupation consisted in constantly stirring up the mass or mess before him with a magnet, which, as often as it came out bristling with resplendent particles of iron of various sizes, he swept clean, and then continued his work until the investigator came out of the heap as clear of iron as it went in. Close to this shop is one in which the models and patterns of the castings are constructed. From a spacious open yard covered with stacks of old scrap-iron, much of which was of the size of common buttons, a door opens into a large shop containing twelve forges solely used for the construction of engine-wheels, which are forced on as well as off their axles by an ingenious machine of extraordinary power. Adjoining the open yard we saw in operation Nasmyth's great steam hammer, on the summit of which there sat perched up a man who could regulate its blow from say twenty-five tons to a little tap sufficient only to drive a common-sized nail. As soon as the furnace-door on one side of this hammer was opened, a large lump of scrap-iron at

a white heat was lifted, and then conducted by a crane on to the anvil beneath. At the same moment, from an opposite furnace, a long iron bar, heated only at one extremity, was by a gentle blow of the hammer no sooner welded to the mass, than the head-smith, using it as a handle, turned and re-turned the lump on the anvil so as to enable the steam hammer to weld its contents into proper form. Of course there has been selected for this extremely heavy work the strongest man that could be obtained. He is of about the height and bulk of the celebrated Italian singer Signor Lablache, with apparently the strength of Hercules, or rather of Vulcan himself; and certainly nothing could be a finer display of muscular power than the various attitudes which this heavy man assumed, as, regardless of the sparks which flew at him, or of the white heat of the lump of iron he was forging, he turned it on one side and then on the other, until at a given signal a small smith in attendance placed a sort of heavy chisel on the iron handle, which by a single blow of the steam-hammer was at once severed from it, in order that it might be piled away and another mass lifted from the fiery furnace to the anvil. Close to this Cyclopean scené there is a shop solely for turning wheels and axles, which, brought here rough from the smiths' forges we have described, never leave this place until they are ready to go under the engine for which they have been made.

"After passing through a grinding shop and a coppersmiths' shop, which we must leave without comment, we entered a most important and interesting workshop, 330 feet in length, by 60 feet in breadth, termed the 'fitting shop,' because the work brought here in various states is all finally finished and fitted for its object. Besides 11 planing-machines, 36 shaping and slotting machines, and 30 turning-lathes, all working by steam-power, we observed, running nearly the whole length of the building, five sets of tables, at which were busily employed in filing, rasping, hammering, &c., eight rows of 'vice-men,' only so called because

they work at vices. The whole of the artificers in this room are of the best description, and the importance of their duties cannot perhaps be more briefly illustrated than by the simple fact that, besides all the requisite repairs of 200 locomotive engines, they were employed in finishing the innumerable details of 30 new ones in progress. Some were wholly engaged in converting bolts into screws; some in fitting nuts; some in constructing brass whistles; in short, in this division of labour almost every 'vice-man' was employed in finishing some limb, joint, or other component part of a locomotive engine destined to draw trains either of goods or passengers.

"After visiting a large store-room, in which all things appertaining to engines, sorted and piled in innumerable compartments, are guarded by a store-keeper, who registers in a book each item that he receives and delivers, we will now introduce our readers to the climax of the establishment, commonly called 'the

Erecting-shop.' Hitherto we have been occupied in following in tedious detail from the foundry to the forge, and from the anvil to the vice, the various items, such as plates, rivets, bolts, nuts, rings, stays, tubes, ferrules, steam-pipes, exhausting-pipes, chimney-pipes, safety-valves, life-guards, axle-boxes, pistons, cylinders, connecting-rods, splashers, leading and trailing-wheels, &c., amounting in number to 5416 pieces, of which a locomotive engine is composed. We have at last, however, reached that portion of the establishment in which all those joints, limbs, and boilers, which have been separately forged, shaped, and finished in different localities, are assembled together for the consummation of the especial object for which, with so much labour and at so great an expense, they have been prepared; indeed, nothing, we believe, can be more true than Mr. Robert Stephenson's well-known maxim – '*A locomotive engine must be put together as carefully as a watch!*'

"Fitting Shop"

"The Erecting Shop" – Grand Junction Railway Engine-Works, at Crewe

"The Erecting-shop at Crewe is a room 300 feet long by 100 feet broad, containing five sets of rails, upon three of which are erected the new engines and tenders – the other two being usually occupied by those under heavy repair. The number of artificers we found employed was 220. In this magnificent building we saw in progress of erection 20 passenger-engines, also 10 luggage-engines; and as this shop has (as we have before stated) turned out a locomotive engine and tender complete on every Monday morning for very nearly a year, and is continuing to supply them at the same rate, we had before us in review locomotive engines in almost every stage of progress; and when we reflected on the innumerable benefits, and even blessings, which resulted to mankind from their power, it was most pleasing to be enabled at one view to see – as it were in rehearsal behind the scenes – performers who were so shortly to appear upon the stage of life.

"At the further end of the line of rails close to the north wall there appeared a long low tortuous mass of black iron-work, without superstructure or wheels, in which the form of an engine bed in embryo could but very faintly be traced; a little nearer was a similar mass, in which the outline appeared, from some cause or other, to be more distinctly marked; nearer still the same outline appeared upon wheels; to the next there had been added a boiler and firebox, without dome, steam escape, or funnel pipe: nearer still the locomotive engine in its naked state appeared, in point of form, complete; and workmen were here busily engaged in covering the boiler with a garment about half an inch thick of hair-felt, upon which others were affixing a covering of inchdeal-plank, over which was to be tightly bound a tarpaulin, the whole to be secured by iron hoops. In the next case the dome of the engine was undergoing a similar toilette, excepting that, instead of a wooden upper garment, it was receiving one of copper. Lastly – (it was on a Saturday that we chanced to visit the establishment) – there stood at the head of this list of recruits a splendid bran-new locomotive engine, completely finished, painted bright green – the varnish was scarcely dry – and in every respect perfectly ready to be delivered over on Monday morning to run its gigantic

The creation of railway workshops represented a new departure in industrial organisation, for the range of skills that were eventually brought together, at least in the larger works like Crewe and Swindon, exceeded anything previously known. But when this article appeared, in March 1849, they were yet to eclipse other manufactories in scale: in the 1840s over 6,000 workers were employed at Sir John Guest's iron-works at Dowlais near Merthyr Tydfil. But this was exceptional, and even in their infancy railway works were considerably larger than all but a handful of industrial enterprises. The workshops at Crewe had been open for six years by 1849 and had replaced the earlier shops of the Grand Junction Railway at Edge Hill. From a village of 148 people in 1831, the town's population mushroomed to 4,571 in 1851. The writer was evidently unfamiliar with railway parlance: hence the quaintly termed 'luggage engines' and the reference to carriages being 'in hospital'. Engines in green livery are described; the colour was the standard livery of the Northern Division of the LNWR until 1873.

course. On other rails within the building were tenders in similar states of progress; and, as the eye rapidly glanced down these iron rails, the finished engine and tender immediately before it seemed gradually and almost imperceptibly to dissolve, in proportion to its distance, until nothing was left of each but an indistinct and almost unintelligible dreamy vision of black iron-work."

The accompanying Illustrations show two of "the Fitting Shops," and "the Erecting Shop."

The Coach Department constructs and maintains, for the traffic on 393 miles of rails, all the requisite passenger-carriages, luggage-vans, travelling post-offices and tenders, parcel vans and parcel-carts, mill-trucks and break-wagons. The total number of carriages of all descriptions maintained at Crewe amounts to 670, of which about 100 at a time are usually in hospital. There are generally from 30 to 40 new carriages in progress; and the number of workmen employed is 260.

[ILN MARCH 24 1849]

RAILWAY EXTENSION

Swindon is described as the "disputed railway territory," from the number of schemes proposing at this point to join the Great Western Railway, or to pass over it with independent lines. It is situated in a very fine part of the county of Wilts, 77 miles from the metropolis (81 by the railway), and 116¾ from Exeter.

The Railway Station, or Stations, – for there is one on each side of the road – are, perhaps, second to none in the kingdom; and their accommodation is of the most elegant and splendid description. Independent of the magnificent Refreshment Rooms, on each side of the line, there are an excellent Hotel and sleeping apartments: they communicate with each other by a covered passage over the railway.

The New Town, which has sprung up within the last two years, is principally occupied by the artisans employed by the Railway Company, who make it a sort of depôt for their various works. The houses are all neatly built of stone, with slated roofs, and arranged in streets. They have

already Bristol, Taunton, Exeter, and Bath streets; and others are fast rising.

The Church, of which we gave an Engraving in our journal of last week, is situated at the west end of the town, and is a very beautiful structure; and the school-houses attached are built in the same style. Numerous other buildings and villas are in progress; all building of stone, which is very plentiful in this neighbourhood. The old town of Swindon is about a mile and a half from the station, on the crown of a hill to the south. The view from it is very commanding, the country being very flat on all sides, but remarkably rich and finely wooded. The old town has all the characteristics of an English market town. The old picturesque houses and cottages are here beginning to make way for the more modern style of architecture; and, if half the projects now in contemplation are completed, the old and new towns will ere long be amalgamated in one.

[ILN OCT 18 1845]

The board resolution to construct the principal locomotive works of the Great Western Railway at Swindon was only passed on 6 October 1840, just over two months before the section of line that passed near the old market town was opened. Not even a station was ready for the opening on 17 December. Between then and the appearance of this article on 18 October 1845, the works and railway village were created. The station buildings were 170ft × 37ft and constructed on three levels: the basement accommodated kitchens and service rooms, the main floor at platform level provided refreshment facilities for first- and second-class passengers while the top floor of the northern building was a hotel and the southern, coffee and sitting rooms. The catering was let on a long lease – a move the GWR was bitterly to regret. Even if the ILN writer was correct in describing the refreshment rooms as magnificent, Brunel had other ideas about their coffee: in a letter to the lessees he wrote, 'I assure you that Mr Player was wrong in supposing that I thought you purchased inferior coffee. I thought I said to him that I was surprised you should buy such bad roasted corn. I did not believe you had such a thing as coffee in the place: I am certain that I never tasted any. I have long ceased to make complaints at Swindon. I avoid taking anything there when I can help it.'

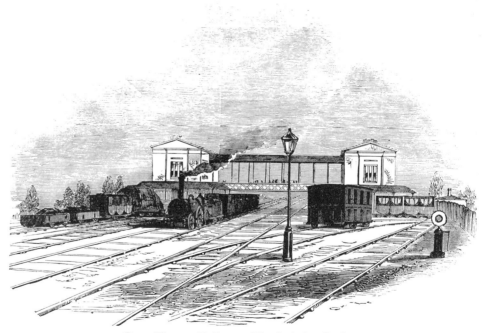

Great Western Railway – The Swindon Station

SIGNALLING

RAILWAY SIGNALS

Obedience to the "signals" used on a railway is indispensable to the safe passage of a train. A moment's inattention to any one of their significant monitions may be followed by the instant death of heedless unsuspecting multitudes, while, on the other hand, a due observance of them at all times, in all seasons, by night as well as by day, divests the speed of even the fastest pleasure train of danger. It is, of course, most important that the servants of a line should become practically familiar with the things signified by the symbols used in their several establishments, but we also deem it to be of much consequence that the public itself should be acquainted with them, for, were such the case, we should cease to hear of the difficulty of obtaining evidence against negligent servants, which on occasions of accident has ordinarily prevailed. Every traveller would then be an observer and a judge of the means used for his preservation, and in proportion to the vigilance of his survey would be the attention of servants entrusted with duties so important to the lives and limbs of passengers.

The signals used on railways are of great variety. Most of the lines have systems peculiar to themselves; and, in consequence, no uniform observance prevails between them, which is a practice much to be regretted, as it tends to confuse the observation of men engaged on different lines, and of

Junction Signal-man at Work

engineers who change one service for another. It cannot, however, be expected that so complicated an operation, and one, too, which has grown up under the management of independent companies, should speedily reach perfection. For the present, the signals are necessarily different on different lines; but we hope to see the day, when the set, which experience has proved the best, shall be universally and compulsorily adopted. We shall now describe the signals used on the more important lines.

Those observed on the London and Birmingham Railway demand the first attention. They consist of Police Signals – Signals shown at Intermediate Stations and the Long Tunnels; and the Engine Signals.

1. POLICE SIGNALS – When the line is clear, and no obstruction in the way of the onward course of the train is either seen or *suspected*, the policeman stands erect, with his flags in his hand, but showing no signal. See Fig. 1. If it be required that the engine should slacken speed, and proceed with caution, from another engine having passed on the same line within five minutes, a Green Flag is held up in the manner shown in Fig. 2. If it be desired that the engine should slacken speed, and proceed with caution, from any defect in the rails, the Green flag is lowered, and held as shown in Fig. 3. But if it be necessary that the engine should stop altogether at any given point, a Red Flag is shown, and waved backwards and forwards, the policeman facing towards the coming engine. At night the same signals are given, by means of coloured lamps. A White Light denotes the line clear: a Green Light requires the use of caution; and when the engine is required to stop, a Red Light is shown, but in place of being held steady, it is waved backwards and forwards. The engine-drivers and guards are, however, warned, that any signal, either by day or night, *violently waved*, denotes danger, and a necessity of stopping.

2. SIGNALS SHOWN AT INTERMEDIATE STATIONS AND THE LONG TUNNELS – Signal posts are erected on the "up" and "down" lines at the Intermediate Stations, and at the entrance of Primrose-hill, Watford, and Kilsby Tunnels, showing a Red Board of a large size, and a Green Board of a smaller size, as day signals. A

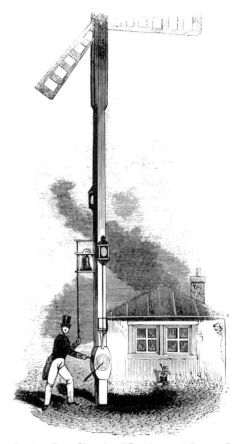

Station Post Signal – "Caution and Danger"

Green or Red Light is substituted as night signals. On a train or engine *passing* an intermediate station, the Green signal is exhibited for the space of *ten* minutes, to denote that a train on the same line has passed within that period, and therefore due caution must be observed on the part of the drivers and guards. On a train *stopping* at an intermediate station, the Red Signal is shown, and continued for five minutes after its departure, when the Green Signal is turned on, to complete the ten minutes' precautionary signal. On a train entering one of the tunnels, the Red signal is shown for the space of ten minutes, to prevent another engine entering within that time; unless the policeman can previously see through that the line is clear, when the Red Signal will be turned off, and the Green shown, to complete the ten minutes' signal. Should the Red Signal be shown an engine passing on that line is ordered invariably to stop on coming up to it.

Birmingham – "All Clear"   "Slacken Speed-Engine"   "Caution – Rails"   Dover – Caution – Rails

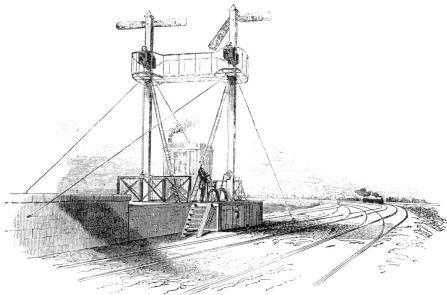

Dover Junction: Danger: Up and Down Lines, Bricklayer's Arms.
Caution, Up Line; Danger, Down Line, London Bridge

It was unusual for the ILN to go into technical details about any aspect of railways; the main exception was the various alternative sources of locomotion to the conventional steam engine (see page 65), but another was this quite involved explanation of the basic elements of signalling. This may have been by way of reassurance to a public that even by 1844 could not have entirely conquered the scepticism or fear that was a common response to the early railways. Nonetheless the writer is not uncritical when he encounters a deficiency, most particularly on the Great Western. The illustration of the junction on the London & Croydon Railway at Bricklayers Arms, where the branch to Bricklayers Arms station left the main line to London Bridge, shows the lever frame that is thought to be the first example of interlocking. A four-lever frame was installed in 1843 to control the signals; the signal wires were connected to stirrups which had to be depressed by the signalman's foot, as seen in the smaller illustration, to clear the signal. The stirrup then prevented the pulling of another lever which would authorise a conflicting movement. It is surprising that the writer does not explain this innovation. A Board of Trade inspector is said to have confounded the system by putting both feet on separate stirrups and managing to clear signals for conflicting routes. The subject of signalling was regarded as being so important that it appeared in several issues.

Junction of the Great Western Railway with the London Branch

Exterior of the A.B. Signal-Box of the South-Eastern Railway at the London Bridge Station

cross, two with the eastern lines, and the central metals are reserved for independent purposes. There is a narrow footway running on each side of the bridge. The greatest care has been taken to adopt as perfect a system of signals as possible. There are sixty semaphores at different points of the locality. The signal-box outside the station and at the point of the bridge is one of the largest and completest that has yet been constructed. It extends from one side of the bridge to the other, and has a range of sixty-seven levers. Two signalmen will be stationed there, except from twelve midnight till six a.m.; but each man will be kept on duty not longer than six hours a day. In the same box there will be stationed a registering clerk and a telegraph clerk.

The two Engravings on pages 240 and 241 of our Supplement show the exterior and the interior of the A. B. signal-box of the South-Eastern Railway, at the entrance to the London Bridge station, which is still more important than the new signal-box at the bridge leading to

the Cannon-street station, as it is used to signal the Brighton, Crystal Palace, and Greenwich trains, besides those of the South-Eastern line. It was fitted up by Messrs. Saxby and Farmer, and is worked entirely under the control of the South-Eastern Company, Mr. Walker the electrician, being employed to superintend the apparatus at all their stations.

The signal-box is a large chamber or pavilion, built of timber, and supported by iron pillars, at a sufficient height directly above the line of railway to allow the trains to pass underneath its floor. The sides of the pavilion are glazed, so that the men within have a perfect view of the trains going up and down. Above the roof of the pavilion are three upright posts, with connecting gangways between them, and a number of projecting arms or blades, which are movable by a simple mechanism from the interior of the pavilion, so that the arm may be either stretched out horizontally, indicating "all right" on the line to which it refers, or else may be sloped to an angle of 45

degrees, which is the signal to stop the train until the arm is again raised to the horizontal position. There are as many as fifty or sixty telegraph wires connected with this signal-box.

On ascending the ladder and entering the pavilion we see placed against the end wall a range of highly-polished spring clicking-levers, working in a metal frame, by which the signalman works the signals and the points. These are uniform in height – about 4 ft. – and each is labelled by a brass plate on the sill, as well as by numbers and letters on the face of the lever. Those that work signals overhead are coloured red; the levers that work points are coloured black. The electric telegraph apparatus, at the other end of the pavilion, is used for communication with the other stations along the line, by the ringing of bells, every stroke of which has its peculiar meaning, well understood and attended to by the telegraph clerk, and registered at the moment with great exactness, in a book kept by a younger clerk for that purpose. It may well be

Interior of the A.B. Signal-Box of the South-Eastern Railway at the London Bridge Station

imagined that the duties of the three persons employed in this signal-box require incessant attention. On Easter Monday as many as 700 or 800 trains are usually signalled at the A. B. station, being at the average rate of about one train in every minute and a half during the eighteen working hours of the day.

[ILN SEPT 8 1866]

A South Eastern Railway terminus on Cannon Street was authorised in June 1861 and opened on 1 September 1866. The ILN combined the report of its opening with a passage on the signalling at nearby London Bridge station. It is particularly interesting to note that in the new box at Cannon Street 'each man will be kept on duty not longer than six hours a day'. This was exceptional in 1866; as late as 1871, a report by the Chief Inspecting Officer of Railways to the Board of Trade could comment that 'eight

hours of continuous duty at very busy signal-cabins and 12 hours in any signal-cabin, are sufficient; but periods of 18, 25, and even 37 hours, for which men have been known to be regularly or periodically employed, principally during exchange of duty, once in two, seven, or thirteen weeks, are inexcusable.' The accident at Thirsk on 2 November 1892 was specifically attributed to the weariness of the signalman, and this led to a reduction in their hours and the system of relief; the appalling head-on collision at Foxcote on the Somerset & Dorset in 1876 had also revealed excessive hours of duty, but legal restrictions were impeded. The stretch of line between London Bridge (the oldest terminus in London and orginally opened by the London & Greenwich Railway in December 1836) and Bricklayers Arms saw a series of signalling innovations. The first use of interlocking has been noted. The semaphore signal made its first appearance on the London & Croydon Railway, which shared

the London & Greenwich's approach to the city from Bricklayers Arms, under the direction of the L&G's engineer, Charles Hutton Gregory, who was later knighted. What is extraordinary in the description of the signalling arrangements at London Bridge is the suggestion that a horizontal board meant that the line was clear and a lowered signal at 45° indicated danger. To the author's knowledge this was never the case, and evidence in the engravings does not suggest that the writer was correct. What was different about early signal operation in most situations was that lines were worked on the 'open' basis on the time interval system, the line being closed for a specified period of time after the passage of a train. The 'normally clear' system continued after the introduction of block working but this was altered after a signal froze in the 'off' position at Abbots Ripton in 1876, causing a double accident. Thereafter lines were 'opened' for the passage of a train and remained 'closed' at other times.

THE MURDER AT SALT-HILL –
THE ELECTRO-MAGNETIC
TELEGRAPH, AT SLOUGH

An extraordinary instance of the working of the newly-applied power of electro-magnetism will be found in the details of the "Murder at Salt-Hill," in another portion of our journal. The eventful circumstance is of such interest as to induce us to submit to our readers a series of illustrations of the detailed means by which the intelligence of a suspected person being in a railway train, has been conveyed from Slough to the metropolis, after the train itself had started from the former place. The instrument of this important result is the Electro-Magnetic Telegraph on the Great Western Railway between Paddington and Slough, a distance of eighteen miles; by which any communication can be made from one point to the other in an almost inappreciably short space of time. To Professor Wheatstone and Mr. Cooke are we indebted for this valuable application of electro-magnetism; they having made an entirely new arrangement of their telegraph, by which it has been greatly simplified, and possesses considerable advantage over the former one.

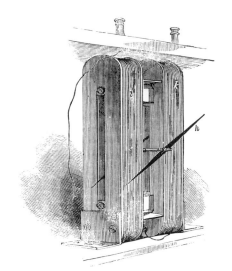

The Coiled Magnets

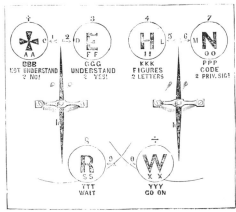

The Index

Arrangements were made before the opening of the Great Western Railway for trials of the new Electric Magnetic Telegraph, devised by Wheatstone and Cooke, between Paddington and West Drayton. The GWR laid at its expense the five wires, insulated with cotton and gutta-percha, in an iron pipe above the ground and beside the line. The agreement envisaged that the railway would, after a period, be entitled to instal the invention throughout the railway without further charge. The five-needle telegraph instruments at Paddington attracted immediate attention, being visited by the Duke of Wellington, Lord Bathurst and Lord Howick in August 1839. Damage to the wires brought the experiment to an end, despite its utility in mitigating some consequences of the frequent locomotive breakdowns in the first years. In 1842–3, the system was overhauled and extended to Slough, using the two-needle instruments illustrated here and with only two wires between the instruments, this time suspended from cast-iron poles, 10–25ft in height. The system was brought to the public's attention by the incident referred to in the article: on New Year's day 1845 John Tawell travelled from Paddington to Slough, murdered a woman using cyanide of potash in a glass of stout and hastily returned to Slough station when the victim's screams alerted neighbours. Tawell was seen leaving the cottage and his description, 'a man in the garb of a Kwaker' – there was no 'Q' in the code at the time – telegraphed to Paddington. From there he was followed and arrested on the following day. Extraordinarily, this second system was also allowed to fall into disuse, so that the GWR, once a pioneer of the telegraph, became one of the most backward of the large railways. This situation was remedied in the 1850s when the telegraph was installed on all major lines.

The Great-Western Electric Telegraph

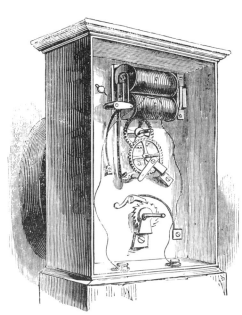

The Striking Apparatus

We have already adverted to the performances of this Telegraph, and have engraved the exterior of the station at Slough, in which the apparatus is worked. We shall now present to our readers the details of such apparatus; before which, however, we shall relate from the evidence on the Coroner's Inquest at Salt-Hill, the steps which led to the successful employment of this novel means of communication.

The Rev. E. T. Champnes, vicar of Upton-cum-Chalvey, examined. Hearing of the suspicious death of the deceased, and that a person in the dress of a Quaker was the last man who had been seen to leave the house, I proceeded to the Slough station, thinking it likely he might proceed to town by the railway. I saw him pass through the office, when I communicated my suspicions to Mr. Howell, the superintendent at the station. He left for London in a first-class carriage. Mr. Howell then sent off a full description of his person, by means of the electric telegraph, to cause him to be watched by the police upon his arrival at Paddington.

Mr. Howell, of the Slough station, deposed as follows: – The prisoner left for town last night by the 7.42 train. I despatched orders by the telegraph to have the prisoner watched on his arrival at Paddington. A few minutes afterwards an answer was returned, stating that the suspected party had arrived, and that Sergeant Williams had left the terminus in the same omnibus for the City.

The words of the communication were precisely as follows:

THE MESSAGE

A murder has just been committed at Salt Hill, and the suspected murderer was seen to take a first-class ticket for London by the train which left Slough at 7h. 42m. p.m. He is in garb of a Quaker, with a brown great coat on, which reaches nearly down to his feet; he is in the last compartment of the second first-class carriage.

THE REPLY

The up-train has arrived; and a person answering, in every respect, the description given by telegraph came out of the compartment mentioned. I pointed the man out to Sergeant Williams. The man got into a New-road omnibus, and Sergeant Williams into the same.

The telegraphic apparatus consists of two wires suspended the length of the line, and attached at either end to the instrument, as seen in Fig. 1, and a branch wire from the instrument, attached to a large metallic surface, imbedded in the earth, for completing the electric circuit. The wire at Paddington is connected with the gas pipe, and that at Slough with the pump-engine. When the instrument is not in motion, the handles, *a a*, are down, as seen in Fig. 1., and the pointers remain in their vertical position. The handles are connected by an arrangement of pins and springs, with the battery and other wires.

[ILN Jan 11 1845]

ACCIDENTS AND DISASTERS

The Victorians, although it would never have been admitted, rather liked the macabre; writers rarely asked their readers to read between the lines. If nothing too awful had happened in an accident, the report would speculate on what could have occurred; in an account of an accident on the Macduff branch between Auchterless and Fyvie in 1888, which was quite bad enough with five deaths, the writer for the ILN *adds: 'There was a quantity of gas tar, and other combustible matter, among the contents of the waggons, and all mixed up with the passenger carriages. If the engine had fallen with them, it is probable that these inflammable materials would have taken fire; and the passengers, unable to extricate themselves, would have been burnt to death.' The* ILN *did not entirely dissociate itself from this ghoulish trait in the human personality but its prose was more restrained than that of some papers which peddled the sensational. It must be remembered that loss of human life on the scale of the worst accidents had been unknown except in time of war; the railway created a potential for disaster on an unprecedented scale. In our own times, when thousands die annually on our roads, it is perhaps difficult to realise the impact such news must have had. Even today, a railway accident, because of its rarity in comparison with other modes of transport, commands headlines while only a major pile-up on the roads would receive more than a few lines.*

Nonetheless a sizeable proportion of the entries concerning railways in the ILN *was devoted to accidents, the frequency of which was, not surprisingly, high until the establishment of interlocked signalling and block or token working on most lines. Serious investigation into the causes of accidents, and recommendations to avoid a similar recurrence, were begun as early as 1840 when railway inspecting officers, appointed by the Board of Trade from the Corps of Royal Engineers, examined an accident at Howden on the Hull & Selby Railway. News of their conclusions was then, as now, confined to the more specialised journals.*

GREAT RAILWAY DISASTER AT NORWICH

On the night of Thursday week, it is our painful task to state, one of the most appalling accidents that ever happened in English railway travelling occurred on the Great Eastern Railway, between Norwich and Brundall, which is a station nearly six miles from Norwich. A train carrying mails to Norwich leaves Great Yarmouth every evening at 8.46, and is joined at Reedham, twelve miles from Norwich, by another train from Lowestoft. The junction was effected that night in the ordinary course, and the combined train proceeded to Brundall, three stations further on. Here it had to wait, because the line is single, until the arrival of the evening express from Norwich to Great Yarmouth, or until permission should be given to the engine-driver to proceed. A mistaken order from Mr. T. Cooper, the night inspector at Norwich station, allowed the down express to leave Norwich, while the combined mail-train from Great Yarmouth was suffered to come on from Brundall. The consequence was that the doomed trains met at Thorpe, nearly two miles from Norwich, and ran headlong into each other. The rails were slippery from rain; there was a slight curve in the line at the fatal spot, so that the lights of neither train could be seen; there was no time to apply the brakes, and the two engines rushed at each other at full speed. The engine drawing the combined mail-train (No. 54) was one of the most approved modern construction and of great power. The engine drawing the train from Norwich was a lighter one, but had acquired, with its train, a considerable momentum. In the crash which followed the collision the funnel of engine No. 54 was carried away, and the engine from Norwich rushed on the top of its assailant, some of the carriages of each train following, until a pyramid was formed of the locomotives, the shattered carriages, and the wounded, dead, or dying passengers. Eighteen persons were killed, and four have since died.

The down train from Norwich was made up, as usual, of two portions. The larger portion, for Yarmouth, formed the first section of the train; after which came the Lowestoft carriages. These two sections would be separated at Reedham,

and each would then travel on its own branch line. The Yarmouth portion of the train consisted of the following carriages: 1, the engine and tender, driven by Clarke and his fireman Sewell (both killed); 2, a horse-box belonging to the Stockton and Darlington Railway Company; 3, a second-class carriage; 4, an open third-class carriage; 5, a first-class carriage; 6, a third-class carriage; 7 and 8, composite carriages; 9 and 10, third-class carriages; 11, brake-van, containing the guard Read. Then came the Lowestoft portion of the train, in the following order: – 12, a second-class carriage; 13, a first-class carriage; 14, a third-class carriage; 15, break-van, containing the guard Black. The two guards escaped with cuts and bruises. They were in the rear part of the train, in carriages which, happily, did not leave the rails, or otherwise the whole of the Lowestoft portion of the train would have fallen into the river Yare, which is here about fifty yards wide. As it was, the Lowestoft carriages remained on the bridge, a wooden one, 69 yards long, adapted for a single line of rails, but in process of widening. Iron girders are being introduced, and there were wide chasms in the bridge. It is a wonder that no passengers were drowned in attempting to get out of these three carriages, for there was no balustrade or railing, and anybody alighting upon the planks of the bridge from the projecting step of a carriage would be likely to fall forward into the water. However, dredging in the river has produced no results. Another reason for thankfulness is that the two engines did not meet upon the bridge. Even if the bridge itself had stood firm, the foremost carriages must have been hurled into the water, and the number of deaths would have been doubled or trebled. A very slight difference in the speed of either train, or a few seconds' difference in the time of starting, would have made the calamity far more dreadful.

It will be seen that there were fourteen carriages behind the engine and tender of the down express. The following was the composition of the up mail one: – Engine and tender, Prior, driver, and Light, fireman (both killed). Then followed the Yarmouth carriages – 2, fish-truck laden with fish; 3, brake-van; 4 and 5, composite carriages; 6, third-class carriage;

Wreck of the Trains after the Collision

7, mail-van, in which was the guard having charge of the mail-bags; 8, composite carriage. Next came the Lowestoft carriages – 9, brake-van; 10, third-class carriage; 11, first-class carriage; 12 and 13, second-class carriages; 14, third-class carriage. Thus there were thirteen carriages behind the engine of the mail, so that the two trains were pretty nearly equal in weight. It is certain, however, that the mail-train must have had a much greater momentum. Both drivers had reason for putting on increased speed, believing as they did that each train was waiting for the other; but the engine of the mail-train was heavier and more powerful than that of the express, besides which there is a slight decline all the way to Brundall. It is thought that the speed of the up mail could not have been less than from thirty to thirty-five miles an hour, while the rate at which the express was travelling would be from twenty to twenty-five miles. Imagination can only faintly conceive the

fearful shock of two such bodies propelled with this velocity, each presenting exactly the same points of contact, and giving and receiving at the same instant the full force of each other's blow. It was, in fact, the meeting of two iron vans, of nearly equal size and power, urged on by steam, with an irresistible weight behind urging them on. The two engines and tenders weighed each forty-five and forty tons. This made some eighty tons of metal hurled almost through the air from opposite points, to say nothing of the dead weight of the train behind. Mathematicians may calculate with this weight and velocity what was the force exerted at the point of impact. People living close by thought they heard a thunder-peal. The darkness of the night, the heavy rain that was falling, and a slight curve round which the mail-train was making its way must have prevented the two drivers from seeing each other's lights till the trains were close together. How this was in reality can never be

The worst head-on collision in the history of British railways occurred on the night of 10 September 1874 between Norwich Thorpe and Brundall stations. As was generally the case human error was to blame, although the Board of Trade inspector criticised the laxity of the system that allowed such mistakes to occur. A series of misunderstandings between the stationmaster, the night inspector and the telegraph clerk, and the dispatch of a message without the required signature resulted in two trains being dispatched from each end of the single line. These three and the ticket collector stood helplessly on the platform at Norwich Thorpe, knowing there was nothing they could do to avert the disaster. The final death toll was twenty-five, and seventy-three were injured; the ILN quotes lower figures.

The Flood at Cowley-Bridge, near Exeter [ILN Jan 27 1866]

The Bristol & Exeter Railway, fully opened in 1844, was built to the broad gauge and became an integral part of the Great Western route to Plymouth and Penzance. Flooding at Cowley Bridge and up the valley of the Exe and Culm along which the railway runs for part of the way, still happens after heavy rain; even the railway is still occasionally inconvenienced.

There is little doubt that our winters have become markedly milder since the nineteenth century when this kind of scene was an almost annual occurrence on the Highland Railway. Trains were regularly brought to a stand by snow and required the assistance of three locomotives with heavy snowplough to extricate them. Huge gangs of labourers were dispatched to dig trains out, and a well-known photograph shows a forest of spades in the snow while the men had a brief respite. The representation of an Allan 2-4-0 is quite reasonable for the time in comparison with other efforts.

Clearing the road through a snow-wreath on the Highland Railway [ILN Mar 24 1866]

CARRIAGES

NEW RAILWAY CARRIAGE

We give a sketch of one of the improved Railway Carriages, just constructed by Messrs. Adams, of Fair Field Works, Bow, for the North Woolwich Branch of the Eastern Counties Railway; and we consider the Directors to have shown judgment in their departure from the common standard to suit an increasing traffic without adding to the length of their trains. These Carriages are forty feet in length, and nine feet in width; the extra width being gained by building the Carriage frames to the width of the ordinary step-boards. The Directors have thus succeeded in accomplishing more on the narrow gauge than has yet been accomplished on the broad gauge, where the carriages are only eight feet six inches in width, by twenty-eight feet in length. The extreme axles are thirty feet apart, and being on eight wheels, these Carriages are obviously safer than those on six wheels or on four. Notwithstanding their length, they will pass a curve of two hundred feet radius by means of the flexibility and arrangement of the springs, which permit the wheels to traverse laterally. The buffer heads are also made to radiate with the springs or curves, so

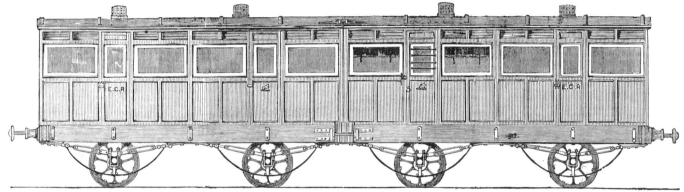

Side view of improved railway carriage

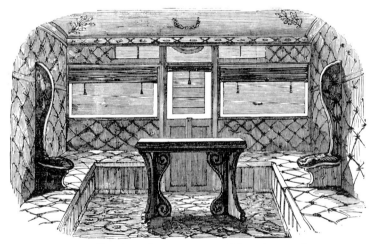

Interior of compartment of first-class carriage

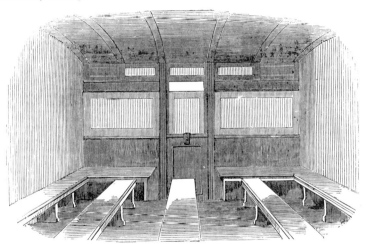

Interior of compartment of second-class carriage

William Bridges Adams was born at Madeley in Staffordshire in 1797, the son of a carriage builder. For a man who was to become a brilliant if unbusinesslike inventor, he had the unlikely background of a supposed misspent youth in South America; ill health had compelled him to go to Chile to recover. He commenced work on railway inventions while out there, and on his return to England, opened the Fairfield Works at Bow in London, later to become Bryant & May's match factory. His most important patent was his radial axlebox which he applied to this carriage for the Eastern Counties Railway. The use of eight wheels was naturally to achieve the steadiness which Crampton also sought in his long wheelbased locomotives. The Adams carriage was semi-rigid, having a manner of hinged joint between the two halves. Side play in the axleboxes was permitted by dispensing with horns. That 110 people were expected to fit into a 40ft coach, the majority of whom would be in the three third-class compartments, gives an idea of how intimate journeys must have been for the less fortunate.

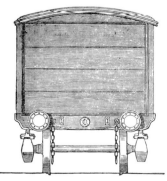

End of carriage

that they press firmly under all circumstances. The Carriages are fitted up in four compartments; one first class with couches all around, and a table in the centre; the other three second class. They will carry about one hundred and ten passengers.

Among the advantages which these improved Carriages present over ordinary Carriages, are–

1. Greater steadiness at high velocities, the great length of the body maintaining its equilibrium independently of the wheels.

2. Diminution of friction, by the easy spring permitting free rolling movement of the wheels, without pressing the flanges against the rails, whether on curves or on nominally straight lines. Also, by diminution of the gross weight of the carriages, as compared with the passengers carried.

3. The proportional diminution of requisite engine-power, equal to fully one-third, as compared with the traction of six-wheeled carriages.

4. Reduction of the length of trains, by increasing the breadth of the carriages.

5. Greater safety; since one wheel breaking out of eight involves far less risk than one out of four or six. The almost impossibility of getting off the rails, on account of the perfect action of the springs, which will keep the wheels always turned to the plane and curves of the rails, whether regular or irregular, instead of confining them to the plane of the carriage.

The allowance of a passage-way through the whole of the interior of the train for the guards, would be important, in case of the illness of a passenger, or a fire, or other accident. In second and third-class carriages, the arrangements for passing through would be as in the pit of a theatre – a passenger could move aside, so as not to lose space. In a first-class carriage, a passenger-way, 1 foot 6 inches wide, would be left, and passengers' cabins arranged on each side, facilitating the use of small private apartments where required for long journeys. The communication through the whole train would permit the collection of tickets during the journey. At present, a journey of fifty miles is frequently performed in little more than an hour, with some additional risk from high speed; and, at the end of the journey, a quarter of an hour is wasted in taking tickets.

[ILN Oct 9 1847]

THE ROYAL RAILWAY CARRIAGE

The carriage constructed for her Majesty's use, by the directors of the London and Birmingham Railway Company, is of a very superior description; and the elegance and convenience combined in the design have scarcely a parallel in the records of coach-building. The following are the details from the *Morning Chronicle*: – "The carriage itself is of an oblong shape, the dimensions being about 13 feet by 7 feet, thus forming a handsome saloon, nearly 8 feet high in the clear. The finest mahogany has been used in its construction; and the body of the carriage is double panelled throughout, and stuffed with felt, in order to lessen the vibration and increase warmth. The carriage is divided externally into three compartments, formed by the door and panels on either side. The body rests upon a bed of the finest ash, a coating of India rubber, three-quarters of an inch in thickness, being placed between, which has the effect of almost destroying the vibration generally attendant on railway carriages. At either end of the state saloon, and entirely unconnected with it, are small compartments, for each a guard, who has the control of a powerful argand lamp, which, on passing through the tunnels along the line, reflects a strong light through a ground-glass of globular form inserted in the panelling. The roof of the carriage projects six inches over the body, and rises in the form of a dome towards the centre, where a ventilating apparatus is fixed, surmounted by a colossal gilt crown, which gives a striking finish to the exterior design. A newly-invented spring has been adopted, one peculiarity attached to it being the insertion of a thin hoop of steel within a leathern belt, which has the effect of increasing the power of tension in a very remarkable degree, and rendering the motion of the carriage perfectly easy. The wheels are of the best construction, having wooden felloes six inches deep, with strong iron centre-pieces, and the inconvenience arising from sudden concussion has been guarded against so far as possible by the finest description of buffer springs. The carriage is painted dark lake (the Queen's colour) relieved with scarlet and gold; the upper quarterings having a broad border of French white round the plate glass windows in either panel. These windows are three feet six inches wide, by two feet six inches high, and have a gilt beading round the exterior, with small gold ornaments at each corner. The lower quarterings are ornamented with the heraldic devices of the royal family. The Queen's coat of arms is emblazoned on the door panel, and the insignia of the Order of the Garter occupy the centre of

Interior of the Royal Railway Carriage

The Royal Railway Carriage and Engine

This carriage was provided by the London & Birmingham Railway for a journey by Queen Victoria from Watford to Tamworth undertaken in late 1843. It was probably the first application of steam heating to a carriage. The locomotive, L&B No 20 was a 2-2-0 built by Haigh Foundry in 1838 with 5ft 6in diameter driving wheels and 12in × 18in inside cylinders.

each side panel. The entrance is made by folding steps with four treads, covered with morocco.

"The interior of the carriage is lined throughout with delicate blue satin, wadded and tufted, and the angles finished with broad fluted pilaster of the same elegant material. The hangings of the windows are light elegant draperies of blue and white satin, tastefully finished with fringe. The cornices are of satinwood, lightly and exquisitely carved, and slightly relieved with gold. One extremity of the saloon is occupied by an ottoman, finished in satin, *en suite* with the curtains. There are also two chairs finished in the same material, the satinwood frames of which are beautifully carved in the Louis Quatorze style. Two console tables and two *encoigneurs* in the same taste complete the furniture, with the exception of the carpet, which is Axminster, of suitable design, and the rich tones of which contrast advantageously with the delicate effect of the other furniture: in the centre of the design are the Royal Arms. It should also be mentioned that by an engenious arrangement

of an elegant curtain, the saloon can be divided into two compartments at pleasure.

"The inconvenience arising from cold in the most carefully constructed railway carriage, where a long journey has to be performed in the winter season, suggested to the directors the necessity of fixing a warming apparatus in the bed of the carriage, and Mr. Perkins, the inventor of the steam gun, has accordingly fitted a very ingenious apparatus for the purpose of heating the carriage, which may be thus briefly described: – a coil of pipe placed near the hinder axle-tree, and supplied with water from a small cistern in the bed of the carriage, is kept heated by means of a lamp with four burners. This pipe is continued round the carriage between the flooring; and the water becoming hot, the heat is communicated through a small brass grating in the floor, the temperature of the carriage being regulated by the ventilator above alluded to.

"The carriage has been built under the superintendence of Mr. Wright, the chief of the company's carriage department; and the interior has been fitted up by Messrs. Gillow, the eminent upholsterers of Oxford-street.

"Throughout Monday, the secretary's office was thronged by ladies and gentlemen, anxious to inspect the carriage, and through the obliging attention of Mr. Creed, and Mr. Lond, his assistant secretary, many hundreds were permitted to do so."

[ILN DEC 2 1843]

RAILWAY SMOKING SALOON

The Directors of the Eastern Counties Railway have just placed on their rails the first of a series of novel Carriages, which will, we think, obtain the lasting preference of the public over the close box system that has hitherto prevailed for the conveyance of first-class passengers.

The Carriage in question consists of an apartment, if we may so phrase it, fifteen feet by seven, applicable to those who prefer a close carriage; and the entrances are through two outer apartments or lobbies, open to the air, for the accommodation of those who may choose an open carriage; each of the outer apartments measuring five feet by seven. The fittings-up of the interior are similar in character to those of a genltleman's plain dining-room. There is a long couch of blue morocco on either side, with a table of polished mahogany down the centre; leaving space sufficient to pass between the table and the sitters. The side windows, provided with crimson silk blinds, are fixtures, consisting of eight sheets of plate glass, half an inch in thickness, (thanks to Sir Robert's repeal of the duty), each about three feet six inches in length by two feet in height, commanding a full view on either hand; and, at each end of the couches, are mirrors, so disposed, that the country passed through, is as well seen as that in front. The doors at each end are provided with plate glass sashes, sliding vertically, so that any amount of air may be admitted or excluded at pleasure. For the purposes of ordinary ventilation, perforated plates of brass are inserted near the roof or ceiling, which is constructed on the plan of an ornamented steamer's cabin, panelled in compartments with dead-white, bordered by gold mouldings.

Interior of smoking saloon, on the Eastern Counties Railway

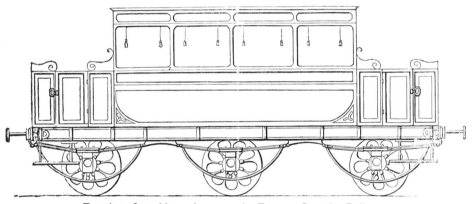

Exterior of smoking saloon, on the Eastern Counties Railway

The Eastern Counties Railway seems to have had more than its fair share of coverage for its carriages, which was not a regular subject for the ILN, *royal carriages apart. Perhaps it was because the ECR had a particularly innovative carriage policy. Smokers were generally disapproved of by the early railway companies which seldom granted then facilities to indulge the habit. The ECR went to the other extreme and provided smokers with the most sumptuous accommodation available to any passengers. The abolition of the excise duty on glass referred to in the text, was one of many duties repealed or reduced following Sir Robert Peel's reintroduction of income tax in 1842, at a rate of 7d in the pound.*

We have never beheld, in carriage-work, a better combination of the plain and simple with the elegant. The table pleasantly garnished with flowers, as we saw it, added much to the effect.

Externally, the Carriage is painted a crimson-lake colour, with gold bandings; the centre being one large massive panel, with the Company's crest in a garter, and their initials on the end doors in Arabesque letters. The mechanical parts of the construction are in plain-black and vermillion. Altogether, it is such a style of carriage as a gentleman with a taste for art, and a taste for driving, might choose for the rail, were railways adapted for private trains, as the sea is for private yachts.

The mechanism of this carriage is

peculiar for England, though well known on the Northern German lines; and we are the more anxious to draw attention to it, because it confirms an opinion formerly expressed by us some time since, when accidents were rife on railways, and disputes ran high as to the respective merits of four and six-wheeled engines – in commendation of a mode of suspension, at that time new, called the Bow Spring, as well adapted to prevent carriages from getting off the rails. A German line – the Hamburg and Bergedorf – opened, at the same time, as an English one, the Dover, and the carriages of both lines were mounted on bow springs. On the Dover, they were condemned; on the Hamburg, they were approved, and were adopted by almost all the new lines of North Germany. The apparent paradox was solved by the knowledge of the fact that the Hamburg carriages were on six wheels, with their extreme axles eighteen feet apart; while the Dover carriages were on four wheels, with the axles eight feet six inches apart. The question, in fact, resolves itself into that of narrow or broad base – position of the centre of gravity. The real base of a railway carriage or engine is, not the road or rail, but the axle bearing; and therefore is it that an engine with outside bearings is more steady than one with inside bearings – the base being thereby extended. An ordinary first-class carriage, on the narrow gauge, stands on a base 6 feet 2 inches by 8 feet 6 inches. The improved Carriage we now speak of stands on a base 6 feet 8 inches by 18 feet 6 inches. The steadiness is thereby so much increased, that additional height may be gained without disadvantage, and a tall man may stand upright in it with his hat on.

But there is yet more connected with this subject. The comfort and safety of the passenger is synonymous, as might have been expected, with the profit of the Railway Companies. We quote from the Engineer's Report at the Half-yearly Meeting of the Eastern Union line:–

"Our carriage stock is spoken of by the public using the line as being more easy and commodious than carriages of the ordinary size and construction; and their smooth and regular motion when travelling, leads me to believe that the repairs in upholding both the road and carriages will be more economical than usual.

"I beg, in connection with the working of our line, to direct your attention to the subject of Adams's Bow springs, which appear admirably adapted for our carrying stock; and from the experience of one passenger carriage which I have had fitted with them, and which has been daily running since the line was opened, I believe that it combines the greatest ease to passengers with the least tractive friction, particularly at high velocities; and if so, such must result in a saving of wear and tear of road, carriages and engines, and is, therefore, well worthy of your consideration, with a view to its extended adoption."

We have no doubt that carriages such as we have described will become very general, and we see no reason why the principle should not be carried out to a still greater extent. There is no mechanical reason to prevent the running of carriages nine feet wide and forty feet long over all the narrow gauge lines in Great Britain, save the paring some three inches here and there from the face of a badly boarded station platform. Want of length in the carriage is the sole obstacle to increased speed, and we understand that it is very practicable to convert the existing short stock into long stock at a trifling expense. What is Colonel Pasley about that he does not look to this? If he would bring it to pass, the public would immortalise him for rescuing them from dog-boxes and un-aired holes – Black-holes of Calcutta in the hot weather – and giving them spacious saloons wherein to move about, and ascertain if any of their kith or kin, friends or connections, be embarked in the same train.

It is said these carriages are for the use of smokers. We do not object to this; smokers and non-smokers should be apart; but why should smokers exclusively be indulged with the use of the best carriages on the line. We would venture a guess, that ladies would especially prefer this to the coops endorsed in gilt letters "For Ladies only."

Be this as it may, the Eastern Counties Railway Company have made a move in the right direction. We believe they are very anxious to obtain the good opinion of the public; and, be it remembered, this improvement is not a mere Royal or exclusive carriage, but one intended for the public.

We were glad to find on inquiry that these new carriages are not proportionately more costly than the old ones. The carriage described, carries twenty-two to twenty-four passengers inside, and fourteen outside.

[ILN SEPT 12 1846]

A CONTRAST IN TRAVEL

The South-Eastern Railway has certainly "moved" a long way in the matter of car-construction since the days when the Duke of Wellington's private coach was considered quite a luxurious vehicle, fit even for the distinguished Warden of the Cinque Ports on his journeys from London to Walmer. The Duke's coach, as our Illustration shows, was an odd sort of cross between a stage-coach and a cattle-truck. We smile at it now, and with some reason, for the South-Eastern Railway Company has just placed upon the rails a vestibule train so elegant and luxurious that even ordinary comfortable rolling stock of to-day (not to mention the old Duke's vehicle) is thrown into the shade by comparison. The train consists of eight cars – one first class drawing-room, one first-class buffet, one second-class, three third-class, and two third-class brakes. Each car is fifty feet long, over corner posts, and the train is furnished with American vestibule connections and couplings of the most recent form. The underframing of the cars is of exceptional strength, and is on the latest and most approved method; electric light, electric bells, and a complete hot-water system for heating add to the passengers' comfort. The decorations are chaste and beautiful. The drawing-room saloon, which is placed in one of the first-class cars, is 32

The train described marked the second attempt of the South Eastern Railway to enter the limelight during the 1890s with carriages of exceptional opulence. The first had been a train of quasi-Pullman cars built in sections at Troy, New York, in 1891–2 and assembled at Ashford. The main departure with the second was the introduction of accommodation for second-class and third-class passengers; moreover they were entitled to use the train without payment of a supplement. The train was so much better than anything then available in the south of England that it must have provoked unfavourable comparison with the typical SER third-class carriage which was among the worst of any British company. The electric light system was Stone's and the hot-water heaters were by Baker. The extraordinary coach used by the Duke of Wellington while he was Lord Warden of the Cinque Ports was designed with a well to prevent the tall duke bumping his head as he entrained. Concern with a low centre of gravity and the custom of placing luggage on coach roofs, covered by tarpaulins, effectively restricted the height of early coaches.

First-Class Saloon of the South-Eastern Railway Company's New Vestibule Train

ft. 5½ in. in length. It accommodates eighteen passengers, who may take their ease upon the most delightfully comfortable revolving and fixed chairs; and midway of the saloon are two fixed settees. In the same car is a particularly dainty ladies' saloon, in which all the upholstery is in tapestry, with a cream-coloured ground of embossed flowers, while the facings and sides of the chairs are of crimson plush velvet. On the floor is a rich Axminster carpet, the window-blinds are of old gold brocaded silk, falling beneath a festooned valance of pale blue and brocaded silk to match the upper panels of the partition. The woodwork is Italian walnut, the style Louis XV.

To avoid the stereotyped has been the object of the designers; accordingly, the other first-class car is treated in the style of Louis XVI. The woodwork here is Spanish mahogany, with beautifully mottled panels of the same wood. In this car are placed a drawing-room saloon and a spacious smoking-saloon, in the former the chairs and settees are upholstered in Gobelin green; in the smoking-saloon a darker tapestry, well covered with flowers, has been employed. Throughout the train the lavatory accommodation is of the finest. In the second-class car richness of design and elegance are again made compatible with the highest degree of comfort. And so, in its degree, of the third-class. The designs are by Mr. Harry S. Wainwright, Carriage and Wagon Superintendent, and were carried out in co-operation with Mr. W. S. Laycock, of Sheffield. The whole train has a magnificent and imposing appearance, and is, indeed, a triumph of vehicular architecture.

[ILN Oct 9 1897]

Carriage used on the South-Eastern Railway by the Duke of Wellington as Warden of the Cinque Ports

SHIPS AND DOCKS

THE CHANNEL RAILWAY FERRY

We lately called attention to the project of a steam railway-ferry from Dover to a point of the opposite French coast, near Cape Grisnez, proposed by Mr. John Fowler, C.E. The question of improving the existing mode of communication between England and the Continent has been under Mr. Fowler's continuous attention for several years, and on two occasions his plans for effecting an improvement have been deposited with the Board of Trade. Apparently, however, the time had not arrived for actual steps to be taken. In the mean time, suggestions for a tunnel were submitted to Mr. Fowler from several quarters, with a request that he would carefully consider such a plan as an alternative to his own proposal of a railway-ferry; and nearly at the same time a scheme was brought forward for a fixed bridge across the Channel. Both these alternatives received Mr. Fowler's attention. The bridge scheme appeared hardly feasible at any cost, and was obviously open to most serious objections on the part of those interested in the navigation of the Channel. The tunnel scheme, from the impossibility of forming any trustworthy estimate of the time or cost required for its completion, did not appear a work likely to be undertaken. The result, therefore, of this reconsideration and of comparison with other projects has been a confirmation of his original idea – the construction of well-sheltered harbours on both coasts, and of vessels so arranged as to make the passage without dependence on tide, wind, or sea; thus providing, for all practical purposes, a continuous communication.

Our Illustrations will show the mode by which the plan of the railway ferry is to be realised. We refer first to a chart of the Channel, showing the proposed harbours at Dover and Andrecelles. We also give a view of the site of the proposed harbour at Dover. This is westward of the existing pier, and is thoroughly sheltered against every gale which could interfere with steamers entering or leaving it. The new harbour will be furnished with a graving-dock, and a covered berth for the steamers, with hydraulic apparatus for transferring the trains from the railway to the steamer, and vice versâ. Combined with this harbour work is to be a short connecting railway by which the London, Chatham, and Dover Railway, equally with the South-Eastern Railway, will be connected with the new harbour and the steamers. No interference with the

Proposed Channel Railway Ferry: Station and Pier at Dover

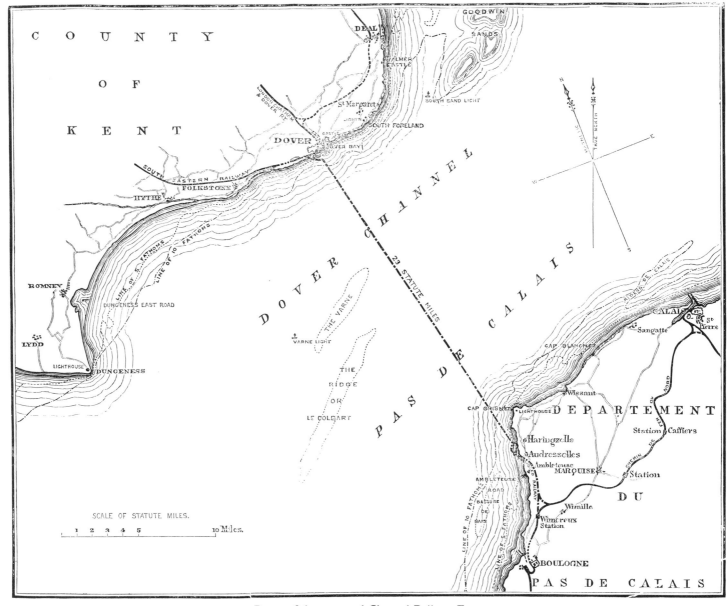

Route of the proposed Channel Railway Ferry

The first public train ferry in the world was introduced by Thomas Bouch on the Firth of Forth in 1850 when the Leviathan, built by Robert Napier, began operation between Granton and Burntisland. A first-class carriage and 20 wagons were carried, but usually only goods wagons and road carriages were carried. A similar service was inaugurated across the Firth of Tay in the following year. As noted elsewhere, the debate about the optimum way to improve communications across the English Channel was almost as old as the nineteenth century, and this was just one of many schemes. What is extraordinary is the confidence that a ship of 450ft would be able to provide a service of 'perfect comfort . . . in all weathers and under all circumstances', and

that 'it is comparatively easy to design vessels of such a size and form as to perform the voyage . . . with scarcely any appreciable pitching and rolling in any state of the weather'. As had been discovered with Brunel's Great Eastern 10 years before, even a ship of almost 700ft was not immune to the power of the sea. One suspects that Fowler was not as enthusiastic about the scheme as Sir Edward Watkin was over the Channel Tunnel: in 1869 he was advising on Egyptian railways and in the following year on Indian railways. No train ferries operated from Britain after the withdrawal of the Tay and Forth vessels until World War I. The first public Anglo-Continental ferry service began in 1924 between Harwich and Zeebrugge, for goods wagons only.

existing harbour or with the pier at Dover will be created by the proposed new works, but a part of the west side of the existing pier will be sheltered and made more available than heretofore. The depth of water at the entrance and within the harbour will be sufficient for the entrance and exit of the steamers at all states of the tide.

On the French coast, much consideration has been given to the locality for the harbour, and great reluctance was felt in being compelled to adopt any place except either Calais or Boulogne. Calais is, however, so exposed to all winds from west to east, and so choked with sand, that it could not possibly comply with the indispensable conditions of the proposed

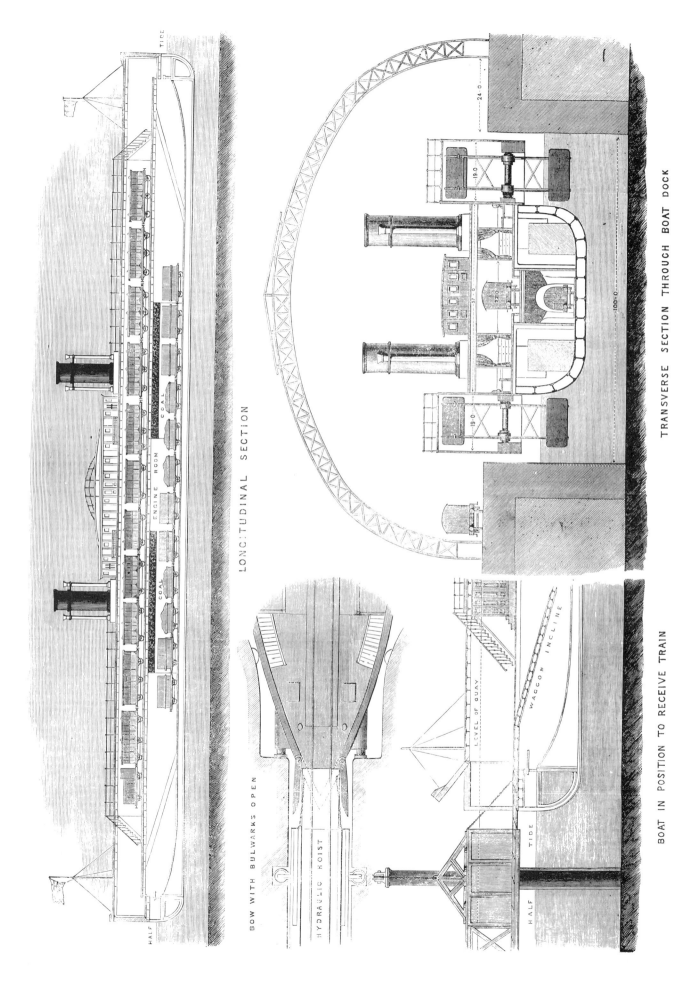

LONGITUDINAL SECTION

TRANSVERSE SECTION THROUGH BOAT DOCK

BOW WITH BULWARKS OPEN

BOAT IN POSITION TO RECEIVE TRAIN

The Channel Railway Ferry: Sections of the proposed Steam-Boat

scheme; and with respect to Boulogne, besides the same natural defect of sand accumulation as at Calais, there was the serious objection of a longer sea voyage, as well as the inconvenience for passengers and goods destined for Germany and the north-eastern part of the Continent. After repeated surveys, a point of the coast at Andrecelles, south of Cape Grisnez and north of Ambleteuse, was selected, which has deep water to the shore, which is sheltered from the north and east by Cape Grisnez, and which is entirely free from any accumulations of sand. The design of this harbour corresponds as nearly as the difference of locality will permit with that already described for Dover, and will be provided with the same convenience for the transfer of passengers between the steamer and the railway.

Connected with the harbour on the French coast will be a short railway (with junctions in both directions) to run up to the Northern (of France) Railway, so as to give continuous communication both to France and to Germany. The decision of all harbour and other works on the French coast must rest with the French Government and their engineers, but it was obviously necessary to any plan of international communication that a practicable harbour on the French coast as well as on the English coast should be discovered, so as to comply with the indispensable physical condition of the work.

Harbours with proper shelter and with sufficient depth of water to afford ingress and egress at all times (irrespective of weather and tide) being provided, it is comparatively easy to design vessels of such a size and form as to perform the voyage in about one hour, and with scarcely any appreciable pitching and rolling in any state of the weather. The vessels, for which a design is prepared, will be 450 ft. in length, with 57 ft. beam, and 85 ft. across the paddle-boxes. They will be luxuriously fitted up with saloons of various kinds, and with every convenience for refreshment or reading, and with private and ladies' cabins. The conditions of a continuous communication would require that at least the mails, luggage, and valuable goods should pass across the Channel and through to their destination without change of carriage. These conditions will give to passengers, especially to invalids and families, at a trifling additional cost, the great comfort of being able to retain their seats in a

railway carriage from London to Paris and other places, without change or disturbance; but when crossing the Channel passengers will have the option of using the saloons, and partaking of refreshment without losing their seats, exactly as passengers now travelling to Edinburgh from London are able to do when stopping for refreshment at Preston or at York.

No doubt, a slight improvement might be made on the existing state of things by lengthening the Dover pier and by improving Boulogne harbour, so that a better class of steamers than the present might be employed; but such a scheme is obviously too imperfect to meet the present and increasing wants of travellers, and would entirely fail to give a continuous railway communication, or to create such an increase of the present traffic as would compensate for a large expenditure.

The practical results of this railway-ferry link of international communication would be, as regards distance, a saving of two miles of water, and fourteen miles of railway between London and Paris; and, as regards time, a saving of at least two hours, partly by greater speed across the Channel, partly by the reduction of distance, and partly in the greatly diminished time required for the transfer of passengers, mails, and luggage. These savings of distance and time are important, but they are comparatively insignificant to the perfect certainty and perfect comfort which will be obtained in all weathers and under all circumstances by the proposed combination of harbours, boats, and mechanical arrangements.

The total expenditure for this great work will be about £2,000,000, and the ferry may be in operation in two years from the time of its commencement, although three years would probably be required for the perfect completion of all the works. Taking the present traffic of mails, passengers, and goods between England, France and part of Germany which might be expected to converge at the proposed railway-ferry, and adding a very small percentage of the clear profits which the railway companies on each side of the Channel would derive from the increased traffic which would be created by the railway-ferry itself, it cannot be doubted that, with a moderate assistance from the two Governments, the work may be carried out by private enterprise.

These works, however, would evidently result in the creation of a monopoly of

mail and passenger communication between England and France, and therefore it might be considered expedient for the English Government to carry out the harbour works on its shore, the French Government the same on the French shore, for each country to possess an equal number of steam ferry-boats, and thus be in all respects on an equal footing. If such arrangement were considered to be the best politically, it would be unusually free from financial objection, as it is not probable that either country would suffer any pecuniary loss by reason of an inadequate return upon their respective expenditure.

We shall give some further Illustrations of the subject next week, including one of the proposed steam-boats to carry the railway trains across the Channel.

[ILN Mar 12 1870]

GREAT GRIMSBY AND ITS DOCKS
The opening of the Great Northern Railway, which gives a railway communication throughout from Great Grimsby to London, and the success which has attended the operation of excluding the water from the coffer-dam and embankments of the Deep Sea Docks, now constructing at Great Grimsby, furnish us with the opportunity of redeeming the promise we made to describe these Docks, when we gave representations of the large pier erected for crossing the Humber ferry, and of the more remarkable points of the line traversed by the section of the Manchester, Sheffield, and Lincolnshire Railway, opened in March last. We now give two views of these important Dock works.

Many of our readers, not ill-versed in the geography of foreign lands, may pause here and ask where is Great Grimsby? Great Grimsby lies on the north-eastern coast of Lincolnshire, at the widest part of the mouth of the Humber, facing the sea, and protected by a curve on the Yorkshire side of the river, known as Spurn Point, from all the storms of the German Ocean. This admirable situation, just out of the sea and at the mouth of the river, with the advantage of a natural breakwater against wind and waves, made it a port of importance in Saxon times, long before Hull was founded.

Macpherson, in his "Annals of Commerce," states that "Grimsby is noted by the Norwegian or Icelandic writers, as an emporium resorted to by merchants from Norway, Scotland,

The Dock Works at Great Grimsby

Orkney, and the Western Islands."

The municipal rights which it still enjoys are said to date from King John. The earliest charter in existence was granted by Edward III., and vested the government of the town in a mayor, two bailiffs, twelve aldermen, and thirty-six burgesses. In that reign Grimsby carried on a considerable trade; and was rich and populous, as is proved by its having furnished eleven ships and one hundred and seventy men to assist at the siege of Calais. From very early times Grimsby returned two members to the House of Commons; but the Reform Bill reduced this privilege one half, by placing the borough in Schedule B.

In the course of time the superior means of internal communication afforded by the Humber raised up Hull, and attracted nearly all the commerce of Grimsby. It then sunk into a mere fishing village, sustained in factitious importance by municipal and parliamentary privileges, until about fifty years ago, when some local landowners formed a company and made a dock, which extends, canal-like, into the town, with a capacity of about fifteen acres. This dock did much toward saving the town from utter decay, and was of considerable advantage, although the tides permitted it to be open but a few hours each day, for local exports and imports.

In 1845, a Company was formed for the purpose of making a Dock at Great Grimsby, worthy of its admirable local position, and to connect it, by the contemplated railway communication, with all the principal towns of England. This Company eventually purchased all the property and privileges of the Old Dock Company at a cheap price.

The promotors of the succession of lines, since amalgamated under the title of the Manchester, Sheffield, and Lincolnshire Railway, made Great Grimsby one of their termini. They had the wisdom soon to see the importance of executing the Dock works upon a scale which would render it a first-rate shipping station. In great towns it has not been unusual to expend vast sums of money upon accommodation for railway stock, land carriages, and merchandise. At Grimsby there was no large population, but there was a natural position most favourable for local, river, coasting, and foreign trade, when once by railways a means of internal communication, equal to the water carriage possessed by Hull was opened. It was determined to provide the best possible accommodation for ships and steamers, as well as land carriages, to attract and create a trade and population, as well as serve the local and general traffic which would naturally flow along the railways.

The Dock Company was amalgamated with the Manchester and Sheffield

The dock referred to in the article as being built 'about fifty years ago' was the Old Dock, engineered by Sir John Rennie and opened in 1801. But to put the port's growth in perspective, Louth remained the more important until discovery of the Dogger Bank fishing grounds gave Grimsby the advantage. Prince Albert did lay the foundation stone, as the ILN writer anticipates, and a costly banquet was held. Opened in 1852, the new docks were immediately prosperous and a weekly steamer service to Hamburg and Rotterdam was inaugurated in the same year. Four years later, a Fish Dock was opened and the Great Northern, the Midland and the Manchester, Sheffield & Lincolnshire railways went into the fishing business, setting up a fishing company, initially with nine boats. By 1890, about 800 trawlers were regularly using the facilities at Grimsby.

Railway; and the works were placed in the hands of Mr. Rendel, the celebrated engineer of Birkenhead Docks and the works at Plymouth; and it was determined to construct docks and warehouses on the most complete scale, as a branch, a feeder, and a water station for the railway.

It will be seen that, in a naval point of view, Great Grimsby occupies a very important position, commanding as it does the mouth of the Humber, and enabling war-steamers to dash into the ocean at a moment's notice. In the last war twelve hundred vessels under convoy were frequently seen at anchor, under the shelter of Spurn Point. In adverse winds nearly as many may be seen taking advantage of this natural protection. The Admiralty were so sensible of the great naval advantages that Grimsby would possess when connected with the interior of the metropolis by railways, that they induced the Woods and Forests to give up a large tract of land of many acres on condition that the lock-gates were increased to a sufficient capacity to receive the largest war-steamers. This the Company consented to do at an additional expense, it is said not far short of £50,000. We believe it is the first instance on record of such a work, for a purely national object, having been undertaken by a private company. The two railways terminate at Great Grimsby – the East Lincolnshire (belonging to the Great Northern) opens up a communication with London through Boston and Peterborough; and the Manchester, Sheffield, and Lincolnshire opens a communication with Hull, Lincoln, and the other towns from which it takes its name. A branch from the station where these two railways unite passes through the town until it reaches the edge of the dock; there it divides into two forks, one of which will traverse the East Wharf to the extremity of the Pier, for the convenience of passengers and goods landed in the out Basin; the other fork will traverse the West Wharf between the quay edge and intended warehouses for the transport of heavy goods.

The Dock works consist of a wet dock, of an area of about thirty acres, walled in on the west side by a wharf 2000 feet long, 200 wide, and 36 feet high, having at the extremity a pier of great length, – making in all a waterside quay and pier about three-quarters of a mile long. This will be the passenger pier for steamers from Hamburgh and the Baltic. The east side wharfing, of the same length, and 670 feet wide, will be partly covered with warehouses, and partly devoted to a goods station, with a perfect communication between the shipping, the warehouses, and the railway, by tramways, – the first example, perhaps, of a complete union of such works.

The passage to the Docks will be through an entrance basin formed by the two piers, area about twenty acres; within which, and alongside the piers, vessels not requiring to enter the Docks may lie. Thus a steamer may discharge passengers and goods in railway carriages and trucks brought right alongside, and taking mails and Manchester silk and cotton goods aboard from other trucks, and go to sea again all in one tide. The communication between the open tidal basin and the Dock will be effected by two locks. The one 300 feet long and 65 feet wide, will admit the largest war-steamer at any time, except an hour before, and an hour after *dead low water*. The other will be 200 feet long, and 45 feet wide. At the lowest tide there will be six feet water on the threshold of these Dockgates. All the ordinary class of vessels and steamers will find water enough enter and lie in shelter in the basin at any hour. At Hull large vessels can only enter an hour before and an hour after high water.

The Dock has capacity for accommodating 700 average ships, and the basin 500, in all 1200 – being a number equal to the accommodation of all the docks open at Hull, where at present the accommodation is insufficient, and Hull merchants are looking for relief to Grimsby Docks.

The Dock dues are fixed at a merely nominal rate. The arrangements for receiving and dispatching goods, either for import or export, require *no intermediate cartage*. Vessels arriving to discharge cargoes for warehousing, will lie under the very warehouse cranes. Those with goods for immediate transmission into the interior, as, for instance, German wool for Leeds or Manchester, will discharge into a line of trucks standing upon the quay. For export the facilities will be equally great; and as the docks and warehouses will be surrounded by a wall, there will be none of that pilferage which occurs at Liverpool and other ports, where the storehouses are at a distance from the quays. Here, as we have said, the sea, the rails, the quays, and warehouses are in most convenient juxtaposition.

Our Baltic and German trade becomes daily of more importance. For the timber trade, Grimsby is peculiarly well situated. Merchants from Hull have already established timber wharfs there; and such is the prospective prosperity of the port, that the Customs duties, without increased facilities, have risen in three years from £3900 to £70,000 a year.

The connexion of Grimsby with Leeds and Manchester is even closer than with London.

The Docks of Grimsby saving twenty miles of river navigation, and lying fifty miles nearer London than Hull, accessible at all hours, will always enable passengers and mails to reach London six hours sooner than by way of Hull. In winter evenings they may be landed the same night, instead of having to lie off until the next morning.

Lincolnshire is the greatest producing county in the kingdom, and therefore requires the largest quantity of bones, oil-cake, and other tillages imported from the Baltic ports. These Docks will also render Great Grimsby the first and best harbour of refuge on the eastern coast.

Endowed with such dock accommodation, forming the port of the greatest producing county, united by railways with Hull, with Leeds, and the clothing district, with Lancashire, the greatest manufacturing county, and with London by a direct line, nearly the most level in the kingdom; not rivalling Hull, but acting as a useful auxiliary and outport for the overflowing Baltic trade, at the same time that it creates a new and profitable commerce of its own, it is impossible to doubt but that Great Grimsby must become one of our most important commercial and naval ports, the mart of a great foreign and home trade. In the unhappy case of war, it must be the station for the fleets which, in the last war, used to lie with so much danger in the Boston-roads – with this difference, that now a few war-steamers will do the watching work of a whole squadron; and we may presume that the national importance of Great Grimsby which has induced Prince Albert to announce his intention of laying the first stone in the spring.

[ILN Nov 18 1848]

ROYALTY

The readiness with which Queen Victoria took to railway travel was of great importance in helping the railways to be accepted. In an age accustomed to space travel, it is difficult to conceive the prejudice and fear that the concept of railway travel aroused among the more impressionable and irrational members of the public. The more hysterical sceptics thought the new mode of travel so unsafe that the chances of survival were limited, that the fleeces of sheep would be ignited from the sparks and buildings burnt to the ground. The knowledge that Her Majesty was sufficiently confident in the new invention to use it reassured the fainthearted. Prince Albert, when still Queen Victoria's suitor, travelled from Slough to Paddington in November 1839, and made frequent use of the railway after his marriage in the following year. The Great Western built a royal saloon in anticipation of Her Majesty's conversion which came in June 1842 when she travelled from Slough to Paddington with Gooch as driver and Brunel on the footplate. There-after Her Majesty used the GWR constantly when travelling between Buckingham Palace and Windsor Castle.

It was common during the early years of railways to request that a member of the royal family open or inaugurate a work of outstanding importance. In 1846, for example, Prince Albert launched the SS Great Britain, and from the opening of the High Level Bridge at Newcastle in 1849, illustrated here, to the opening of the Forth Bridge in 1890 by the Prince of Wales, opening ceremonies were often performed by royalty. Work began on the famous High Level Bridge across the Tyne at Newcastle in 1845, the first pile being driven under the supervision of Robert Stephenson in April 1846. Carrying three lines of railway and, 20ft below, a 20ft roadway flanked by two 6ft footpaths, the bridge was opened by Queen Victoria on 28 September 1849. Her Majesty was so delighted with the reception she received from the Geordies, that she agreed to return the following year to open John Dobson's magnificent Central station and the final link in the East Coast main line, the Royal Border Bridge at Berwick. A toll was payable on the road across the High Level Bridge, collected by NER employees. The High Level Bridge was the only rail bridge at Newcastle until 1906 when the King Edward Bridge was opened.

Presentation of the Addresses to the Queen, on the High Level Bridge, Newcastle-upon-Tyne [ILN Oct 6 1849]

TRAIN SERVICES

PARLIAMENTARY TRAINS

RAILWAY CARRIAGES FOR CONVEYING THIRD-CLASS PASSENGERS AT OR UNDER ONE PENNY PER MILE

A most interesting Report has just been published, by order of the House of Commons, on this important subject. It includes a series of lithographic plates of the carriage or carriages either already sanctioned, recommended, or most approved of by the Railway Department of the Board of Trade, for the conveyance of third-class passengers under the poor man's penny-a-mile clause of the Railway Act; and a statement in detail, showing the number of passengers the carriage or carriages are constructed to hold, with the length, breadth, and height of the same, and the sizes and situations of the spaces provided for admitting air and light; and whether glass is used in any and in which of the said spaces. Also, a copy of the rules or regulations, if any, which the Railway Department of the Board of Trade have issued or recommended for carrying out the law applicable to the carriages on those railways which come under the penny-a-mile clause; and stating whether the locking of any of the doors of these carriages is in practice; and also the times of these carriages starting, the time of their arrival at their various destinations, the entire time on the road, and the distance travelled in each case respectively.

From this report it appears, that the comfort and despatch of third-class passengers have, as yet, been only imperfectly secured.

The conveniences sought by the legislature in the construction and transit of a "parliamentary carriage" are–

1. Free admission of light and air.
2. Protection against wind, wet, and cold.
3. Lamps for night journeys.
4. Seats with backs, and of sufficient depth to permit all persons to sit with ease.
5. Windows for "look-outs."
6. Doors in sufficient numbers on each side to prevent confusion in getting in and out, and to provide means of ready escape in case of accidents.
7. Moderate proportion in the size of the carriages.
8. Acceleration of speed.

But the report shows that these requirements have not been fully considered. In no case have they been strictly obeyed; and, in many instances, they fall sadly short of them. The consequences to the poor traveller are sufficiently obvious to make it unnecessary for us to do more than hint at a few of them. The want of "look-out" deprives the trip of its instructive pleasures; the deficient ventilation and exposure to bad weather become fertile sources of disease; slow rates of travelling add to the difficulties of the poor in competing with the class above them; and the want of light at night converts the carriage into a den of infamy.

We do not throw great blame on the authors of these unnecessarily parsimonious arrangements. Experience is of slow growth; and the wants of the poor are ordinarily the last to be discovered. A model of a carriage, placed in the board-room of a company, looks a very pretty affair, and one like it is ordered to be built; but, when the great carriage itself comes upon the line, many important things are often found to have been overlooked in the tiny and very nice design. In this way we believe many of the evils exposed in the report to have originated.

We look with confidence to a great improvement in the construction and management of the poor man's train; and are glad to learn that, on the South Eastern Line, it has been determined to run it at the same rate as the higher priced trains.

The following is an abstract of the detailed information given in the report.

ARBROATH AND FORFAR

The carriages have no night lamps. In bad weather the small openings over the doors for the admission of air are closed, and the ventilation seriously impeded. The doors, which are placed on one side only, are furnished with small squares of glass; and in bad weather, when it is necessary to close the shutters in the doors on the opposite side, light is very imperfectly admitted.

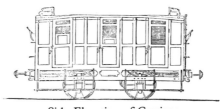

Side Elevation of Carriage

BRIGHTON, CROYDON, AND DOVER

No night lamp; one door only on each side. In bad weather, when the shutters are closed, the carriage is badly lighted by Venetian apertures, and the passengers shut from the view of the beautiful country through which the line passes.

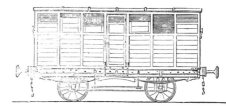

Side Elevation of Carriage

BRISTOL AND GLOUCESTER

No night lamp; one door only on each side. A sight of the country is confined to the passengers who are fortunate enough to get near the door. No provision is made for the admission of air in bad weather, when the doors and windows are closed. This badly lighted and badly ventilated carriage carries fifty-four passengers.

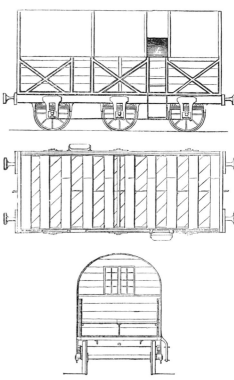

Side Elevation, Plan, and Transverse Section

EASTERN COUNTIES

No night lamp; when the shutters are closed there is no look-out, and no air but that which steals its way through four Venetian blinds.

Side Elevation

GREAT WESTERN

No night lamp. No look-out for seated passengers. When the shutters are closed the carriage is badly lighted by Venetians. One door only on each side.

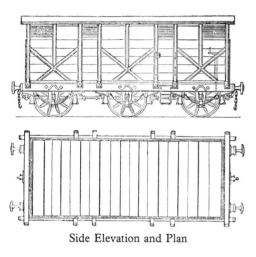

Side Elevation and Plan

LANCASTER AND PRESTON JUNCTION

On this line two kinds of carriages are used, one for twenty-four passengers and another for forty passengers. No night lamp in either of them. The large one has only a single door on each side. Ventilation, when the doors and windows are closed, wholly stopped.

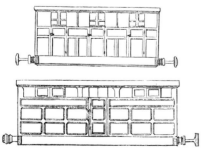

Side Elevation of the Small and Large Carriages

GREAT NORTH OF ENGLAND

No night lamp; four small fixed windows for the admission of light; and no ventilation when the door shutters are closed, except three narrow openings over each window. One door only on each side.

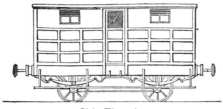

Side Elevation

LONDON AND BIRMINGHAM AND GRAND JUNCTION

No night lamp. When the door shutters are closed it is badly lighted by Venetians, and has no look-out.

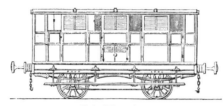

Side Elevation

LONDON AND SOUTH-WESTERN

No night lamp. No provision for ventilation when the curtains are drawn over the openings; and, in bad weather, no adequate protection, and no look-out.

Side Elevation

MANCHESTER AND BIRMINGHAM

Only one door on each side, and but two small windows on each side, beside those in the doors.

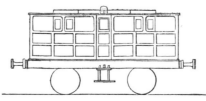

Side Elevation

MANCHESTER, BOLTON, AND BURY

No lamp at night; no means of ventilation in bad weather; and one door only on each side.

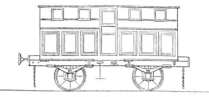

Side Elevation

MANCHESTER AND LEEDS

No night lamp. The only entrances for light are two small fixed windows on each side. No ventilation in bad weather, but by three narrow openings on each side.

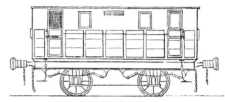

Side Elevation

MIDLAND

No ventilation when the glasses in the doors are closed.

Side Elevation

NEWCASTLE AND DARLINGTON

No night lamp. Daylight parsimoniously admitted by two small windows on each side; and only one door on each side.

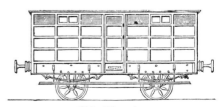

Side Elevation

NEWCASTLE-UPON-TYNE AND NORTH SHIELDS – NO. I AND II.

Two kinds used, one for fair, and another for foul weather. No night lamp in either of them. In the former no protection from sudden emergencies of wet and cold, and in the latter no ventilation when the blinds are drawn.

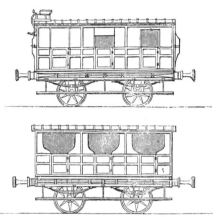

Elevations of Nos. I and II

NORTH UNION

No night lamp. No ventilation when the glasses are closed.

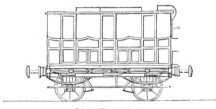

Side Elevation

SHEFFIELD AND MANCHESTER

No night lamp; and no ventilation when the shutters are closed.

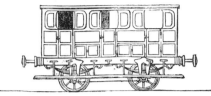

Side Elevation

YARMOUTH AND NORWICH

No night lamp; and when the shutters are closed, badly lighted by Venetians.

Side Elevation

YORK AND NORTH MIDLAND

No night lamp. Daylight only allowed to struggle through two small windows on each side; and no ventilation when the doors are closed. One door only on each side.

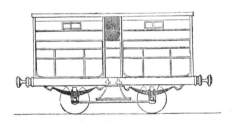

Side Elevation
[PICTORIAL TIMES SEPT 13 1845]

As the writer of this article comments, facilities to make the lot of the third-class passenger comfortable were only 'imperfectly secured' in the early years of railways. The railway companies were initially reluctant to carry the 'lower orders'; many were concerned about the political and social consequences of the working class moving about the place, but interestingly Parliament insisted on provision for their needs with the Regulation of Railways Act 1844. This ruled that at least one train a day in each direction should call at all stations and offer covered third-class seated accommodation at a fare not exceeding a penny a mile and at a minimum average speed of 12mph. So loathe were some railway companies to comply with the enforced running of 'Parliamentary trains' that they deliberately operated them at inconvenient times. The squalor of the carriages provided is the subject of the article; a journey on a wet night in a crowded carriage may well be imagined – holes had to be drilled in the floors so that at least the rainwater would not collect inside the carriage. The accident in Sonning cutting in 1841 revealed the awful conditions in which third-class passengers had to travel: the coaches did not have a roof, were open sided, had seat planks just 18in above the floor and the sides and ends enclosed to a height of only 2ft. Passengers travelling the whole length of the line from Paddington to Bristol had to endure such conditions for 9½ hours. The accident at Sonning, in which eight passengers died, was the catalyst for reform of third-class travel, although companies were slow to respond to government decree, as this article indicates. It is interesting to note that the best carriage illustrated is that of the Midland Railway. Much of the credit for reform of third-class conditions must go to the Midland's enlightened general manager, James Allport, who foresaw and initiated the abandonment of the three class system. In the 1850s he ran first and third class only trains on the Manchester, Sheffield & Lincolnshire Railway, and from April 1872 catered for third class on all Midland trains. In January 1875, the MR abolished the second class and reduced first-class fares to those of the previous second class. The standard of comfort provided for second-class passengers became the prerogative of the third class, and the carriages of T.L. Clayton, the Midland's carriage and wagon superintendent, set the standard which other companies had to achieve if they were to compete.

Arrival of the Workmen's Penny Train at the Victoria Station

THE WORKMEN'S PENNY TRAIN FROM LUDGATE-HILL TO THE VICTORIA STATION

The Metropolitan Extension of the London, Chatham, and Dover Railway Company, which connects Blackfriars and Ludgate-hill with the Victoria station at Pimlico by a line through Walworth, Camberwell, Brixton, Stockwell, and Battersea-fields, has been made the scene of an interesting experiment in social economics during the last two months. On Monday, the 27th of February, commenced the running of two trains daily throughout the week, from each terminus of this line to the other, for the exclusive accommodation of "artisans, mechanics, and daily labourers, both male and female," going to their work, or returning from work to their homes. Every passenger is required to be the holder of a weekly ticket, price one shilling, to be obtained, either at Ludgate-hill or Victoria, not later than the Thursday before the week for which the ticket is to be used; and, to prevent any abuse of the privilege of the cheap trains, the ticket-holder must not only give his own name, address, and occupation, but likewise that of his employer. With this ticket he is entitled to travel once a day, in both directions, to and from Ludgate-hill and Victoria, or either of those two stations and any of the intermediate stations – namely, Blackfriars Bridge, the Borough-road, the Elephant and Castle, Camberwell-gate, Camberwell New-road, Loughborough-road, Brixton, North Stockwell or Clapham, Stewart's-lane, and Battersea Park – but he is not allowed to vary the journey from one day to another, and must go over the same portion of the line daily throughout the week. The morning trains from each end of the line start at five minutes before five o'clock, and arrive at the other end shortly before six. The evening trains, on five days of the week, start at a quarter past six, but on Saturdays at half-past two in the afternoon. No luggage may be conveyed but the workman's basket of tools or implements of labour, not exceeding 28lb. in weight for each passenger. The Engraving on the next page is from a sketch of the scene witnessed upon the arrival of one of these trains at the Victoria station, between five and six in the morning, early in the month of March, when the lamps were still kept alight at that hour. There can be no mistake about the bona-fide working-class character of the honest people who are here seen trooping along the railway platform to their respective places of daily labour, having travelled from their suburban lodgings, a distance of several miles, for the small charge of one penny. The example of the London, Chatham, and Dover Railway Company, which deserves much commendation, has been followed by the Metropolitan Railway Company upon their line (the Underground), from Paddington or Hammersmith to Farrington-street, where daily return-tickets, price twopence, are now supplied to passengers of this class. We shall be glad to hear that the adoption of this system has been profitable, or at least remunerative, to the railway companies. It certainly promises to remedy, in a great degree, the temporary distress caused in some neighbourhoods by the wholesale demolition of houses formerly inhabited by people of the working class.

[ILN APRIL 22 1865]

The early opposition of railway companies to the idea of catering for workers was soon shown to have been poor business sense, as receipts from third class grew to exceed those of the other two classes by 1860. The first commuters were not such by choice; they had been displaced from their homes by demolition, usually for railways, and had been compelled to move further away from their work. There was a good deal of sympathy for their plight and in 1854 the Great Eastern Railway was ordered by Parliament to carry workers from Edmonton and Walthamstow to its Bishopsgate terminus for 2d return. The GER embraced the idea and, to quote Sir William Acworth, set out to become 'the poor man's line'. The success of the GER suburban services accelerated the need for a new terminus, leading to the opening in 1874 of Liverpool Street which became the busiest terminus in London. The 1865 experiment by the London, Chatham & Dover Railway described in the article was still considered a novel idea. Coercion on this occasion was unnecessary since the company had volunteered to run the trains, albeit a response to public concern for the workers' situation. Workmen's tickets became a normal arrangement, particularly after the principle of assisting workers in reaching their work was enshrined in the Artisans' and Labourers' Dwellings Act of 1868.

The Eastern Counties Railway had an appalling reputation for its unpunctuality, poor quality of service, high scale of charges and frequency of accidents; the creation of the Great Eastern Railway in 1862 gradually redeemed the quality of rail travel in East Anglia. The station depicted is almost certainly the Bishopsgate terminus of the ECR, designed by Braithwaite and opened in July 1840 in one of the most squalid areas of London, renowned for its pickpockets, prostitutes and criminals. Originally named Shoreditch, the station had been renamed in 1844 but unsurprisingly remained the butt of acid criticism. There were only two platforms with three centre carriage roads, surmounted by a corrugated wrought-iron roof off which water drained through 34 cast-iron columns. This picture was drawn after a new frontage had been put up in the Italianate style by Sancton Wood. A new London terminus was one of the first priorities of the GER, sanction for the extension to Liverpool Street being given a year after its formation, although it was to be more than 10 years before the new station opened.

(see page 112)

Snobbery and class prejudice is exemplified in these cameos of the three classes going off to the Derby in 1842; even the second-class passengers are given faces more befitting to Neanderthal man. The first-class carriage has a coupé compartment at the end; on some railways these were locked when next to the engine. In 1842 passengers for Epsom races would have de-trained at Stoat's Nest, between the later Purley and Coulsdon North stations, and continued by road to Epsom; in 1847 the line from West Croydon was extended to Epsom.

[ILN MAY 14 1892]

Arrival of Christmas Train, Eastern Counties Railway – Drawn by Duncan [ILN Dec 21 1850]

First Class

Second Class

Third Class

England in 1842: Going to the Derby

BATTLE OF THE GAUGES

One of the major dilemmas of early railway history was the conflict between the broad and narrow ('standard') gauge railway companies. As the tenor of the ILN writer's comments implies, the broad gauge was superior whether safety, speed, stability or accommodation were considered; the only drawbacks were higher initial investment and that fewer lines had been built with 7ft 0¼in as the gauge, and that it is obviously impossible to adapt narrow gauge civil engineering structures for broad gauge whereas the reverse is relatively easy. The technical considerations and niceties which the two camps marshalled in support of their case were wasted on the Gauge Commissioners, appointed as arbiters by Parliament in 1845. They acknowledged the superiority of the broad gauge on several counts but ruled against it on purely practical grounds, although the terms of the Gauge Act of 1846 were not as severe as once proposed. It took until 1892 for the broad gauge to be gradually replaced, but expansion of 7ft lines continued until the 1860s, with 1,040 miles at its apogee.

THE GAUGES

The Gauge Question has at last been brought formally before Parliament, and the Government has made an attempt to solve this – perhaps the most difficult and momentous of the social problems of the day. We are in a curious position with regard to our present means of communication, and all we can do is but a shift and compromise between two great powers. We are paying a penalty of inconvenience for having progressed, and for having done, perhaps, too much in an early stage of a great invention.

All that the advocates of the Broad Gauge can prove as to the superiority of that system will not help the country out of the dilemma. The elaborate experiments, in which every ounce of weight and every foot of speed are calculated with mathematical nicety, to show with what safety a rate of speed can be obtained of which the first railroad engineers never dreamed; all the flying along the double lines of iron, with the speed of an arrow and the smoothness of a billiard ball, leaves the "great difficulty" just where it stood; it only serves to increase our regret that we had not begun on the "Broad" foundation, instead of arriving at it now, trammelled and fettered by another system, which has taken such firm root among us, that to alter it, to what may perhaps be more advantageous, is an impossibility.

Every proof and demonstration that can be given of the superiority of the "Broad Gauge," even if admitted, is a vexation; men dislike being told of the good things they cannot enjoy it does not require a Board of Directors, a Chairman, a Banquet, and exultant speeches, to prove that seventy miles an hour, as the rate of speed, is better than half that amount, or any amount, indeed, less than it. Everybody grants the advantage of saving time and shortening distance. But, if the trains could be shot along the line with the speed of a message along the wires of the Electric Telegraph, with perfect safety (and it would be rash to pronounce even this impossible), unless the improvement could be applied to every line in the kingdom, the benefit would remain an abstraction, a thing proved to be possible, but not possible for *us*, with the physical means we at present have at our disposal. No experiment, no science, no reports, nor any number of speeches at dinners, can do away with that enormous "fact," the one thousand six hundred miles of railroad already made upon the Narrow Gauge. There they lie upon the surface of the country, stretching in every direction, interesecting at every possible angle; where they do join with the "Broad" line that has succeeded it in the course of time, with some points of practical advantage in its favour, the inconvenience, trouble, confusion, and, consequently, expense are awful drawbacks upon that system. What would it be with some score of trunk lines of the "Broad" system driven among that net-work of the "Narrow" railways which overspreads the North? Every point of junction would become an affliction and a nuisance, destructive to the time or property of all men. The delays and accidents of Gloucester, multiplied by forty or fifty, would be too much for human patience to bear.

If any mechanical means can be found of rendering the difference of the rails of no importance to the carriages that run upon them, the conflict will cease; but, if all prospect of such an expedient must be relinquished, some compromise between the two systems must be effected. To this the resolutions of the House of Commons amount. The continuation of the Great Western into Cornwall, and all its branches southward to the coast, will be on its own gauge, of necessity; but, north of that line, no railway will be made on any gauge but the narrow. This is for the future; but it leaves the evil actually existing unprovided for; in fact, here Parliament is powerless; it cannot undo the past: if the difficulty is ever got rid of, it will be by the same energy that has brought out railway system to what it is. Except drawing up intricate and absurd standing orders, which have multiplied the expences of railway bills to a ruinous amount, encouraging litigation, and placing the best and the worst lines on a footing of equality, the Government has done nothing during the development of modern railway enterprise, that entitles it to the slightest respect. That it repents its carelessness now, may be true; but it seems to lack either the skill or the courage to grapple with the difficulty effectually. We, of course, mean by the term Government, the Executive, without regard to parties.

The present state of things, that is, the existence of two conflicting systems, cannot be charged against either the Government or private parties. The Narrow system was the best when it was adopted; the speed attainable on it was thought the maximum that could be gained; but mankind never will rest contented even with a good thing when something a degree better is shown them, though undoubtedly sufficient for all practical purposes. The Broad Gauge does not differ in its superiority, if even that is conceded, so much in kind as in degree; it resolves itself into a calculation of less or more on all points; less oscillation, more speed, and so forth. But the motion of the Narrow Gauge is very bearable, and its speed not to be despised; the very highest speed attainable on any line will never be made the general average; thus the advantages of the two systems will, in the long run, approximate pretty nearly. If we were beginning our career, with our present experience, it would be right to choose that system which presented even the smallest shade of superiority; but, as it is, circumstances have decided for us, and bound us down, for better for worse, to one principle over the greater part of the country. The question now is, which shall be accommodated to the other? The larger can, of course, be altered to the smaller; a Narrow Gauge could be worked on a Broad Gauge line with comparatively little outlay; but no conceivable sum would effect the converse. It would be unjust to compel the Broad lines to alter their rails to the Narrow at their own expense; but the addition of an intermediate line of rail would do all that is required; and the Government itself, which has done so little, might attempt this without finding it ruinous. The tendency of present proceedings is evidently to a compromise, as the only way of getting rid of a daily increasing difficulty. This is proved by the following extract from a leading morning journal:

And here we would throw out another suggestion for abolishing, if possible, the bugbear of "Break of Gauge." Let proclamation be issued for the encouragement of mechanical genius, offering a handsome premium for any invention that shall either remedy or rectify the evil. Who knows but that, in the inventory of events, some succedaneum may be found in science? It will be admitted by either partisans that neither Gauge as yet has had sufficient probation. The ordeal years of the Railway System do not yet equal the years of our own infants. Neither Gauge comes down to us as of anointed nativity, and no one is necromancer enough to affirm that time may discover unrevealed virtues in the Narrow Gauge, however much probability may be against the prediction, which the Broad Gauge does not possess. Both are pioneers of a new process of improvement. At any rate, the Broad Gauge up to the present period has proved itself the Demiurgus, or mechanical wonder of the age. True it is, that the one has the advantage over the other in genealogy. if the one dates its ancestry from the dark ages of railways, the other links its lineage with the reformed locomotion of later days. The one seeks to catholicise the Gauge of the country, and to suppress the competition of a great system, while that great system is struggling to introduce its *novum organum* of Gauge with its Atlantas of speed and its Titans of traction. On this hinges the fate of the two great confederacies – the Guelphs and Ghibellines of the railway economy. The Broad Gauge, it can not be denied, is an invigoration of the old railway system, on

a gigantic and energetic scale. It is, nevertheless, doubtful whether, if the question were reopened, either would be pronounced the Optimist Gauge, since we are greatly swayed to the conclusion that the intermediate of six feet would be looked on as the happy medium.

[ILN JUN 20 1846]

THE BREAK OF GAUGE AT GLOUCESTER
NATIONAL UNIFORMITY OF GAUGE

No public question at first sight ever seemed so inapt for pictorial illustration as that of the Railway Gauges, being nothing more than parallel lines, essentially stiff, mechanical, and monotonous; yet no one has yielded better pictures than those which we publish to-day. It is another proof that the commonest everyday incidents present good subjects for pictures if we *will* but to seek them. As universal chroniclers, we could not give this question the "go by," uninviting as it appeared; and so we dispatched our Artist to Gloucester, where the strongest evidence on this subject is said to be made palpable every day and hour. At Gloucester, two different railways unite; one running southwards, from Birmingham; the other northwards, from Bristol. The first has a width of 4 feet 8½ inches between its rails; the last, 7 feet: and an effect like this which we here make manifest in straight lines takes place.

Gloucester	
From Bristol	To Birmingham

The Gauge, or width of the rails, is *broken* or interrupted: hence the term we now hear so much of – "*Break* of Gauge." Gentle Reader, you have now a theory of what "Break of Gauge" is. If you chance to travel yourself between Birmingham or Cheltenham and Bristol, you will sensibly *feel* it. The Gauge being thus broken, your journey is brought to a dead halt. With all your baggage and rattle-traps, whatever they be in number and size, you are obliged to shift from one carriage to another. Make the journey, and you will have practical experience of what our Artist has so vividly presented. You will hear the Railway Policeman bawling into the deaf Passenger's ear that he must dismount; you will see the anxious Mamma hastening her family in its transit from carriage to carriage, dreading the penalty of being too late; your dog will chance to have his foot crushed be-

tween wheel barrows and porters' baskets – howling more terrifically than the engine itself; the foreigner "Got dams," in broken English, at the stolid porter who is carrying off his luggage; the best glass decanters to be presented to your host, fall and are cracked to atoms; your wife's medicine-chest is broken, and rhubarb, grey powder, and castor oil unnaturally mixed before their time; the orphans going to school at Cheltenham, lose their way in the crowd; and the old maid and her parrot are screeching at honest John for his passive inactivity amidst the turmoil. The reality far surpasses the bustle of our illustration. If your carriage-horses accompany you, they, too, must be shifted by dint of whip and cajollery – perchance "Highflyer," over-restive and impatient at the prospect of another Railway trip, protests so vehemently against a second caging, that he must needs be left behind; you resolve that no consideration will ever tempt you to bring your horses again by Railway, where there is "Break of Gauge".

The removal of goods, owing to the "Break of Gauge," is even more irksome than that of passengers. Where it does not absolutely prohibit the traffic, the transhipment involves loss, pilferage, detention, besides a money tax of from 1s. 6d. to 2s. 6d. per ton, as we learn from the statements of Messrs. Pickford and Horne, the greatest carriers in the world. An old carrier thus graphically speaks of the contents of a goods train, and the shifting of them:

It is found at Gloucester, that to transship the contents of one waggon full of miscellaneous merchandise to another, from one Gauge to the other, takes about an hour, with all the force of porters you can put to work upon it! An ordinary train of waggons, laden with promiscuous goods, may be composed of the following descriptions, namely, loose commodities, such as bricks, slates, lime or limestone, and chalk, flags, clay, manure, salt, coal and coke, timber and deals, dyewoods, iron, iron ore, lead and metals, cast-iron pots, grates and ovens, grindstones, brimstone, bones and hoofs, bark, hides, and seal skins, oil cake, potatoes, onions, and other vegetables, cheese, chairs and furniture, hard-ware, earthenware, dry salteries, groceries, provisions, cotton wool, oils, wines, spirits, and other liquids, manufactured goods, fish and eggs, ripe fruit &c. &c. &c. Now let us contemplate the loss by damage done to the goods on this one train alone, by reason of the Break of Gauge causing the removal of every article. In the hurry the bricks are miscounted, the slates chipped at the edges, the cheeses cracked, the ripe fruit and vegetables crushed and spoiled; the chairs, furniture, and oil cakes, cast iron pots, grates and ovens, all more or less broken; the coals turned into slack, the salt short of weight, sundry bottles of wine deficient, and the fish too late for market. Whereas, if there had not been any interruption of Gauge, the whole train would, in all probability, have been at its destination long before the transfer of the last article, and without any damage or delay.

The pigs decidedly object to Break of Gauge, and oxen resist terrifically [sic]; two hours have been spent in transshipping one.

Palliatives have been proposed, but they are pronounced, by greatly preponderating evidence, to be decidedly impracticable. It was suggested, for example, to have loose carriages, removable, by a lifting machine, from one truck to another. It is answered, first, that "loose" carriages, for coals, &c., have already been tried on the Liverpool and Manchester, and Midlands, and given up. And, as respects the lifting machine, it is but *one* operation out of many requisite; and, to transship a train of 100 waggons, would require a man and horses to travel 50 miles! to bring up each waggon to the lifting machine.

Such are the results of interrupting the uniformity of the Railway Gauge. At present there is only *one* Break – at Gloucester; but, as the newly-sanctioned railways would at once increase the one to *ten*, and the projected increase the ten to *thirty*, Parliament stepped in, and, at its advice, the Crown appointed a Commission, which, as we informed our readers weeks ago, reported in favour of the necessity for having a Uniform Gauge. There being already above 1900 miles of 4 feet 8½ inch gauge, and only 270 miles of 7 feet gauge, and as the broader gauge can be easily reduced whilst the smaller cannot be enlarged, and as the respective merits were, if not balanced, rather in favour of the Narrow Gauge for general purposes, the recommendation of the Commission was that the 4 feet 8½ inch gauge should henceforth be declared the National Gauge, and all railways made upon it.

It should not, however, be withheld that the Broad Gauge has been found to insure certain advantages over the Narrow: these are the increased power and speed of the engines, and the stability and convenience of the carriages; all which are strikingly evident on the Great Western Railway.

THE BREAK OF GAUGE
RHYMES ON A RAIL

Grand Opening Chorus by All Hands

Smash! dash! splash! crash!
Fowling! scowling! howling! growling!
Bawling, squalling, over-hauling,
Tearing, swearing, de'il-may-caring,
Rushing, crushing, ladies blushing,
Crockery breaking, babies shrieking,
Boilers steaming, parents screaming,
Earthly pandemonia seeming.
    Oh! the Gauge, the Gauge,
    The Break of Gauge.
The *crack* improvement of our age:

Aria

How sweet are the pleasures of training
    From London to Liverpool town, Sirs,
Though, when you're half way I am
        meaning
    At Brummagen – there you go down,
        Sirs.
Arous'd from your slumber – your
        number
    Forgotten – your baggage is trundled
Perhaps twenty miles o'er the Humber,
    While you are towards Holyhead
        bundled!
    Chorus – Smash, crash – as above.

Here comes a dowager duchess
    With page and her parrot and charley,
An Alderman deaf as his crutches,
    A maestro in furious parly.
The sweet little maid and her brother –
    Poor orphans! Fear, Love, hand in
        hand locks:
Here's a babe roaring lusty – her mother
Amazed at the smash of her bandbox!
    Chorus "conjerio" – Smash &c.

Such scenes our best feelings must
        harrow,
    Or else they must speedily harden:
The dog's gout is cured by the barrow;
    Smashed phials ("*with care*") from
        the Garden,*
Pour out their sauce for the fishes;
    While over their innocent basket,
Rattle down glasses and dishes,
    Roll'd off by the man in the casquette.
    Chorous – Smash, ad. lib.

And now have the passengers entered
    Their cribs, and away on the journey:
Poor, peasant, steed, ox, are con centred;
    Dogs, hogs, and a stagging attorney.

Through tunnels the steam vent is
        screeching;
    They drive like the hurricane blind,
        sirs;
And now they're the terminus reaching,
    With half of their luggage behind, sirs.

Finale

Smash – dash – splash – mash;
Bawling – squalling – overhauling;
Neighing – braying – not obeying;
Barking – larking – swell mob sharking;
Hogs unshipping – jarvies whipping;
Cabs and busses – glorious fusses;
Steaming – scheming – fightin –
        screaming –
Earthly Pandemonia seeming:
    Oh! the Break – the Break –
    The Break of Gauge –
    The crack dodge of the Railing rage!

* Id. est. – Hatton. – *Vide Boxum*
                [ILN JUNE 6 1846]

Gloucester was the embodiment of the gauge problem: there the broad gauge from Bristol and narrow (standard) gauge from Birmingham met, causing delay, breakages and higher costs. It is ironic to note that the engineer of the Bristol & Gloucester, Brunel, had assured the directors that 'a very simple arrangement may effect the transfer of the entire load of goods from the waggon of one Company to that of the other'. The reality was very different; the 'simple arrangement' was either not forthcoming or failed to work, for delays and frustration with the arrangements mounted. Naturally the Gauge Commissioners visited the transfer sheds where the narrow-gauge party, in the shape of J. D. Payne, Goods Manager of the Birmingham Railway, made sure that mayhem reigned: 'Fearing lest the extent of the transfer work might be too small to impress the Committee, he arranged for the unloading of two trains already dealt with, as an addition to the usual work, and when the Members came to the scene, they were appalled by the clamour arising from the well arranged confusion of shouting out addresses of consignments, the chucking of packages across from truck to truck, the enquiries for missing articles, the loading, unloading and reloading, which his clever device had brought into operation.'

Trans-Shipment of goods from the Broad Gauge to the Narrow Gauge Carriages

GEORGE HUD[...]

Mr. Hudson, "the [...]
until recently, a li[...]
which city he h[...]
Mayor. In his busi[...]
fortune, and inherit[...]
His career in railwa[...]
it is well kno[...]
unprecendented su[...]
no trivial degree, to[...]
and integrity. On[...]
him, we understan[...]
pense for his adm[...]
their affairs. At [...]
enormous; and he[...]
the last year a co[...]
the Duke of Devo[...]

Mr. Hudson [...]
popularity in his o[...]
of all ranks would [...]
sum of money t[...]
speculative enterp[...]
has not blunted[...]
disposition. It is [...]
visiting a broth[...]
fortunes had been [...]
he proposed to him[...]
in a particular r[...]
which his poor fri[...]
asserting his utte[...]
consequent incapa[...]
the offer. "Never [...]
will arrange that f[...]
period he called ag[...]
with a cheque [...]
pounds, the fruits [...]

Mr. G. Hudson, M[...]

THE LATE
GEORGE STEPHENSON, ESQ.

In our Obituary of last week we briefly recorded the death of this eminent engineer, whose high destiny it has been "to be, (says the *Daily News*,) the main instrument in effecting one of the greatest revolutions our revolutionary era has witnessed, by that combination of the railway and the locomotive steam-engine to which Europe and America owe their railway systems."

George Stephenson was born in the village of Wylam, on the banks of the Tyne, about nine miles west of Newcastle, in April, 1781; and at the time of his death was in his 68th year. His father was a workman at the Wylam Colliery, and he himself worked in the same humble way, having been sent into the pit at a very early age. At the age of fourteen, or fifteen, he was employed as a brakesman, on the waggon way between Wylam and Newburn; his father having removed to Wabbottle, about a mile north-west of the latter village. Young Stephenson also occasionally worked at the ballast quay of Messrs. Nixon and Co. at Willington, about five miles east of Newcastle.

After having been some years employed at Wylam, Mr. Stephenson removed to Killingworth Colliery, the property of Lord Ravensworth and partners, where he was still employed as a brakesman. At Killingworth he married his first wife, by whom he had one son, the celebrated engineer, Mr. Robert Stephenson, M.P.

The earliest indication of George Stephenson's genius for mechanics showed itself at Killingworth, where he effectually repaired his own eight-day house clock, that was out of order; and he thenceforth became the watchmaker of the village, an occupation to which he devoted many leisure hours. Soon after this, a large condensing machine erected at the colliery for pumping water from the pit got out of order, and various ineffectual attempts were made to repair it. At length Mr. Stephenson's attention was directed to the engine, and having carefully examined its working parts, he thought he discovered where the defects lay: he was allowed to "try his hand," and succeeded in repairing the engine, and even introducing some improvement into its construction. His employers were so

satisfied with this result, that he was at once promoted from a brakesman to an engineer, and was entrusted with the entire management of the engine. Here he had many opportunities of self-improvement; and his progress was soon developed in the discovery of the Safety Lamp. Several claims have been made to the merit of this invention, and to the present day the exact amount of credit due to each remains a matter of controversy.

Mr. Stephenson's claims were warmly and liberally supported by many of the most respectable coal-owners and others in the Newcastle district, who maintained that to his ingenuity the mining interest is indebted for the discovery of the principle on which the safety-lamp is constructed. On the very day that Mr. Stephenson was making his first experiment (Oct. 21, 1815), a letter was received by the Rev. John Hodgson from Sir Humphry Davy, announcing that he had discovered that explosive mixtures of mine-damp would not pass through small apertures or tubes; and that, if a lamp were made air-tight on the sides, and furnished with apertures, it would not communicate flame to the outward atmosphere. The coincidence of this communication with Stephenson's experiment is very extraordinary. To remunerate him for the invention, a meeting was held in November, 1818, and a subscription opened, which eventually amounted to one thousand pounds; this sum, together with a piece of plate, was presented to Mr. Stephenson, at a public dinner, held in the Assembly Rooms, Newcastle.

From this period, Mr. Stephenson's advancement was rapid; and thenceforth his career became more particularly identified with the locomotive engine. In 1804, Trevethick and Vivian's machine drew carriages at Merthyr-Tydvil, at the rate of five miles an hour. In 1811 appeared Blenkinsop's engine, and in 1812 Chapman produced one; both which were defective. In 1814, Mr. Stephenson constructed for the Killingworth Colliery an engine which was used on the colliery railroad with almost perfect success. This did not, however, please the engineer, and he subsequently constructed another engine for the same place, which answered much better, and laid the foundation of the existing system of railroads.

In 1824 Mr. Stephenson established on engine manufactory in Newcastle, in partnership with the Messrs. Pease (of Darlington), Mr. Robert Longridge, and Mr. Robert Stephenson. This concern is situated on the Forth banks, and continues to prosper under the firm of Messrs. Robert Stephenson and Co. The first locomotive railway for the purpose of travelling, according to the present principles of traction, was laid between Stockton and Darlington; and was opened in 1825. Mr. Stephenson has been known to confess that his ideas and anticipations of the capabilities of this mode of transit, both as to the speed and the effect which it would produce when generally adopted (as he foresaw it must be ultimately), were such as he did not even dare to express, for fear of being pronounced insane. At that time he talked of reaching a velocity of twenty miles an hour, but his inward thoughts said sixty or one hundred miles. It was not, however, till the formation of the Liverpool and Manchester Railway, in 1829, that Mr. Stephenson was brought prominently before the public as an engine builder. In that year the directors of the above line offered a premium of £500 for the best locomotive engine to run on their railway; when George Stephenson entered the lists, and constructed his celebrated engine "the Rocket," which won the prize. This achievement gave a decisive stamp to Mr. Stephenson's reputation as a railway engineer; and he was subsequently employed in the construction of most of the principal lines of railway in the kingdom. He was also engaged in constructing lines in Belgium, Holland, France, Germany, Italy, and Spain; and he had the honour to receive a knighthood from Leopold of Belgium, for railway services. We are indebted for the substance of these details to a memoir in the *Newcastle Journal*.

The best evidence of the true greatness of Mr. Stephenson's character is the unwavering faith in his own theoretical conclusions, combined with sound practical judgment, that he manifested throughout his career. About a year ago he said at a public dinner at Newcastle – "At Liverpool I pledged myself to attain a speed of ten miles an hour. I said I had no doubt it would go much faster, but we

The Signalman's Christmas Dinner on the Railway Line [ILN Dec 27 1890]

It is surprisin
a special sup
George Steph
obituary notic
biography pro
his life after
his son's ach
Birmingham
Newcastle an
Stephenson's
good educatio
The controve
miner's safe
unpleasant a
the worst in
biography o
that it seems
same ends
Stephenson r
ing a dignif
marked cont
to prove his
at his ho
Chesterfield,
serious attac

The cessation of railway services over Christmas did not occur until 1960 and this depiction of 'the signalman's Christmas dinner' was doubtless to remind readers of the discomfort endured by some to maintain them. To call the character a signalman would seem to be misleading, since signals and points had long been worked by a centrally located enclosed frame in 1890; he may well have been a Signal & Telegraph Dept worker, whose function would be to prevent signals and their wires, points and their rodding from becoming inoperative through snow or ice, or a fog signalman repeating the indications of the semaphore signals with hand signals, required during falling snow.

ABORTIVE SCHEMES

THE CHANNEL TUNNEL

We present a series of Sketches and Illustrations of the Channel Tunnel Works at Dover, recently commenced by the Submarine Continental Railway Company, of which Sir Edward Watkin, Bart., M.P., Chairman of the South-Eastern Railway Company, is the presiding director. On Saturday, the 18th inst., Sir Edward Watkin conducted a party of thirty or forty gentlemen from London to inspect these works, the Lord Mayor of London being one of the party. They descended the shaft, walked a thousand yards under the sea, and admired the working of Colonel Beaumont's compressed-air boring machine. They had the electric light, by which the tunnel was illuminated from end to end. In anticipation of this visit Sir Edward had directed a luncheon to be prepared in the tunnel, which was partaken of in a chamber cut in the side of the heading, tables and stools being set there for the occasion. This chamber is subsequently to be converted into a siding. The party spent upwards of an hour in the tunnel, and then went to Dover, where a luncheon, to which the Mayor and some of the members of the Dover Corporation had been invited, was provided at the Lord Warden Hotel.

The Channel Tunnel was again opened to another party of London visitors on Tuesday of last week, when Sir E. Watkin could not be present, but his place was taken by Mr. Miles Fenton, general manager of the South-Eastern Railway, aided by Mr. Shaw, Secretary to that Company. Under the guidance of Mr. Francis Brady, C.E., engineer of the Channel Tunnel, and Colonel Beaumont, R.E., the visitors, six at a time, having put on rough overalls to save their clothes from dust, descended into the shaft by means of an iron cage, such as is used in coal-mines. The shaft is sunk in the chalk cliff at the foot of the "Shakespeare Cliff," between Folkestone and Dover, and is about one hundred and sixty feet in depth. The opening is circular, with boarded sides, and the descending apparatus is worked by a steam-engine. At the bottom of this shaft is a square chamber dug in the grey chalk, the sides of which are protected by heavy beams; and in front is the experimental boring, a low-roofed circular tunnel, about seven feet in diameter the floor of which is laid with a double line of tram-rails. This tunnel is admirably ventilated, and on visiting days is lighted with electric lamps, the steam-power at the mouth of the shaft being sufficient for all purposes. The stratum through which the experimental borings have been made is the lower grey chalk. This material, while perfectly dry, and very easily worked, is sufficiently hard to dispel any apprehensions of crumbling or falling in. The main feature of the Channel Tunnel scheme, as designed by the engineers of the Submarine Continental Railway Company, is that of constructing the tunnel altogether in the lower measure of the grey chalk. In this respect it differs from the scheme of a rival Company, whose tunnel would reach the lower measure of grey chalk two or three miles eastward of Dover, necessitating an approach through the white chalk, which is heavily charged with water, and from which stratum, in fact, the town of Dover get its water supply.

The length of the Submarine Continental Railway Company's Tunnel, under sea, from the English to the French shore, will be twenty-two miles; and, taking the shore approaches at four miles on each side, there will be a total length of thirty miles of tunnelling. The approach tunnel descends from the daylight surface by an inclosed gallery, with an incline of 1 in 80, towards Dover, to a point on the Southern Railway Company's line, about two miles and a half from Folkestone. The exact point is at the western end of the Abbot's Cliff tunnel, at which point the gault clay out-crops to the sea level. Half a mile of heading has been driven, by machinery, from this point; after which, the works were suspended, to enable them to be resumed at a point nearer to Shakespeare's Cliff, where the tunnel passes under the sea. It is the shaft at this point that is represented in our Engraving. This shaft is 160 ft. deep. It is sunk close to the western end of Shakespeare's Cliff. The opening is situated on a plateau, formed by the débris which was blown down by the famous blast that took place in the construction of the South-Eastern Railway between Folkestone and Dover, some years ago. The shaft passes through about 40 ft. of overlying débris; it then just touches the white chalk, which is pervious to water; after which it goes down to the beginning of the tunnel, which is here 100 ft. below the surface of the sea. The small amount of water observed in the shaft above, when the party of visitors descended, came from the white chalk already mentioned. A heading, now three quarters of a mile long, has been driven in the direction of the head of the Admiralty Pier, entirely in the grey chalk, near its base, and a few feet above the impermeable strata formed by the gault clay. The idea of the projectors is so to localise the tunnel, not only in the part already made, but also when it passes out under the sea, that it shall have the body of the grey chalk above it, and that of the gault clay below it; both these strata being in themselves impervious to water, and both alike having heavily watered strata on each side of them; namely, the white chalk, as shown in our Section, above the grey chalk; and the lower greensand below the gault clay. This condition, together with that of providing sufficient roof between the top of the tunnel and the sea, which roof has a thickness of 150 ft., will necessitate the tunnel being turned in a curved line.

The present heading is 7 ft. in diameter. Machinery is being constructed by which this 7 ft. hole can be enlarged to 14 ft., by cutting an annular space, 3 ft. 6in. wide, around it. This will be done by machinery similar to that already described, but furnished with an upper bore-head, suitable for dealing with chalk, to make an annular cutting, instead of acting like the first machine, which makes the 7 ft. cutting. The one machine will follow the other, at a proper interval; and the débris from the cutting by the first will be passed out through the second machine. The compressed air, likewise, which is necessary to work the advanced machine, will be similarly passed through the machine coming behind. There will be no difficulty in speeding the machines so that they shall work along the tunnel at the same rate of progress; and the larger machine can, as well as the smaller one, do its work with a minimum of manual labour; only two men are at present needed for each machine.

At the end of the tunnel the visitors

The East Lancashire Railway, in connecting Manchester and a number of prospering towns in the Bolton and Bury area with the West Riding of Yorkshire, was naturally seen by the Lancashire & Yorkshire Railway as a substantial threat. The only section of line not owned by the ELR, which co-operated with the Midland Railway to reach West Yorkshire, was between Clifton Junction and Salford. Matters came to a head over one particular issue, the tolls paid by the ELR for the passengers conveyed over LYR metals between Clifton Junction and Salford, with the results described in this article. The sight of the opposing companies' engines trying to push each other out the way must have been rather ludicrous, if entertaining, recalling for modern memories a comparable episode in The Titfield Thunderbolt. *Relations between the companies continued to be acrimonious, even leading to the ELR proposing a line of its own, parallel to the LYR, between the two points; in the event the section became jointly owned. Conduct of this kind, obviously at the management's behest, was fortunately not typical, although there were some amusing contretemps: at Havant in 1858 the London & South Western Railway captured a London, Brighton & South Coast engine during a dispute over running powers between Havant and Portcreek Junction; this is the subject of the* ILN *report for 8 January 1859.*

---

withdrew the obstruction, and the various trains were allowed to pass onwards, fortunately without accident or injury to the passengers, though it must be confessed to have been a dangerous experiment.

[ILN MARCH 17 1849]

THE LATE RAILWAY FRACAS

The extraordinary scene which occurred last week at the Clifton Railway Station, and of which we gave the full particulars in our last, ought not to be allowed to drop from memory without the indignant reprobation of the public. Our police regulations will not tolerate that two rival omnibus drivers should back up a street to impede traffic, and endanger life by their quarrels, neither should the infinitely more dangerous blockade of a line of railway be allowed to pass unpunished. By all acts authorizing the formation of railways, the directors are empowered to punish any person who

Railway Blockade at Clifton Station, near Manchester

may wilfully place obstruction on the rails; and that, too, whether damage to property or loss of life have or have not occurred. A wilful obstruction on the part of railway officials themselves is an offence still more flagrant and dangerous. Were there such a functionary in England as a public prosecutor, the blockade at Clifton would fall under his special cognizance; but, in the absence of such a functionary, it is to be hoped that some means will be found to bring within reach of the law the railway officials who acted in the highly culpable manner to which we have alluded. These railway gentry, who seemed inclined to carry things with so high a hand, both in their relations with other companies and with the public, should remember, too, in their own interest, that railway dividends are not entirely composed of fares received from persons who travel on business, but that large numbers of their best customers travel for pleasure and recreation. This class are very sensitive to danger, and will transfer their favours to other lines, where civil war is not raging, and where there is no more than the ordinary risk to life and limb. The everyday casualties of railway travelling are quite sufficient of themselves to deter the timid from all unnecessary travelling. It is a suicidal policy, as well as a public

offence, to increase these risks by such reckless conduct as was exhibited at Clifton.

PORTSMOUTH – THE RAILWAY DISPUTE

Circumstances have recently occurred in reference to the means of transit to the chief naval arsenal of Great Britain which render the View of Portsmouth which we give in this week's Number of our Journal appropriate. The island of Portsea, on the south-west shore of which the town of Portsmouth is situated, lies between two inlets of the sea – Portsmouth Harbour, west, and Langston Harbour, east – which send out narrow creeks meeting together four miles north of Portsmouth. The town consists of two parts, joining each other, but each surrounded on the land side by separate lines of fortification – Portsmouth and Portsea – on the last of which is the dockyard. On the west side of the harbour is Gosport, where are the victualling yard, reservoirs, &c.; and opposite its mouth, between it and the Isle of Wight, expands the famous roadstead of Spithead. The fortifications of Portsmouth and Portsea have been stated to be the most complete in Europe; but nevertheless we every now and then

126

hear of plans for improving and strengthening them. However the fact of their strength may be, it is certain that the ramparts and batteries connected with them command some charming views. On the land side the ramparts are planted with trees, and form an agreeable terrace walk. From the Platform Battery, near the harbour, one of the best views of Portsmouth, with the harbour and Spithead, is to be obtained. The dockyard of Portsmouth, the largest in the kingdom, is in fact a town in itself, occupying over one hundred and twenty acres. It is situated in the east side of the harbour, and is supplied with all the necessary means for building, repairing, and fitting out ships of war. Besides being a great naval station, Portsmouth is a large garrison, always occupied by a considerable number of troops, and is the head-quarters of the western military district. This being so, it need hardly be said that communication between so important a place and the metropolis is constant, goods and passenger traffic continuous, and transit by railway indispensable. The right to supply this necessity is at present the subject of dispute between the Brighton and South Coast and South-Western Railway Companies.

As far as can be ascertained, the following is a correct version of the matter. The first railway into Portsmouth was constructed by the Brighton Company. It was an extension of their coast-line from Chichester, passing through Havant, entering the fortifications at Hilsea, and terminating at the present station at Portsmouth. The South-Western Company afterwards obtained powers to construct a line from Fareham to join the Brighton line at Hilsea, running into Portsmouth on the Brighton line; and the two companies obtained powers by which one half share of the line from Hilsea into Portsmouth, called the Joint Line, was sold to the South-Western, who thus became joint owners thereof. After this a line, called the Portsmouth Railway, was constructed from Godalming to Havant, and was to have been opened on the 1st inst. To the company possessing this line Parliament granted running powers over the lines from Havant into Portsmouth; but they were prohibited from using the joint station at Portsmouth, except upon agreement with both the Brighton and South-Western Companies; and as regards the Brighton line from Havant to Hilsea, the

running powers were to be used under terms and conditions to be fixed by arbitration in case of difference. The South-Western Company a short time since took a lease of the Portsmouth line at a rent of £18,000 a year, and the Portsmouth Company brought before an arbitrator its case as to the terms and conditions under which their traffic should run over the Brighton Company's line between Havant and Hilsea. The award has not yet been made, and in the meantime the Brighton Company intimated to the South-Western that they could not allow the latter to carry the traffic of the Portsmouth railway into the joint station at Portsmouth.

The South-Western Company advertised the opening of the line for the 1st of January, communicated the fact to the Brighton Company, and on the 24th of December that Company received a notice that, on and after the 28th of December, a goods train from the Portsmouth line would arrive at Havant at 9.58 a.m., and proceed thence, via Hilsea, to Portsmouth, returning from Portsmouth, via Hilsea and Havant, to the Portsmouth railway at 5.45 p.m. The Brighton Company, as the award was not made and the terms of admission into the Portsmouth station not fixed, wrote on the 27th of December to the South-Western stating that, in the absence of proper regulations for the use of the line, they could not permit any train from or to the Portsmouth railway to run over the Brighton line from Havant to Hilsea.

On the following morning, notwithstanding this notice, the South-Western Company's principal officers arrived at Havant from Petersfield, not at 9.58 a.m., but between six and seven a.m., before it was light, bringing with them a goods train, with an engine behind as well as one in front, a supply of water and provisions, a barrel of beer, and a force of about eighty men. The tongue of the junction points had been taken out, and a rail at the junction removed the previous evening by the Brighton Company, so as to render access impossible, and an engine had been placed at the Havant station, on the up line leading to the Junction, so as to prevent any train coming down the up line, and thus obtaining access. The only servants of the Brighton Company on the spot were – the station-master, engine-driver and fireman, signalman, and one or two platelayers. From these the South-Western people unsuccessfully demanded

the production of the missing rails. They then jumped upon the engine, over-powered the driver and fireman, and forcibly drove the engine into an adjacent siding, and at once, in the face of the danger signals, drove their own train down the up line, till the engine reached the down line, where its further progress was impeded, because the Brighton officials immediately removed some other rails on the Portsmouth side of the Havant station, and thus the attempt made by the South-Western Company to obtain the desired access was frustrated. The South-Western train remained standing across both the up and the down lines of the Brighton Company, and the communication between Brighton and Portsmouth was thus cut off, and all the passengers of the Brighton Company were obliged to be shifted from train to train during the whole period, for the South-Western Company continued for six hours refusing to withdraw the obstruction. In the meantime the Brighton Company had summoned a large number of their employees and some powerful engines, and the South-Western officials, feeling that it would be prudent to withdraw, took their departure, and the public traffic was resumed.

[ILN JAN 8 1859]

The idea of wage or salary reductions has only recently been revived, but it has been tied to the welfare of the company concerned – a case of accepting a wage reduction to save the company's very existence. In the nineteenth century, wages were closely allied to food prices, and in times of cheap food following good harvests, it was common for wages to be correspondingly reduced. The years 1848–50 were such a period; hence the claim by G. B. Paget that the men could afford a cut.

STRIKES ON THE MIDLAND RAILWAY

A series of strikes, of various classes of workmen employed by the Midland Railway Company, have for some time been pending, and at length the goods guards and porters have ceased work at every principal station, thereby putting an entire stop to the goods traffic throughout the lines. The strike at Derby station commenced on Monday morning, and was so universal that all the goods sheds were instantly closed, and it was found impossible to collect together hands sufficient to send off even one luggage train, although a great variety of parcels and packages, some of which contained articles of an extremely perishable nature, required forwarding to their destinations without delay. This general cessation from labour is owing to the directors reducing the wages of one class of men – the goods guards – from 19s. to 17s. weekly, and of goods porters from 17s. to 16s. The strikes commenced at Nottingham about a fortnight ago, when four men threw up their situations rather than submit to the reduction. The knowledge of this was immediately communicated to their fellow-labourers in every direction, and more general strikes followed at Leeds, Bradford, and Derby. The engine-drivers and firemen, until within the last few days, have also been upon the eve of striking, in consequence of the directors wanting them to travel three journeys at the same rate of wages they have hitherto received for two journeys; but they were too unanimous amongst themselves to be forced to submit to the new terms. They are 203 in number, and all, except three, would have struck within six hours had not the company consented to allow the old engagements to remain in force. As soon as danger from the pending strike appeared to be over, Mr. G. B. Paget brought down a number of new men to displace the ring-leaders; but their comrades were true to their friends, and threatened to leave in a body at a moment's notice if even one were dismissed for taking part in the movement. The consequence has been that not one man has been discharged. Mr. G. B. Paget, in addressing the men, urged upon them to accept the reduction, the very low price of provisions well enabling them to do so; and he promised, if they would, that, as the price of food rose at any future time, he would see that their rate of remuneration was increased. On Wednesday the goods guards and porters at Derby, some hundreds in number, returned to their employment, the former at their original rate of remuneration, and the latter for the present at reduced wages, but with a promise of an advance whenever the price of food becomes higher. Although the directors strained every nerve, from Monday morning until Tuesday night, they found themselves unable to carry on their business without the assistance of their old goods guards; but, by extensive importations of agricultural labourers, who for many miles around may be had for very little remuneration, the had pretty nearly swamped the more humble class of goods porters, and they have been compelled to seek and accept a compromise. The policemen and pointsmen, who a week or two ago had their salaries reduced 5 per cent., and who were too scattered in small numbers along the whole extent of the various lines to act in concert, have petitioned the board to restore to them the small modicum which, they say, without their consent, has been stopped out of their weekly wages, and declare their intention of giving up their situations simultaneously if their petition be not complied with. Should this really occur, the greatest danger to the company's traffic will be the result; so much property and so many lives constantly depending upon the discretion of these officials, especially of the pointsmen.

[ILN DEC 29 1849]